Search and Seizure Checklists

Clark Boardman's Criminal Law Library

Searches & Seizures, Arrests and Confessions
by William E. Ringel

Eyewitness Identification:
Legal and Practical Problems
by Nathan R. Sobel

Prisoners' Rights Sourcebook:
Theory/Litigation/Practice
edited by Ira P. Robbins

Rights of Juveniles: The Juvenile Justice System
by Samuel M. Davis

Plea Bargaining and Guilty Pleas
by James E. Bond

The Law of Electronic Surveillance
by James G. Carr

Representation of Witnesses Before
Federal Grand Juries
by National Lawyers Guild

Police Misconduct: Law and Litigation
by National Lawyers Guild

Federal Rules of Criminal Procedure
with Practice Comments by Michele G. Hermann

Prosecutorial Misconduct
by Bennett L. Gershman

Search and Seizure Law Report
articles, cases & comments/published monthly

Drug Abuse and the Law Sourcebook
by Gerald F. Uelmen and Victor G. Haddox

Police Misconduct and Civil Rights Law Report
articles, cases & comments/published quarterly

Drug Law Report
articles, cases & comments/published bimonthly

Please write for further information about these publications.
Clark Boardman Company, Ltd., 435 Hudson Street, N.Y., N.Y. 10014

Search and Seizure Checklists

Fourth Edition

by Michele G. Hermann

Clark Boardman Company, Ltd.
New York, New York

Copyright 1985 by Clark Boardman Company, Ltd.

Library of Congress Cataloging in Publication Data:

Hermann, Michele G.
   Search and seizure checklists.

   1. Searches and seizures—United States—Outlines,
syllabi, etc.   I. Title.
KF9630.Z9H47   1983   345.73′0522   83-15529
ISBN 0-87632-348-4   347.305522

Preface

Search and Seizure Checklists—Fourth Edition is an outline of Fourth Amendment law. It is designed to be a quick reference to doctrines and cases.

The format of the *Checklists* is a topical analysis of the Fourth Amendment which identifies what is required to obtain search or arrest warrants and the situations which justify warrantless searches and seizures. Major federal cases are quoted for each of the legal propositions to illustrate the application and source of the rules. These citations are not exhaustive but represent leading or significant cases in the area, with a heavy concentration on the United States Supreme Court. Cases cited are through the 1983–84 Term of the U.S. Supreme Court.

The outlines of each doctrine of criminal-constitutional law can be taken as elements which must be proved in order to prevail in justifying a search. Thus, where appropriate, burdens of proof are also discussed.

I would like to express my gratitude for the work of my research assistants who have made substantial contributions to this project, which could not have succeeded without them.

Michele Hermann
University of New Mexico
School of Law
Albuquerque, New Mexico

Contents

Chapter 1

Basic Definitions: Search, Seizure, and the Exclusionary Rule

A. Constitutional Law: The Fourth Amendment, as applied to the states through the Fourteenth Amendment, governs searches and seizures.

1. "The right of the people to be secure in their persons, houses, papers, and effects, against unreasonable searches and seizures, shall not be violated and no warrants shall issue, but upon probable cause, supported by oath or affirmation, and particularly describing the place to be searched, and the persons or things to be seized." U.S. Const. amend. IV.

2. "Since the Fourth Amendment's right of privacy has been declared enforceable against the States through the Due Process Clause of the Fourteenth [Amendment], it is enforceable against them by the same sanction of exclusion as is used against the Federal Government." *Mapp v. Ohio,* 367 U.S. 643, 655 (1961).

B. Interests Protected: The Fourth Amendment protects the legitimate privacy interests of individuals, not merely their property rights.

1. "[T]he Fourth Amendment protects people, not places. What a person knowingly exposes to the public, even in his own home or office, is not a subject of Fourth Amendment

protection.... But what he seeks to preserve as private, even in an area accessible to the public, may be constitutionally protected." *Katz v. United States,* 389 U.S. 347, 351-52 (1967).

2. "[C]apacity to claim the protection of the Fourth Amendment depends not upon a property right in the invaded place but upon whether the person who claims the protection of the Amendment has a legitimate expectation of privacy in the invaded place." *Rakas v. Illinois,* 439 U.S. 128, 143 (1978).

3. "The Fourth Amendment protects legitimate expectations of privacy rather than simply places. If the inspection by police does not intrude upon a legitimate expectation of privacy, there is no 'search' subject to the Warrant Clause." *Illinois v. Andreas,* 463 U.S. 765,____(1983).

4. "Although *Katz* recognized that the Fourth Amendment 'protects people, not places,' it is still necessary to consider the nature of the place—whether private or public, residential or commercial—in which legitimate privacy expectations are being asserted. For instance,...'a man's home is, for most purposes, a place where he expects privacy.'... On the other hand,... '[i]t is a fair generalization...that business and commercial premises are not as private as residential premises, and that consequently there are various police investigative procedures which may be directed at such premises without the police conduct constituting a Fourth Amendment search.'" *United States v. Reed,* 733 F.2d 492, 500-01 (8th Cir. 1984).

C. Seizable Items: The Fourth Amendment governs searches for contraband, fruits, instrumentalities, and evidence of crime.

1. "The requirements of the Fourth Amendment can secure the same protection of privacy whether the search is for 'mere evidence' or for fruits, instrumentalities or contraband. There must, of course, be a nexus...between the item to be seized and criminal behavior. Thus in the case of 'mere evidence,' probable cause must be examined in terms of cause to believe that the evidence sought will aid in a particular apprehension or conviction." *Warden v. Hayden,* 387 U.S. 294, 306-07 (1967).

2. "Under existing law, valid warrants may be issued to search *any* property, whether or not occupied by a third party, at which there is probable cause to believe that fruits, instrumentalities, or evidence of a crime will be found." *Zurcher v. Stanford Daily*, 436 U.S. 547, 554 (1978).

D. Scope of Seizure: Seizure includes the collection of evidence and the detention of individuals.

1. "A seizure affects only the person's possessory interests; a search affects a person's privacy interests." *Segura v. United States,* 468 U.S.____,____(1984).

2. "Although in the context of personal property, and particularly containers, the Fourth Amendment challenge is typically to the subsequent search of the container rather than to its initial seizure by the authorities, our cases reveal some general principles regarding seizures. In the ordinary case, the Court has viewed a seizure of personal property as *per se* unreasonable within the meaning of the Fourth

Amendment unless it is accomplished pursuant to a judicial warrant issued upon probable cause and particularly describing the items to be seized.... Where law enforcement authorities have probable cause to believe that a container holds contraband or evidence of a crime, but have not secured a warrant, the Court has interpreted the Amendment to permit seizure of the property, pending issuance of a warrant to examine its contents, if the exigencies of the circumstances demand it or some other recognized exception to the warrant requirement is present.... [W]hen an officer's observations lead him reasonably to believe that a traveler is carrying luggage that contains narcotics, the principles of *Terry [v. Ohio,* 392 U.S. 1 (1968)] and its progeny would permit the officer to detain the luggage briefly to investigate the circumstances that aroused his suspicion, provided that the investigative detention is properly limited in scope." *United States v. Place,* 462 U.S. 696,____(1983).

3.   "It is quite plain that the Fourth Amendment governs 'seizures' of the person which do not eventuate in a trip to the station house and prosecution for crime—'arrests' in traditional terminology. It must be recognized that whenever a police officer accosts an individual and restrains his freedom to walk away, he has 'seized' that person." *Terry v. Ohio,* 392 U.S. 1, 16 (1968).

4.   "[T]he detention of the respondent against his will constituted a seizure of his person, and the Fourth Amendment guarantee of freedom from 'unreasonable searches and seizures' is clearly implicated.... 'Nothing is more clear than that the Fourth Amendment was meant to prevent wholesale intrusions upon the personal security of our citizenry, whether these intrusions be termed "arrests" or "investigatory detentions." ' " *Cupp v. Murphy,* 412 U.S. 291, 294 (1973).

E. Probable Cause Defined: Probable cause is supplied by evidence which would lead a reasonable person to believe that an offense has been or is being committed.

1. "[Probable cause] mean[s] more than bare suspicion: Probable cause exists where 'the facts and circumstances within their [the officers'] knowledge and of which they had reasonably trustworthy information [are] sufficient in themselves to warrant a man of reasonable caution in the belief that' an offense has been or is being committed." *Brinegar v. United States,* 338 U.S. 160, 175 (1949).

2. "If the facts and circumstances before the officer are such as to warrant a man of prudence and caution in believing that the offense has been committed, it is sufficient." *Stacey v. Emery,* 97 U.S. 642, 645 (1878).

3. "'The substance of all the definitions' of probable cause 'is a reasonable ground for belief of guilt'.... And this 'means less than evidence which would justify condemnation' or conviction...." *Brinegar v. United States,* 338 U.S. 160, 175 (1949).

4. "[P]robable cause is a flexible, common-sense standard. It merely requires that the facts available to the officer would 'warrant a man of reasonable caution in the belief'...that certain items may be contraband or stolen property or useful as evidence of a crime; it does not demand any showing that such belief be correct or more likely true than false. A 'practical, nontechnical' probability that incriminating evidence is involved is all that is required." *Texas v. Brown,* 460 U.S. 730, 742 (1983).

5. "[P]robable cause is a fluid concept—turning on the assessment of probabilities in particular factual contexts—

not readily, or even usefully, reduced to a neat set of legal rules.... While an effort to fix some general, numerically precise degree of certainty corresponding to 'probable cause' may not be helpful, it is clear that 'only the probability, and not a prima facie showing, of criminal activity is the standard of probable cause.'" *Illinois v. Gates,* 462 U.S. 213,____(1983).

6.   "Probable cause is the 'sum total of layers of information and the synthesis of what police have heard, what they know, and what they observed as trained officers.... Each individual layer of information is not to be weighed. Rather, the "laminated total" of the facts available is the source of the justification for a vehicle search without a warrant.'" *United States v. Orozco,* 715 F.2d 158, 160 (5th Cir. 1983).

F. Remedy: A major remedy for unconstitutional police action may be to exclude the illegally procured evidence from admission in a criminal prosecution.

1.   "Whether the exclusionary sanction is appropriately imposed in a particular case, our decisions make clear, is 'an issue separate from the question whether the Fourth Amendment rights of the party seeking to invoke the rule were violated by police conduct.'" *United States v. Leon,* 468 U.S.____,____ (1984).

2.   "In the absence of an allegation that the magistrate abandoned his detached and neutral role, suppression is appropriate only if the officers were dishonest or reckless in preparing their affidavit or could not have harbored an objectively reasonable belief in the existence of probable cause." *United States v. Leon,* 468 U.S.____,____(1984).

3. "[S]uppression of evidence obtained pursuant to a warrant should be ordered only on a case-by-case basis and only in those unusual cases in which exclusion will further the purposes of the exclusionary rule." *United States v. Leon,* 468 U.S. _____, _____ (1984).

4. "[T]he exclusionary rule should not be applied when the officer conducting the search acted in objectively reasonable reliance on a warrant issued by a detached and neutral magistrate that subsequently is determined to be invalid...." *Massachusetts v. Sheppard,* 468 U.S. _____, _____(1984).

5. "If letters and private documents can thus be seized and held and used in evidence against a citizen accused of an offense, the protection of the Fourth Amendment declaring his right to be secure against such searches and seizures is of no value, and...might as well be stricken from the Constitution. The efforts of the courts and their officials to bring the guilty to punishment, praiseworthy as they are, are not to be aided by the sacrifice of those great principles established by years of endeavor and suffering which have resulted in their embodiment in the fundamental law of the land.... To sanction such proceedings would be to affirm by judicial decision a manifest neglect if not an open defiance of the prohibitions of the Constitution, intended for the protection of the people against such unauthorized action." *Weeks v. United States,* 232 U.S. 383, 393-94 (1914).

6. "The Government cannot violate the Fourth Amendment—in the only way in which the Government can do anything, namely through its agents—and use the fruits of such unlawful conduct to secure a conviction.... Nor can the Government make indirect use of such evidence for its case, ...or support a conviction on evidence obtained

through leads from the unlawfully obtained evidence.... All these methods are outlawed, and convictions obtained by means of them are invalidated, because they encourage the kind of society that is obnoxious to free men." *Walder v. United States,* 347 U.S. 62, 64-65 (1954).

7.   "The deterrent purpose of the exclusionary rule necessarily assumes that the police have engaged in willful, or at the very least negligent, conduct which has deprived the defendant of some right. By refusing to admit evidence gained as a result of such conduct, the courts hope to instill in those particular investigating officers, or in their future counterparts, a greater degree of care toward the rights of an accused." *Michigan v. Tucker,* 417 U.S. 433, 447 (1974).

8.   "But it is not deterrence alone that warrants the exclusion of evidence illegally obtained—it is 'the imperative of judicial integrity'.... The exclusion of an illegally procured confession and of any testimony obtained in its wake deprives the Government of nothing to which it has any lawful claim and creates no impediment to legitimate methods of investigating and prosecuting crime. On the contrary, the exclusion of evidence causally linked to the Government's illegal activity no more than restores the situation that would have prevailed if the Government had itself obeyed the law." *Harrison v. United States,* 392 U.S. 219, 224 n.10 (1968).

G.   Exceptions: A number of exceptions to the exclusionary rule have been developed.

1.   "[T]he exclusionary rule is designed to deter police misconduct rather than to punish the errors of judges and

magistrates. . . . [T]here exists no evidence suggesting that judges and magistrates are inclined to ignore or subvert the Fourth Amendment or that lawlessness among these actors requires application of the extreme sanction of exclusion." *United States v. Leon,* 468 U.S. _____, _____ (1984).

2.   "[T]he Fourth Amendment exclusionary rule should be modified so as not to bar the use in the prosecution's case-in-chief of evidence obtained by officers acting in reasonable reliance on a search warrant issued by a detached and neutral magistrate but ultimately found to be unsupported by probable cause." *United States v. Leon,* 468 U.S. _____, _____ (1984).

3.   "Suppression . . . remains an appropriate remedy if the magistrate or judge in issuing a warrant was misled by information in an affidavit that the affiant knew was false or would have known was false except for his reckless disregard of the truth. The exception. . .will also not apply in cases where the issuing magistrate wholly abandoned his judicial role; . . . in such circumstances, no reasonably well-trained officer should rely on the warrant. Nor would an officer manifest objective good faith in relying on a warrant based on an affidavit 'so lacking in indicia of probable cause as to render official belief in its existence entirely unreasonable.'" *United States v. Leon,* 468 U.S. _____, _____ (1984).

4.   "[D]espite the broad deterrent purpose of the exclusionary rule, it has never been interpreted to proscribe the introduction of illegally seized evidence in all proceedings or against all persons. As in the case of any remedial device, 'the application of the rule has been restricted to those areas where its remedial objectives are thought most

efficaciously served.' " *Stone v. Powell,* 428 U.S. 465, 486-87 (1976).

5. "[T]he Constitution guarantees a defendant the fullest opportunity to meet the accusation against him. He must be free to deny all the elements of the case against him without thereby giving leave to the Government to introduce by way of rebuttal evidence illegally secured by it, and therefore not available for its case in chief. Beyond that, however, there is hardly justification for letting the defendant affirmatively resort to perjurious testimony in reliance on the Government's disability to challenge his credibility." *Walder v. United States,* 347 U.S. 62, 65 (1954).

6. "[I]t does not follow from *Miranda [v. Arizona,* 384 U.S. 436 (1966)] that evidence inadmissible against Hass in the prosecution's case in chief is barred for all purposes, always provided that 'the trustworthiness of the evidence satisfies legal standards'.... [T]he shield provided by *Miranda* is not to be perverted to a license to testify inconsistently, or even perjuriously, free from the risk of confrontation with prior inconsistent utterances." *Oregon v. Hass,* 420 U.S. 714, 722 (1975).

7. "[A] defendant's statements made in response to proper cross-examination reasonably suggested by the defendant's direct examination are subject to otherwise proper impeachment by the government, albeit by evidence that has been illegally obtained that is inadmissible on the government's direct case, or otherwise, as substantive evidence of guilt." *United States v. Havens,* 446 U.S. 620, 627-28 (1980).

8. "Any incremental deterrent effect which might be achieved by extending the rule to grand jury proceedings is uncertain at best. Whatever deterrence of police miscon-

duct may result from the exclusion of illegally seized evidence from criminal trials, it is unrealistic to assume that application of the rule to grand jury proceedings would significantly further that goal. Such an extension would deter only police investigation consciously directed toward the discovery of evidence solely for use in a grand jury investigation. The incentive to disregard the requirement of the Fourth Amendment solely to obtain an indictment from a grand jury is substantially negated by the inadmissibility of the illegally seized evidence in a subsequent criminal prosecution of the search victim." *United States v. Calandra,* 414 U.S. 338, 351 (1974).

9.   "[W]here the State has provided an opportunity for full and fair litigation of a Fourth Amendment claim, a state prisoner may not be granted federal habeas corpus relief on the ground that evidence obtained in an unconstitutional search or seizure was introduced at his trial. In this context the contribution of the exclusionary rule, if any, to the effectuation of the Fourth Amendment is minimal and the substantial societal costs of application of the rule persist with special force." *Stone v. Powell,* 428 U.S. 465, 494-95 (1976).

10.   "[T]he supervisory power does not authorize a federal court to suppress otherwise admissible evidence on the ground that it was seized unlawfully from a third party not before the court. Our Fourth Amendment decisions have established beyond any doubt that the interest in deterring illegal searches does not justify the exclusion of tainted evidence at the instance of a party who was not the victim of the challenged practices." *United States v. Payner,* 447 U.S. 727, 735 (1980).

11.   "[W]e requested the parties to address an additional question: Whether the rule requiring the exclusion at a

criminal trial of evidence obtained in violation of the Fourth Amendment... should to any extent be modified, so as, for example, not to require the exclusion of evidence obtained in the reasonable belief that the search and seizure at issue was consistent with the Fourth Amendment. We decide today, with apologies to all, that the issue we framed for the parties was not presented to the Illinois courts and, accordingly, do not address it." *Illinois v. Gates,* 462 U.S. 213,____(1983).

12.   "The 'body' or identity of a defendant or respondent in a criminal or civil proceeding is never itself suppressible as a fruit of an unlawful arrest, even if it is conceded that an unlawful arrest, search, or interrogation occurred." *Immigration and Naturalization Service v. Lopez-Mendoza,* 468 U.S.____,____(1984).

13.   "Important as it is to protect the Fourth Amendment rights of all persons, there is no convincing indication that application of the exclusionary rule in civil deportation proceedings will contribute materially to that end." *Immigration and Naturalization Service v. Lopez-Mendoza,* 468 U.S.____,____(1984).

14.   "Henceforth in this circuit, when evidence is sought to be excluded because of police conduct leading to its discovery, it will be open to the proponent of the evidence to urge that the conduct in question, if mistaken or unauthorized, was yet taken in a reasonable, good-faith belief that it was proper. If the court so finds, it shall not apply the exclusionary rule to the evidence." *United States v. Williams,* 622 F.2d 830, 846-47 (5th Cir. 1980), *cert. denied,* 449 U.S. 1127 (1981).

15.   "[W]e reach this decision without embracing or rejecting the terms 'inevitable discovery' and 'good faith' as

exceptions to the exclusionary rule. In this complicated area, it is wiser to let the cases speak for themselves and to encourage careful analysis and argument than to endorse vague headings which add little to our understanding of the problems and which, because of their symbolic impact, may lead inadvertently to a weakening of the Fourth Amendment's protection. In various ways, the issues of causation and good faith will undoubtedly enter into the court's handling of the exclusionary rule. . . . But the law as it stands is flexible enough to accommodate the sound disposition of cases without '[t]he announcement of a radical change in the scope of the exclusionary rule [which] creates a host of interpretive problems.'" *United States v. Alvarez-Porras,* 643 F.2d 54, 60 (2d Cir.), *cert. denied,* 454 U.S. 839 (1981).

Chapter 2

Search

**A.   Scope of Protection: The Fourth Amendment pro-
hibition against unreasonable searches protects an
individual's legitimate expectation of privacy.**

1.   "A 'search' occurs when an expectation of privacy that
society is prepared to consider reasonable is infringed."
United States v. Jacobsen, 466 U.S.____,____(1984).

2.   "In assessing the degree to which a search infringes
upon individual privacy, the Court has given weight to such
factors as the intention of the Framers of the Fourth
Amendment,... the uses to which the individual has put a
location,... and our societal understanding that certain
areas deserve the most scrupulous protection from government invasion." *Oliver v. United States,* 466 U.S.____,
____(1984).

3.   "The Fourth Amendment protects legitimate expectations of privacy rather than simply places. If the inspection
by police does not intrude upon a legitimate expectation of
privacy, there is no 'search' subject to the Warrant
Clause." *Illinois v. Andreas,* 463 U.S. 765,____(1983).

4.   "[T]he Fourth Amendment protects people, not places.
What a person knowingly exposes to the public, even in his
own home or office, is not a subject of Fourth Amendment
protection.... But what he seeks to preserve as private,
even in an area accessible to the public, may be constitu-

tionally protected." *Katz v. United States,* 389 U.S. 347, 351-52 (1967).

5. "[C]apacity to claim the protection of the Fourth Amendment depends not upon a property right in the invaded place but upon whether the person who claims the protection of the Amendment has a legitimate expectation of privacy in the invaded place." *Rakas v. Illinois,* 439 U.S. 128, 143 (1978).

6. "[The] capacity to claim the protection of the Amendment depends not upon a property right in the invaded place but upon whether the area was one in which there was a reasonable expectation of freedom from governmental intrusion." *Mancusi v. DeForte,* 392 U.S. 364, 368 (1968).

7. "The person in legal possession of a good seized during an illegal search has not necessarily been subject to a Fourth Amendment deprivation. . . . [L]egal possession of a seized good is not a proxy for determining whether the owner had a Fourth Amendment interest, for it does not invariably represent the protected Fourth Amendment interest. This Court has repeatedly repudiated the notion that 'arcane distinctions developed in property tort law' ought to control our Fourth Amendment inquiry." *United States v. Salvucci,* 448 U.S. 83, 91 (1980).

8. "[T]he Fourth Amendment protects people, not places, and. . . police action which intrudes upon and invades an individual's justifiable expectation of privacy constitutes a search within the meaning of the Fourth Amendment." *United States v. Venema,* 563 F.2d 1003, 1006 (10th Cir. 1977).

9. "Three principles guide our inquiry. First, 'the Fourth Amendment protects people, not places'.... Thus, the question we must answer is not whether the room and closet were somehow 'private spaces' in the abstract, but whether [Defendant] had a reasonable expectation of privacy therein.... Second, a privacy interest, in the constitutional lexicon, consists of a reasonable expectation that uninvited and unauthorized persons will not intrude into a particular area. One may freely admit guests of one's choosing—or be legally obliged to admit specific persons—without sacrificing one's right to expect that a space will remain secure against all others.... Third, an expectation of privacy, strictly speaking, consists of a belief that uninvited people will not intrude *in a particular way.*" *United States v. Lyons,* 706 F.2d 321, 325-26 (D.C. Cir. 1983).

10. " 'Legitimation of expectations of privacy by law must have a source outside of the Fourth Amendment, either by reference to concepts of real or personal property law or to understandings that are recognized and permitted by society.' To identify which expectations merit fourth amendment protection, the courts have pointed to a number of factors. Most obvious among these is an individual's possessory or proprietary interest in the place or thing. However, a property right alone is not determinative.... 'Other factors to be weighed include whether the defendant has a possessory interest in the thing seized or the place searched, whether he has the right to exclude others from that place, whether he has exhibited a subjective expectation that it would remain free from governmental invasion, whether he took normal precautions to maintain his privacy and whether he was legitimately on the premises.' " *United States v. Cassity,* 720 F.2d 451, 456 (6th Cir. 1983).

11.   "[I]n order for the government to prove the constitutionality of its intrusion against an individual's claim of a violation of a reasonable expectation of privacy, it must demonstrate that: (1) the place where the intrusion occurred is one where the individual did not have a justified expectation of privacy; (2) the intrusion was not aided by mechanical or electronic means; and (3) the investigating officer was situated where an individual should anticipate that another person might have a right to be." *United States v. Mankani,* 738 F.2d 538, 544 (2d Cir. 1984).

B.   Test: The individual must exhibit an expectation of privacy which is reasonable.

1.   "[T]his Court uniformly has held that the application of the Fourth Amendment depends on whether the person invoking its protection can claim a 'justifiable,' a 'reasonable,' or a 'legitimate expectation of privacy' that has been invaded by government action.... This inquiry...normally embraces two discrete questions. The first is whether the individual, by his conduct, has 'exhibited an actual (subjective) expectation of privacy'.... The second question is whether the individual's subjective expectation of privacy is 'one that society is prepared to recognize as "reasonable,"' whether...the individual's expectation, viewed objectively, is 'justifiable' under the circumstances." *Smith v. Maryland,* 442 U.S. 735, 740 (1978).

2.   "We simply decline to use possession of a seized good as a substitute for a factual finding that the owner of the good had a legitimate expectation of privacy in the area searched." *United States v. Salvucci,* 448 U.S. 83, 92 (1980).

3.   "[T]here is a twofold requirement, first that a person have exhibited an actual (subjective) expectation of privacy and, second, that the expectation be one that society is prepared to recognize as 'reasonable.' Thus a man's home is, for most purposes, a place where he expects privacy, but objects, activities, or statements that he exposes to the 'plain view' of outsiders are not 'protected' because no intention to keep them to himself has been exhibited. On the other hand, conversations in the open would not be protected against being overheard, for the expectation of privacy under the circumstances would be unreasonable." *Katz v. United States,* 389 U.S. 347, 361 (1967) (Harlan, J., *concurring*).

4.   "While the agents' assertion of dominion and control over the package and its contents did constitute a 'seizure,' that seizure was not unreasonable. The fact that, prior to the field test, respondents' privacy interest in the contents of the package had been largely compromised is highly relevant to the reasonableness of the agents' conduct in this respect. The agents had already learned a great deal about the contents of the package from the Federal Express employees, all of which was consistent with what they could see. The package itself, which had previously been opened, remained unsealed, and the Federal Express employees had invited the agents to examine its contents. Under these circumstances, the package could no longer support any expectation of privacy." *United States v. Jacobsen,* 466 U.S.____,____(1984).

5.   "Although *Katz* recognized that the Fourth Amendment 'protects people, not places,' it is still necessary to consider the nature of the place—whether private or public, residential or commercial—in which legitimate privacy expectations are being asserted.... For instance,...'a man's home is, for most purposes, a place where he

expects privacy....' On the other hand,... '[i]t is a fair generalization...that business and commercial premises are not as private as residential premises, and that consequently there are various police investigative procedures which may be directed at such premises without the police conduct constituting a Fourth Amendment search.' " *United States v. Reed,* 733 F.2d 492, 500-01 (8th Cir. 1984).

6. "Much of the apparent force of the Government's argument is lost, however, when one takes into account the limited relevance of legal entitlements when identifying legitimate expectations of privacy. It has long been recognized that rights defined by positive law, though they sometimes figure in the constitutional calculus, do not control it.... The crucial factor is whether a person's expectations are founded on 'understandings that are recognized and permitted by society.'... The expectation that one's dwelling is secure from invasion by strangers surely is one that society is willing to recognize and respect." *United States v. Lyons,* 706 F.2d 321, 327 (D.C. Cir. 1983).

7. "The objection aspect [*sic*] of justifiable reliance, that the expectation be one recognized as reasonable by the current society, bars the bizarre, the freakish and the weird expectations.... The test applied as to society's tolerance of the search rests, as it has for years, upon 'the facts and circumstances—the total atmosphere of the case.' " *United States v. Fisch,* 474 F.2d 1071, 1077-78 (9th Cir.), *cert. denied,* 412 U.S. 921 (1973).

8. "When the defendant initially rented the locker he was advised by the manager of [the] [s]torage company that...from time to time she allowed the police on the premises and permitted them to use their dogs for the

purpose of detecting marijuana, and that should he store marijuana in his locker, he did so at his own risk. In view of such warning, ... the defendant is in poor position to assert that he had a justifiable expectation to privacy in the areaway outside his locker." *United States v. Venema,* 563 F.2d 1003, 1006 (10th Cir. 1977).

C. Exceptions: There are a number of intrusions which do not constitute searches protected by the Fourth Amendment.

1.   "It is ... beyond dispute that [the policeman's] action in shining his flashlight to illuminate the interior of [Defendant's] car trenched upon no right secured to the latter by the Fourth Amendment.... Numerous other courts have agreed that the use of artificial means to illuminate a darkened area simply does not constitute a search, and thus triggers no Fourth Amendment protection." *Texas v. Brown,* 460 U.S. 730, 739-40(1983).

2.   "[T]he particular course of investigation that the agents intended to pursue here—exposure of respondent's luggage, which was located in a public place, to a trained canine—did not constitute a 'search' within the meaning of the Fourth Amendment." *United States v. Place,* 462 U.S. 696,____(1983).

3.   "[D]id monitoring the beeper signals complained of by respondent invade any legitimate expectation of privacy on his part?... [W]e hold they did not. Since they did not, there was neither a 'search' nor a 'seizure' within the contemplation of the Fourth Amendment." *United States v. Knotts,* 460 U.S. 276, 285(1983).

4. "[P]etitioner in all probability entertained no actual expectation of privacy in the phone numbers he dialed, and ... even if he did, his expectation was not 'legitimate.' The installation and use of a pen register, consequently, was not a 'search,' and no warrant was required." *Smith v. Maryland,* 442 U.S. 735, 745-46 (1979).

5. "Respondent urges that he has a Fourth Amendment interest in the records kept by the banks. ... Even if we direct our attention to the original checks and deposit slips, rather than to the microfilm copies actually viewed and obtained by means of the subpoena, we perceive no legitimate 'expectation of privacy' in their contents." *United States v. Miller,* 425 U.S. 435, 442 (1976).

6. "[O]bservation of objects and activities inside a person's home by unenhanced vision from a location where the observer may properly be does not impair a legitimate expectation of privacy. However, any enhanced viewing of the interior of a home does impair a legitimate expectation of privacy and encounters the Fourth Amendment's warrant requirement, unless circumstances create a traditional exception to that requirement." *United States v. Taborda,* 635 F.2d 131, 139 (2d Cir. 1980).

7. "A specific exception to the Fourth Amendment's warrant and probable cause requirements is that a search conducted pursuant to a valid consent is constitutionally permissible. ... Once consent has been obtained from one with authority to give it, any expectation of privacy has been lost." *United States v. Rubio,* 727 F.2d 786, 796, 797 (9th Cir. 1984).

8. "An individual has no legitimate expectation that the person to whom he is speaking will not relate the conversation to the legal authorities, either by repetition or by the

recording of the conversation." *United States v. Haimowitz,* 725 F.2d 1561, 1582 (11th Cir. 1984).

9.   "Permissible techniques of surveillance include more than the five senses of officers and their unaided physical abilities. Binoculars, dogs that track and sniff out contraband, searchlights, fluorescent powders, automobiles and airplanes, burglar alarms, radar devices, and bait money contribute to surveillance without violation of the Fourth Amendment in the usual case. On the other hand, wiretaps, breaking and entering, and many other searches and seizures fall on the other side of the line." *United States v. Dubrofsky,* 581 F.2d 208, 211 (9th Cir. 1978).

10.   "[D]iscovery of evidence does not constitute a 'search' within the meaning of the Fourth Amendment if an officer, standing in a place where he has a right to be, merely sees what is in plain view before him." *United States v. Finnegan,* 568 F.2d 637, 640 (9th Cir. 1977).

11.   "Because no one owns or possesses abandoned property, no one can claim a Fourth Amendment interest in it. . . . The very notion of abandonment. . .implies a renunciation of any reasonable expectation of privacy." *United States v. Alden,* 576 F.2d 772, 777 (8th Cir.), *cert. denied,* 439 U.S. 855 (1978).

12.   "Although the expectations [of privacy] test has done away with outmoded property concepts no longer satisfactory for fourth amendment analysis. . . the distinction between open fields and curtilage is still helpful in determining the existence or not of reasonable privacy expectations." *United States v. Williams,* 581 F.2d 451, 453 (5th Cir. 1978), *cert. denied,* 440 U.S. 972 (1979).

13.   "[T]he search of these packages was a private one, conducted by the air carrier's employees without government intervention, and is therefore not subject to the Fourth Amendment." *United States v. Gumerlock,* 590 F.2d 794, 796 (9th Cir.) (en banc), *cert. denied,* 441 U.S. 948 (1979).

Chapter 3

Seizure

A. Significance: Once a seizure of a person occurs, Fourth Amendment protections are invoked.

1. "It is quite plain that the Fourth Amendment governs 'seizures' of the person...." *Terry v. Ohio,* 392 U.S. 1, 16 (1968).

2. "If there is no detention—no seizure within the meaning of the Fourth Amendment—then no constitutional rights have been infringed." *Florida v. Royer,* 460 U.S. 276, 285(1983).

3. "The simple language of the [Fourth] Amendment applies equally to seizures of persons and to seizures of property." *Payton v. New York,* 445 U.S. 573, 585 (1980).

4. "[D]etention of the respondent against his will constituted a seizure of his person, and the Fourth Amendment guarantee of freedrom from 'unreasonable searches and seizures' is clearly implicated." *Cupp v. Murphy,* 412 U.S. 291, 294 (1973).

5. "The first tier of police-citizen encounters involves no restraint of the liberty of the citizen involved, but rather, the voluntary cooperation of the citizen is elicited through non-coercive questioning. This type of contact does not rise to the level of a seizure and therefore is outside the realm of fourth amendment protection. The second category, the investigative stop, is limited to brief, non-intrusive detention

during a frisk for weapons or preliminary questioning. This type of encounter is considered a 'seizure' sufficient to invoke fourth amendment safeguards, but because of its less intrusive character requires only that the stopping officer have specific and articulable facts sufficient to give rise to reasonable suspicion that a person has committed or is committing a crime. The third type of police-citizen encounters, arrests, are [*sic*] characterized by highly intrusive or lengthy search or detention. The fourth amendment requires that an arrest be justified by probable cause to believe that a person has committed or is committing a crime." *United States v. Armstrong*, 722 F.2d 681, 684 (11th Cir. 1984).

B. Test: A person has been seized if, under the totality of the circumstances, a reasonable person would not believe himself free to go.

1. "It is quite plain that the Fourth Amendment governs 'seizures' of the person which do not eventuate in a trip to the station house and prosecution for crime—'arrests' in the traditional terminology.... Only when the officer, by means of physical force or show of authority, has in some way restrained the liberty of a citizen may we conclude that a 'seizure' has occurred." *Terry v. Ohio*, 392 U.S. 1, 16, 19 n.16 (1968).

2. "[I]t is submitted that the entire encounter was consensual and hence [Defendant] was not being held against his will at all. We find this submission untenable. Asking for and examining [Defendant's] ticket and his driver's license were no doubt permissible in themselves, but when the officers identified themselves as narcotics agents, told [him] that he was suspected of transporting narcotics, and

asked him to accompany them to the police room, while retaining his ticket and driver's license and without indicating in any way that he was free to depart, [Defendant] was effectively seized for the purposes of the Fourth Amendment. These circumstances surely amount to a show of official authority such that 'a reasonable person would have believed he was not free to leave.'" *Florida v. Royer,* 460 U.S.491, 501-02 (1983).

3.   "We conclude that a person has been 'seized' within the meaning of the Fourth Amendment only if, in view of all of the circumstances surrounding the incident, a reasonable person would have believed that he was not free to leave. Examples of circumstances that might indicate a seizure, even where the person did not attempt to leave, would be the threatening presence of several officers, the display of a weapon by an officer, some physical touching of the person of the citizen, or the use of language or tone of voice indicating that compliance with the officer's request might be compelled .... In the absence of some such evidence, otherwise inoffensive contact between a member of the public and the police cannot, as a matter of law, amount to a seizure of that person." *United States v. Mendenhall,* 446 U.S. 544, 554-55 (1980).

4.   "What is apparent from [*Florida v.*] *Royer* [460 U.S. 491 (1983)] and *Brown* [*v. Texas,* 443 U.S. 47 (1979)] is that police questioning, by itself, is unlikely to result in a Fourth Amendment violation. While most citizens will respond to a police request, the fact that people do so, and do so without being told they are free not to respond, hardly eliminates the consensual nature of the response....Unless the circumstances of the encounter are so intimidating as to demonstrate that a reasonable person would have believed he was not free to leave if he had not responded, one cannot say that the questioning resulted in

a detention under the Fourth Amendment. But if the person refuses to answer and the police take additional steps...then the Fourth Amendment imposes some minimal level of objective justification to validate the detention or seizure." *Immigration and Naturalization Service v. Delgado,* ____U.S.____,____(1984).

5. "[The test is] whether, under the totality of the circumstances, a reasonable person would have thought he was not free to leave.... [D]etermination of whether such freedom of choice exists involves a 'refined judgment,' especially when no force, physical restraint, or blatant show of authority is involved.... This judgment may involve looking at matters as nebulous as the tone of an officer's question." *United States v. Lara,* 638 F.2d 892, 896 (5th Cir. 1981).

6. "[*United States v.*] *Berry* [670 F.2d 583 (5th Cir. 1982)] points to some specific factors that may indicate whether a police-citizen contact is consensual or a seizure. Blocking a citizen's path or impeding his progress is an indicator that a seizure has occurred. Similarly, retaining his ticket or identification may indicate a seizure if his freedom is thereby restrained. An officer's statement that the individual is the focus of an investigation or that a truly innocent person would cooperate with police tends to indicate lack of consent and therefore a seizure. The Supreme Court has suggested still other factors: the suspect's age, education and intelligence; the length of the suspect's detention and questioning; the number of police officers present; the display of weapons; any physical touching of the suspect; and the language and tone of voice of the police." *United States v. Puglisi,* 723 F.2d 779, 783 (11th Cir. 1984).

7. "[A] request by police that a suspect accompany them to a separate office raises the presumption of a seizure:

'Only exceptionally clear evidence of consent should overcome a presumption that a person requested to accompany an agent to an office no longer would feel free to leave.'" *United States v. Waksal,* 709 F. 2d 653, 659 (11th Cir. 1983).

C. Justification to Seize—Arrest: An arrest or its functional equivalent must be based on probable cause.

1. "[T]he general rule [is] that every arrest, and every seizure having the essential attributes of a formal arrest, is unreasonable unless it is supported by probable cause." *Michigan v. Summers,* 452 U.S. 692, 700 (1981).

2. "[T]he general rule [is] that seizures of the person require probable cause to arrest." *Florida v. Royer,* 460 U.S. 491, 499 (1983).

3. "Nothing is more clear than that the Fourth Amendment was meant to prevent wholesale intrusions upon the personal security of our citizenry, whether these intrusions be termed 'arrests' or 'investigatory detentions.'" *Davis v. Mississippi,* 394 U.S. 721, 726-27 (1969).

4. "[D]etention for custodial interrogation—regardless of its label—intrudes so severely on interests protected by the Fourth Amendment as necessarily to trigger the traditional safeguards against illegal arrest." *Dunaway v. New York,* 442 U.S. 200, 216 (1979).

5. "[T]he entry into a home to conduct a search or make an arrest is unreasonable under the Fourth Amendment

unless done pursuant to a warrant." *Steagald v. United States,* 451 U.S. 204, 211 (1981).

6. "[P]robable cause to arrest [Defendant] did not exist at the time he consented to the search of his luggage. The facts are that a nervous young man with two American Tourister bags paid cash for an airline ticket to a 'target city.' These facts led to inquiry, which in turn revealed that the ticket had been bought under an assumed name. The proffered explanation did not satisfy the officers. We cannot agree with the State, if this is its position, that every nervous young man paying cash for a ticket to New York City under an assumed name and carrying two heavy American Tourister bags may be arrested and held to answer for a serious felony charge." *Florida v. Royer,* 460 U.S. 491, 507(1983).

7. "Requiring an individual to accompany police to an office indicates a detention for a time period longer than that permitted in a seizure; cuts the individual off from the outside world, without indication of when he might be allowed to leave; places him in unfamiliar surroundings; may subject him to increased implicit police pressure; and leaves him without third parties to confirm his story of events that may have occurred, should his story differ from that of police. Such a detention, if not by consent—and, as we noted earlier, courts should scrutinize exceptionally closely whether consent in fact was voluntary in such situations—we believe is only constitutional if accompanied by probable cause." *United States v. Berry,* 670 F.2d 583, 602 (5th Cir. 1982).

8. "[A]n investigative stop does not become an arrest merely because the detaining officer directs the subject out of a vehicle. Nor does an officer's display of a weapon necessarily convert an investigative stop into an arrest."

United States v. Aldridge, 719 F.2d 368, 371 (11th Cir. 1983).

D.   Justification to Seize—Stop: A stop must be based on reasonable suspicion.

1.   "[A] police officer may in appropriate circumstances and in an appropriate manner approach a person for purposes of investigating possible criminal behavior even though there is no probable cause to make an arrest." *Terry v. Ohio,* 392 U.S. 1, 22 (1968).

2.   "[T]he Court...acknowledge[s] the authority of the police to make a *forcible stop* of a person when the officer has reasonable, articulable suspicion that the person has been, is, or is about to be engaged in criminal activity." *United States v. Place,* 462 U.S. 696, ____(1983).

3.   "[N]ot all seizures of the person must be justified by probable cause to arrest for a crime.... [C]ertain seizures are justifiable under the Fourth Amendment if there is articulable suspicion that a person has committed or is about to commit a crime.... Detentions may be 'investigative' yet violative of the Fourth Amendment absent probable cause. In the name of investigating a person who is no more than suspected of criminal activity, the police may not carry out a full search of the person or of his automobile or other effects. Nor may the police seek to verify their suspicions by means that approach the conditions of arrest." *Florida v. Royer,* 460 U.S. 491, 498(1983).

4.   "The Fourth Amendment applies to seizures of the person, including brief investigatory stops such as the stop of the vehicle here.... An investigatory stop must be

justified by some objective manifestation that the person stopped is, or is about to be, engaged in criminal activity." *United States v. Cortez,* 449 U.S. 411, 417 (1981).

5.   "When the officers detained appellant for the purpose of requiring him to identify himself, they performed a seizure of his person subject to the requirements of the Fourth Amendment.... In the absence of any basis for suspecting appellant of misconduct, the balance between the public interest and appellant's right to personal security and privacy tilts in favor of freedom from police interference." *Brown v. Texas,* 443 U.S. 47, 50 (1979).

6.   "[T]he Fourth Amendment allows a properly limited 'search' or 'seizure' on facts that do not constitute probable cause to arrest or to search for contraband or evidence of crime.... [W]hen an officer's observations lead him reasonably to suspect that a particular vehicle may contain aliens who are illegally in the country, he may stop the car briefly and investigate the circumstances that provoke suspicion." *United States v. Brignoni-Ponce,* 422 U.S. 873, 881 (1975).

7.   "An investigatory stop, allowable on the mere suspicion of criminal activity, must be limited in scope and duration. The importance of these requirements cannot be overstated for it is the limited and transitory nature of the stop that justifies the elimination of the probable cause requirement typically accompanying fourth amendment seizures." *United States v. Ilazi,* 730 F.2d 1120, 1125 (8th Cir. 1984).

8.   "The legality of an investigatory stop depends on (1) the nature and extent of the government's need for the stop, which must be judged according to the importance of its law enforcement interests under the circumstances, and

(2) the reasonableness of the stop, which depends mainly on the degree of police intrusion on the defendants' freedom of movement.... The longer and more intrusive the stop, the stronger must be the justification for it." *United States v. Pelusio,* 725 F.2d 161, 165 (2d Cir. 1983).

9. "[T]he degree of intrusiveness of stops that do not rise to the level of arrests may vary, and in order to be lawful in a given case it must be proportional to the degree of suspicion that prompted the intrusion. When little or no suspicion exists, therefore, very little intrusion is tolerable." *United States v. Berryman,* 717 F.2d 651, 657 (1st Cir. 1983), *cert. denied,* ____U.S. ____ (1984).

E. Justification to Seize—Lesser Intrusions: Some restrictions on a person's freedom of movement are permitted in the absence of probable cause or reasonable suspicion.

1. "[F]or Fourth Amendment purposes, we hold that a warrant to search for contraband founded on probable cause implicitly carries with it the limited authority to detain the occupants of the premises while a proper search is conducted.... [I]t was lawful to require respondent to re-enter and to remain in the house until evidence establishing probable cause to arrest him was found...." *Michigan v. Summers,* 452 U.S. 692, 705 (1981).

2. "Against this important interest [officer safety] we are asked to weigh the intrusion into the driver's personal liberty occasioned not by the initial stop of the vehicle, which was admittedly justified, but by the order to get out of the car. We think this additional intrusion can only be described as *de minimis.* The driver is being asked to

expose to view very little more of his person than is already exposed. The police have already lawfully decided that the driver shall be briefly detained; the only question is whether he shall spend that period sitting in the driver's seat of his car or standing alongside it. Not only is the insistence of the police on the latter choice not a 'serious intrusion upon the sanctity of the person,' but it hardly rises to the level of a 'petty indignity.' . . . What is at most a mere inconvenience cannot prevail when balanced against legitimate concerns for the officer's safety." *Pennsylvania v. Mimms,* 434 U.S. 106, 111 (1977).

3. "[A] requirement that stops on major routes inland always be based on reasonable suspicion would be impractical because the flow of traffic tends to be too heavy to allow the particularized study of a given car that would enable it to be identified as a possible carrier of illegal aliens. . . . While the need to make routine checkpoint stops is great, the consequent intrusion on Fourth Amendment interests is quite limited. . . . Accordingly, we hold that the stops and questioning at issue may be made in the absence of any individualized suspicion at reasonably located checkpoints." *United States v. Martinez-Fuerte,* 428 U.S. 543, 557, 562 (1976).

4. "[T]he Fourth Amendment is [not] offended when Customs officials, acting pursuant to this statute and without any suspicion of wrongdoing, board for inspection of documents a vessel that is located in waters providing ready access to the open sea." *United States v. Villamonte-Marquez,* 462 U.S. 579, ____(1983).

5. "[It is possible that] the requirements of the Fourth Amendment could be met by narrowly circumscribed procedures for obtaining, during the course of a criminal investigation, the fingerprints of individuals for whom there

is no probable cause to arrest." *Davis v. Mississippi,* 394 U.S. 721, 728 (1969).

F.   Non-Seizures: Some encounters between civilians and police do not constitute seizures.

1.   "Obviously, not all personal intercourse between policemen and citizens involves 'seizures' of persons. Only when the officer, by means of physical force or show of authority, has in some way restrained the liberty of a citizen may we conclude that a 'seizure' has occurred." *Terry v. Ohio,* 392 U.S. 1, 19 n.16 (1968).

2.   "[L]aw enforcement officers do not violate the Fourth Amendment by merely approaching an individual on the street or in another public place, by asking him if he is willing to answer some questions, by putting questions to him if the person is willing to listen, or by offering in evidence in a criminal prosecution his voluntary answers to such questions.... Nor would the fact that the officer identifies himself as a police officer, without more, convert the encounter into a seizure requiring some level of objective justification.... The person approached, however, need not answer any question put to him; indeed, he may decline to listen to the questions at all and may go on his way.... He may not be detained even momentarily without reasonable, objective grounds for doing so; and his refusal to listen or answer does not, without more, furnish those grounds." *Florida v. Royer,* 460 U.S. 491, 497, 498 (1983).

3.   "We conclude that a person has been 'seized' within the meaning of the Fourth Amendment only if, in view of all of the circumstances surrounding the incident, a reason-

able person would have believed that he was not free to leave. Examples of circumstances that might indicate a seizure, even where the person did not attempt to leave, would be the threatening presence of several officers, the display of a weapon by an officer, some physical touching of the person of the citizen, or the use of language or tone of voice indicating that compliance with the officer's request might be compelled .... In the absence of some such evidence, otherwise inoffensive contact between a member of the public and the police cannot, as a matter of law, amount to a seizure of that person." *United States v. Mendenhall,* 446 U.S. 544, 554-55 (1980).

4.   "[A]irport stops of individuals by police, if of extremely restricted scope and conducted in a completely non-coercive manner, do not invoke the Fourth Amendment. The interest of the government in terminating drug smuggling is, on the one hand, very substantial. The toll on our society in lives made wretched, in costs to citizens, and in profits of gross size funnelled to the most odious criminals, is staggering.... Considering on the other hand the intrusion on the individual, we believe that an airport stop need not necessarily be of so coercive a nature that communication with police cannot be voluntary. We find it possible, at least under certain circumstances, for no significant intrusion to occur." *United States v. Berry,* 670 F.2d 583, 594-95 (5th Cir. 1982).

G. Seizure of Personal Property: Personal property may be subject to a limited warrantless seizure if there is reasonable suspicion that it contains seizable items.

1.   "A 'seizure' of property occurs when there is some meaningful interference with an individual's possessory

interests in that property." *United States v. Jacobsen,* 466 U.S._____,_____(1984).

2.   "In the ordinary case, the Court has viewed a seizure of personal property as *per se* unreasonable within the meaning of the Fourth Amendment unless it is accomplished pursuant to a judicial warrant issued upon probable cause and particularly describing the items to be seized. . . . Where law enforcement authorities have probable cause to believe that a container holds contraband or evidence of a crime, but have not secured a warrant, the Court has interpreted the Amendment to permit seizure of the property, pending issuance of a warrant to examine its contents, if the exigencies of the circumstances demand it or some other recognized exception to the warrant requirement is present." *United States v. Place,* 462 U.S. 696, _____ (1983).

3.   "[I]t is. . .well settled that objects such as weapons or contraband found in a public place may be seized by the police without a warrant. The seizure of property in plain view involves no invasion of privacy and is presumptively reasonable, assuming that there is probable cause to associate the property with criminal activity." *Payton v. New York,* 445 U.S. 573, 586-87 (1980).

4.   "[T]he Government asks us to recognize the reasonableness under the Fourth Amendment of warrantless seizures of personal luggage from the custody of the owner on the basis of less than probable cause, for the purpose of pursuing a limited course of investigation, short of opening the luggage, that would quickly confirm or dispel the authorities' suspicion. Specifically, we are asked to apply the principles of *Terry v. Ohio,* [392 U.S. 1 (1969)], to permit such seizures on the basis of reasonable, articulable suspicion, premised on objective facts, that the luggage

contains contraband or evidence of a crime. In our view, such application is appropriate." *United States v. Place,* 462 U.S. 696, _____ (1983).

5. "Given the fact that seizures of property can vary in intrusiveness, some brief detentions of personal effects may be so minimally intrusive of Fourth Amendment interests that strong countervailing governmental interests will justify a seizure based only on specific articulable facts that the property contains contraband or evidence of a crime." *United States v. Place,* 462 U.S. 696, _____(1983).

6. "[W]hen the police seize luggage from the suspect's custody, we think the limitations applicable to investigative detentions of the person should define the permissible scope of an investigative detention of the person's luggage on less than probable cause. Under this standard, it is clear that the police conduct here exceeded the permissible limits of a *Terry*-type investigative stop. The length of the detention of respondent's luggage alone precludes the conclusion that the seizure was reasonable in the absence of probable cause." *United States v. Place,* 462 U.S. 696, _____ (1983).

7. "[W]here officers, having probable cause, enter premises, and with probable cause, arrest the occupants who have legitimate possessory interests in its contents and take them into custody and, for no more than the period here involved, secure the premises from within to preserve the status quo while others, in good faith, are in the process of obtaining a warrant, they do not violate the Fourth Amendment's proscription against unreasonable seizures." *Segura v. United States,* 468 U.S. _____,_____ (1984).

H. Seizure of Homes: A dwelling may be secured while a search warrant is obtained.

1.   "As we have noted, however, a seizure affects only possessory interests, not privacy interests. Therefore, the heightened protection we accord privacy interests is simply not implicated where a *seizure* of premises, not a search, is at issue. We hold, therefore, that securing a dwelling, on the basis of probable cause, to prevent the destruction or removal of evidence while a search warrant is being sought is not itself an unreasonable seizure of either the dwelling or its contents." *Segura v. United States,* 468 U.S.____, ____(1984).

2.   "Securing of the premises from within, however, was no more an interference with the petitioners' possessory interests in the contents of the apartment than a perimeter 'stakeout.' In other words, the intial entry—legal or not— does not affect the reasonableness of the seizure. Under either method—entry and securing from within or a perime- ter stakeout—agents control the apartment pending arrival of the warrant; both an internal securing and a perimeter stakeout interfere to the same extent with the possessory interests of the owners." *Segura v. United States,* 468 U.S.____,____(1984).

Chapter 4

Arrest

A.   Definition: An individual has been arrested when he is not free to go, whether or not formal words of arrest are used.

1.   "Nothing is more clear than that the Fourth Amendment was meant to prevent wholesale intrusions upon the personal security of our citizenry, whether these intrusions be termed 'arrests' or 'investigatory detentions.'" *Davis v. Mississippi,* 394 U.S. 721, 726-27 (1969).

2.   "The officers had [Defendant's] ticket, they had his identification, and they had seized his luggage. [He] was never informed that he was free to board his plane if he so chose, and he reasonably believed that he was being detained. At least as of that moment, any consensual aspects of the encounter had evaporated. . . . As a practical matter, [Defendant] was under arrest. Consistent with this conclusion, the State conceded. . .that [Defendant] would not have been free to leave the interrogation room had he asked to do so." *Florida v. Royer,* 460 U.S. 491, 503 (1983).

3.   "[D]etention for custodial interrogation—regardless of its label—intrudes so severely on interests protected by the Fourth Amendment as necessarily to trigger the traditional safeguards against illegal arrest." *Dunaway v. New York,* 442 U.S. 200, 216 (1979).

4. "[W]here the defendant is transported to the police station and placed in a cell or interrogation room he has been arrested, even if the purpose of the seizure is investigatory rather than accusatory. Because such a seizure constitutes an arrest, it must be supported by probable cause." *Gonzales v. City of Peoria,* 722 F.2d 468, 477 (9th Cir. 1983).

5. "[T]he determination of whether an arrest has occurred for Fourth Amendment purposes does not depend upon whether the officers announced that they were placing the suspects under arrest.... An action tantamount to arrest has taken place if the officers' conduct is more intrusive than necessary for an investigative stop." *United States v. Rose,* 731 F.2d 1337, 1342 (8th Cir. 1984).

6. "[W]hen [the agent] requested [Defendant] to come with him to the Delta office, the interrogation could no longer be characterized as 'brief' or 'on-the-spot.' Rather, the request signaled the beginning of a more extended interrogation which was to occur in a place other than where it began. Second, ... [Defendant] was never informed that he was 'free to go,' and the circumstances surrounding the request indicate that [he] would have been physically restrained if he had refused to accompany [the agent] or had tried to escape his custody. Third, ...the circumstances indicate that the detention involved here was for the purpose of interrogation. In sum, the scope of the intrusion involved in [the agent's] request for [Defendant] to accompany him to the Delta office was significantly greater than that involved in a brief *Terry* stop, and therefore amounted to an arrest." *United States v. Hill,* 626 F.2d 429, 435-36 (5th Cir. 1980).

7. "Even if we were to find the initial stop of appellants to have been justified, the following detention of appellants

clearly went beyond the scope of *Terry,* which justifies only a very limited detention 'reasonably related in scope to the justification for [its] initiation'. . . . Appellants were not free to leave at any point after the initial stop by the agents. . . . 'It does not take formal words of arrest or booking at a police station to complete an arrest. . . .' When appellants were taken to the private office and were not free to leave, the arrest was clearly complete." *United States v. McCaleb,* 552 F.2d 717, 720 (6th Cir. 1977).

B. Standard: An arrest must be based on probable cause.

1. "[T]he general rule [is] that every arrest, and every seizure having the essential attributes of a formal arrest, is unreasonable unless it is supported by probable cause." *Michigan v. Summers,* 452 U.S. 692, 700 (1981).

2. "Where the standard is probable cause, a search or seizure of a person must be supported by probable cause particularized with respect to that person. This requirement cannot be undercut or avoided by simply pointing to the fact that coincidentally there exists probable cause to search or seize another or to search the premises where the person may happen to be." *Ybarra v. Illinois,* 444 U.S. 85, 91 (1979).

3. " '[P]robable cause' to justify an arrest means facts and circumstances within the officer's knowledge that are sufficient to warrant a prudent person, or one of reasonable caution, in believing, in the circumstances shown, that the suspect has committed, is committing, or is about to commit an offense." *Michigan v. DeFillippo,* 443 U.S. 31, 37 (1979).

4.   "[G]ood faith on the part of the arresting officers is not enough. Probable cause exists if the facts and circumstances known to the officer warrant a prudent man in believing that the offense has been committed." *Henry v. United States,* 361 U.S. 98, 102 (1959).

5.   "[P]robable cause to arrest [Defendant] did not exist at the time he consented to the search of his luggage. The facts are that a nervous young man with two American Tourister bags paid cash for an airline ticket to a 'target city.' These facts led to inquiry, which in turn revealed that the ticket had been bought under an assumed name. The proffered explanation did not satisfy the officers. We cannot agree with the State, if this is its position, that every nervous young man paying cash for a ticket to New York City under an assumed name and carrying two heavy American Tourister bags may be arrested and held to answer for a serious felony charge." *Florida v. Royer,* 460 U.S.491, 507(1983).

6.   "In order for an officer to have probable cause to make an arrest without a warrant it is not necessary that he have personal knowledge of all items of information which taken together constitute probable cause. The court looks to the collective knowledge and information of all of the officers involved." *United States v. Rose,* 541 F.2d 750, 756 (8th Cir. 1976), *cert. denied,* 430 U.S. 908 (1977).

7.   "Although flight alone will not provide probable cause [to believe] that a crime is being committed, in appropriate circumstances it can supply the 'key ingredient justifying the decision of a law enforcement officer to take action.' 'Flight invites pursuit and colors conduct' that might otherwise appear innocent." *United States v. Bowles,* 625 F.2d 526, 535 (5th Cir. 1980).

8. "Any facts developing after arrest cannot relate back to legitimize an arrest already made without probable cause." *Riley v. Wyrick,* 712 F.2d 382, 387 (8th Cir. 1983).

9. [W]hen state officers arrest for a federal crime, the legality of the arrest is determined by the law of the state in which the arrest takes place, subject to federal constitutional standards." *United States v. Mahoney,* 712 F.2d 956, 958 (5th Cir. 1983).

C. Arrests in Public Places: A warrant is not required to arrest in a public place, even if obtaining one was feasible.

1. "[I]f probable cause exists, no warrant is required to apprehend a suspected felon in a public place." *Steagald v. United States,* 451 U.S. 204, 221 (1981).

2. "[A] warrantless arrest in a public place is valid if the arresting officer had probable cause to believe the suspect is a felon." *Payton v. New York,* 445 U.S. 573, 590 (1980).

3. "Law enforcement officers may find it wise to seek arrest warrants where practicable to do so, and their judgments about probable cause may be more readily accepted where backed by a warrant issued by a magistrate. . . . But we decline to transform this judicial preference into a constitutional rule when the judgment of the Nation and Congress has for so long been to authorize warrantless public arrests on probable cause. . . ." *United States v. Watson,* 423 U.S. 411, 423 (1976).

4. "[W]arrantless arrests based on probable cause and made in a public place are permissible under the Fourth

Amendment." *United States v. Costa,* 691 F.2d 1358, 1361 (11th Cir. 1982).

D.   Arrests in Homes: An arrest warrant is required to make a routine felony arrest in a residence.

1.   "[T]he Fourth Amendment to the United States Constitution ...prohibits the police from making a warrantless and nonconsensual entry into a suspect's home in order to make a routine felony arrest .... [T]he Fourth Amendment has drawn a firm line at the entrance to the house. Absent exigent circumstances, that threshold may not reasonably be crossed without a warrant...." *Payton v. New York,* 445 U.S. 573, 576, 590 (1980).

2.   "[T]he Fourth Amendment prohibits the police from making a warrantless and nonconsensual entry into a suspect's home to make a routine felony arrest." *United States v. Johnson,* 457 U.S. 537, 538-39 (1982).

3.   "In the absence of exigent circumstances, we have consistently held that...judicially untested determinations are not reliable enough to justify an entry into a person's home to arrest him without a warrant, or a search of a home for objects in the absence of a search warrant.... We see no reason to depart from this settled course when the search of a home is for a person rather than an object. A contrary conclusion—that the police, acting alone and in the absence of exigent circumstances, may decide when there is sufficient justification for searching the home of a third party for the subject of an arrest warrant—would create a significant potential for abuse." *Steagald v. United States,* 451 U.S. 204, 213-15 (1981).

4. "It is axiomatic that 'the physical entry of the home is the chief evil against which the wording of the Fourth Amendment is directed.' And a principal protection against unnecessary intrusions into private dwellings is the warrant requirement imposed by the Fourth Amendment on agents of the government who seek to enter the home for purposes of search or arrest." *Welsh v. Wisconsin,* 466 U.S.____,____(1984).

5. "The existence of probable cause to arrest, however, does not justify entering a suspect's home without either consent or a warrant.... [A] warrantless forcible entry to effect an arrest is impermissible unless required by exigent circumstances." *United States v. Gray,* 626 F.2d 102, 105 (9th Cir. 1980).

6. "[W]arrantless entries to effect an arrest of a third person are unreasonable absent exigent circumstances or consent." *United States v. Collazo,* 732 F.2d 1200, 1204 (4th Cir. 1984).

E. Exigent Circumstances: Hot pursuit of fleeing suspects justifies warrantless arrests in homes.

1. " '[H]ot pursuit' means some sort of a chase, but it need not be an extended hue and cry 'in and about [the] public streets.' The fact that the pursuit here ended almost as soon as it began did not render it any the less a 'hot pursuit' sufficient to justify the warrantless entry into [Defendant's] house. Once [Defendant] saw the police, there was likewise a realistic expectation that any delay would result in destruction of evidence.... [A] suspect may not defeat an arrest which has been set in motion in a

public place...by the expedient of escaping to a private place." *United States v. Santana,* 427 U.S. 38, 43 (1976).

2. "[There is] no element of 'hot pursuit' in the arrest of one who was not in flight, was completely surrounded by agents before she knew of their presence, who claims without denial that she was in bed at the time, and who made no attempt to escape." *Johnson v. United States,* 333 U.S. 10, 16 n.7 (1948).

3. "[T]he nature of the underlying offense is an important factor to be considered in the exigent-circumstances calculus... [I]t is difficult to conceive of a warrantless home arrest that would not be unreasonable under the Fourth Amendment when the underlying offense is extremely minor. We therefore conclude that the commonsense approach utilized by most lower courts is required by the Fourth Amendment prohibition on 'unreasonable searches and seizures,' and hold that an important factor to be considered when determining whether any exigency exists is the gravity of the underlying offense for which the arrest is being made." *Welsh v. Wisconsin,* 466 U.S.____,____ (1984).

4. "[W]here a warrantless arrest in a private dwelling is challenged, the government has the burden of proving that exigent circumstances existed at the time which justified such an arrest.... The most common examples of exigent circumstances are the hot-pursuit, fleeing-suspect, and destruction-of-evidence cases.... [T]he following factors [are] relevant in a fleeing-suspect case: (1) the gravity of the offense committed; (2) the belief that the suspect was armed; and (3) the likelihood that the suspect would escape in the absence of swift police action." *United States v. Williams,* 612 F.2d 735, 739 (3d Cir. 1979), *cert. denied,* 445 U.S. 934 (1980).

5.   "The ultimate test is whether there is such a compelling necessity for immediate action as will not brook the delay of obtaining a warrant." *United States v. Adams,* 621 F.2d 41, 44 (1st Cir. 1980).

F.   Entering Homes After Arrests: Police may accompany an arrested person into his home after a lawful arrest.

1.   "[I]t is not 'unreasonable' under the Fourth Amendment for a police officer, as a matter of routine, to monitor the movements of an arrested person, as his judgment dictates, following the arrest. The officer's need to ensure his own safety—as well as the integrity of the arrest—is compelling." *Washington v. Chrisman,* 455 U.S. 1, 7 (1982).

2.   "Here, the officer had placed [Defendant] under lawful arrest, and therefore was authorized to accompany him to his room for the purpose of obtaining identification." *Washington v. Chrisman,* 455 U.S. 1, 6 (1982).

3.   "Law enforcement officers who have lawfully apprehended a suspect on a portion of a structure (here it was an open porch built as a part of the home) which they have reason to believe contains dangerous third persons who might pose a threat to their safety have a right to conduct a reasonable security check of such premises." *United States v. Burgos,* 720 F.2d 1520, 1526 (11th Cir. 1983).

4.   "We know of no principle of Fourth Amendment law that would forbid [the Agent] who had made...a lawful arrest from maintaining custody of [the Defendant] during a peaceful entry into the house where [Defendant] lived while

the latter found his passport." *United States v. Rodriguez,*
532 F.2d 834, 838 (2d Cir. 1976).

5. "[S]earch warrants are directed against evidence of
crime and not persons. The fact that there is probable
cause to arrest a person for a crime does not automatically
give police probable cause to search his residence or other
area in which he has been observed for evidence of that
crime." *United States v. Savoca,* 739 F.2d 220, 225 (6th
Cir. 1984).

Chapter 5

Search Warrant Requirements

A. Issuance: The warrant must be issued by a disinterested magistrate.

1. "[I]nferences [must] be drawn by a neutral and detached magistrate instead of being judged by the officer engaged in the often competitive enterprise of ferreting out crime." *Johnson v. United States,* 333 U.S. 10, 14 (1948).

2. "[T]he participation of a detached magistrate in the probable-cause determination is an essential element of a reasonable search or seizure...." *Steagald v. United States,* 451 U.S. 204, 216 (1981).

3. "A magistrate failing to 'manifest that neutrality and detachment demanded of a judicial officer when presented with a warrant application' and who acts instead as 'an adjunct law enforcement officer' cannot provide valid authorization for an otherwise unconstitutional search." *United States v. Leon,* 468 U.S.____,____(1984).

4. "[T]he Town Justice did not manifest that neutrality and detachment demanded of a judicial officer when presented with a warrant application for a search and seizure.... [H]e was not acting as a judicial officer but as an adjunct law-enforcement officer." *Lo-Ji Sales, Inc. v. New York,* 442 U.S. 319, 326-27 (1979).

5. "The justice is not salaried. He is paid, so far as search warrants are concerned... for his *issuance* of the warrants

and he receives nothing for *denial* of the warrant.... [T]he issuance of the search warrant by the justice of the peace ...effected a violation of...the Fourth and Fourteenth Amendments...." *Connally v. Georgia*, 429 U.S. 245, 250-51 (1977).

6.   "Inherent in the concept of a warrant is its issuance by a neutral and detached magistrate.... [T]he Fourth Amendment does not contemplate the executive officers of Government as neutral and disinterested magistrates." *United States v. U.S. District Court*, 407 U.S. 297, 316-17 (1972).

7.   "[T]he state official who was the chief investigator and prosecutor in this case...was not the neutral and detached magistrate required by the Constitution." *Coolidge v. New Hampshire*, 403 U.S. 443, 453 (1971).

8.   "[A] neutral and detached magistrate is inserted between the government's agents and the object of the search. It is the magistrate's duty to hold the balance steady between the protection of individual privacy on the one hand and the public need to recover evidence of wrongdoing on the other. The magistrate should first satisfy himself as to the adequacy and reliability of the facts set forth in the application before him." *United States v. Travisano,* 724 F.2d 341, 345 (2d Cir. 1983).

9.   "Unlike officers in the field, a magistrate is not entitled to rely on the judgment of law enforcement officials. He or she is expected to review the material submitted and make a detached, independent judgment as to the existence of probable cause." *United States v. Davis,* 714 F.2d 896, 900 (9th Cir. 1983).

B. Standard: The magistrate must find probable cause that the place to be searched contains items connected with criminal activity.

1. "[A]n officer may not properly issue a warrant to search...unless he can find probable cause therefor from facts or circumstances presented to him under oath or affirmation." *Nathanson v. United States*, 290 U.S. 41, 47 (1933).

2. "A search warrant...is issued upon a showing of probable cause to believe that the legitimate object of a search is located in a particular place, and therefore safeguards an individual's interest in the privacy of his home and possessions against the unjustified intrusion of the police." *Steagald v. United States*, 451 U.S. 204, 213 (1981).

3. "[T]he grounds for a search must satisfy objective standards which ensure that the invasion of personal privacy is justified by legitimate governmental interests.... The governmental interests to be served in the detection or prevention of crime are subject to traditional standards of probable cause to believe that incriminating evidence will be found." *Torres v. Puerto Rico*, 442 U.S. 465, 471 (1979).

4. "The validity of a search warrant depends upon the sufficiency of what is found within the four corners of the underlying affidavit. An affidavit is sufficient if it establishes probable cause; that is, if the stated facts would reasonably allow a magistrate to believe that the evidence will be found in the stated location." *United States v. Taylor,* 716 F.2d 701, 705 (9th Cir. 1983).

5. "In determining probable cause the magistrate is not required to determine whether *in fact* the items to be

searched for are located at the premises to be searched, but only whether there is *reasonable ground* to believe [that] they are there." *United States v. Solario*, 577 F.2d 554, 555 (9th Cir. 1978).

6. "An affidavit need only 'enable the magistrate to conclude that it would be reasonable to seek the evidence in the place indicated by the affidavit. The nexus between the place to be searched and the items to be seized may be established by the type of crime, the nature of the items, and the normal inferences where a criminal would likely hide [the evidence].'" *United States v. Jacobs,* 715 F.2d 1343, 1346 (9th Cir. 1983).

C. Probable Cause Defined: Probable cause is supplied by evidence which would lead a reasonable person to believe that an offense has been or is being committed.

1. "[T]he term 'probable cause,' according to its usual acceptation, means less than evidence which would justify condemnation; and, in all cases of seizure, has a fixed and well known meaning. It imports a seizure made under circumstances which warrant suspicion." *Locke v. United States*, 7 Cranch 339, 348 (1813).

2. "[Probable cause] mean[s] more than bare suspicion: Probable cause exists where 'the facts and circumstances within their [the officers'] knowledge and of which they had reasonably trustworthy information [are] sufficient in themselves to warrant a man of reasonable caution in the belief that' an offense has been or is being committed." *Brinegar v. United States*, 338 U.S. 160, 175 (1949).

3. "If the facts and circumstances before the officer are such as to warrant a man of prudence and caution in believing that the offense has been committed, it is sufficient." *Stacey v. Emery*, 97 U.S. 642, 645 (1878).

4. "[P]robable cause is a flexible, common-sense standard. It merely requires that the facts available to the officer would 'warrant a man of reasonable caution in the belief'...that certain items may be contraband or stolen property or useful as evidence of a crime; it does not demand any showing that such belief be correct or more likely true than false. A 'practical, nontechnical' probability that incriminating evidence is involved is all that is required." *Texas v. Brown,* 460 U.S. 730, 742 (1983).

5. "[P]robable cause is a fluid concept—turning on the assessment of probabilities in particular factual contexts—not readily, or even usefully, reduced to a neat set of legal rules.... While an effort to fix some general, numerically precise degree of certainty corresponding to 'probable cause' may not be helpful, it is clear that 'only the probability, and not a prima facie showing, of criminal activity is the standard of probable cause.'" *Illinois v. Gates,* 462 U.S. 213,____(1983).

6. "[P]robable cause is the sum total of layers of information and the synthesis of what the police have heard, what they know, and what they observe as trained officers. We weigh not individual layers but the 'laminated' total. It has often been repeated, but it bears repetition, that 'In dealing with probable cause,...as the very name implies, we deal with *probabilities.* These are not technical; they are the factual and practical considerations of everyday life on which reasonable and prudent men, not legal technicians, act.'" *Smith v. United States,* 358 F.2d 833, 837 (D.C. Cir. 1966), *cert. denied,* 386 U.S. 1008 (1969).

**D. Description: The warrant must describe with suffi-
cient particularity the person or the place to be
searched and the items to be seized.**

1. "The requirement that warrants shall particularly describe the things to be seized...prevents the seizure of one
thing under a warrant describing another. As to what is to
be taken, nothing is left to the discretion of the officer
executing the warrant." *Marron v. United States*, 275 U.S.
192, 196 (1927).

2. "[W]arrants must particularly describe the 'things to be
seized,' as well as the place to be searched." *Dalia v.
United States*, 441 U.S. 238, 255 (1979).

3. "The warrant...[requires] a 'particular description' of
things to be seized." *Coolidge v. New Hampshire*, 403 U.S.
443, 467 (1971).

4. "Where the standard is probable cause, a search or
seizure of a person must be supported by probable cause
particularized with respect to that person." *Ybarra v.
Illinois*, 444 U.S. 85, 91 (1979).

5. "[T]he warrant left it entirely to the discretion of the
officials conducting the search to decide what items were
likely obscene and to accomplish their seizure. The Fourth
Amendment does not permit such action.... Nor does the
Fourth Amendment countenance open-ended warrants, to
be completed while a search is being conducted and items
seized or after the seizure has been carried out." *Lo-Ji
Sales, Inc. v. New York*, 442 U.S. 319, 325 (1979).

6. "In the instant case, the warrant did not relate the
documents sought to any particular offense, individual
transaction, or even to a specific provision of the U.S.

Code. We therefore hold that the search warrant, having no particularity in its description of the records to be searched and seized, constituted a general warrant violating the fourth amendment." *In re Grand Jury Proceedings,* 716 F.2d 493, 499 (8th Cir. 1983).

7. "When a police officer conducting a valid search inadvertently comes across an article not specified in the warrant, but one nevertheless having an incriminating character, it is well established that he may seize that article as well as any others that are specified in the warrant." *United States v. Jefferson,* 714 F.2d 689, 694 (7th Cir. 1983).

8. "A search warrant must contain a description of the place to be searched. The place must be described with sufficient particularity as to enable the executing officer to locate and identify it with reasonable effort. Such specificity is required in order to avoid any reasonable probability that another place might mistakenly be searched." *United States v. Alberts,* 721 F.2d 636, 639 (8th Cir. 1983).

E. Showing: To enable the magistrate to make an independent evaluation, the affidavit must contain more than mere conclusions.

1. "An affidavit must provide the magistrate with a substantial basis for determining the existence of probable cause, and [a] wholly conclusory statement fail[s] to meet this requirement. . . . Sufficient information must be presented to the magistrate to allow that official to determine probable cause; his action cannot be a mere ratification of the bare conclusions of others." *Illinois v. Gates,* 462 U.S. 213, _____(1983).

2. "Under the Fourth Amendment, an officer may not properly issue a warrant to search a private dwelling unless he can find probable cause therefor from facts or circumstances presented to him under oath or affirmation. Mere affirmance of belief or suspicion is not enough." *Nathanson v. United States*, 290 U.S. 41, 47 (1933).

3. "The Commissioner must judge for himself the persuasiveness of the facts relied on by a complaining officer to show probable cause. He should not accept without question the complainant's mere conclusion that the person whose arrest is sought has committed a crime.... The complaint contains no affirmative allegation that the affiant spoke with personal knowledge of the matters contained therein; it does not indicate any sources for the complainant's belief; and it does not set forth any other sufficient basis upon which a finding of probable cause could be made." *Giordenello v. United States*, 357 U.S. 480, 486 (1958).

4. "This is not to say that probable cause can be made out by affidavits which are purely conclusory, stating only the affiant's or an informer's belief that probable cause exists without detailing any of the 'underlying circumstances' upon which that belief is based." *United States v. Ventresca*, 380 U.S. 102, 108-09 (1965).

5. "The affidavit need only establish the *probability* of criminal activity and presence of evidence on specific premises, not proof beyond a reasonable doubt. It is not required that the affidavit allege direct observation of criminal activity in order to justify the issuance of a warrant." *United States v. Packer,* 730 F.2d 1151, 1155 (8th Cir. 1984).

6. "To credit a confidential source's information in making a probable cause determination, the affidavit should support an inference that the source was trustworthy and that the source's accusation of criminal activity was made on the basis of information obtained in a reliable way." *United States v. Landis,* 726 F.2d 540, 543 (9th Cir.), *cert. denied,* _____ U.S. _____ (1984).

F. Hearsay: A warrant may issue based on affidavits containing only hearsay when the totality of the circumstances presented to the magistrate constitutes probable cause.

1. "[W]e conclude that it is wiser to abandon the 'two-pronged test' established by our decisions in *Aguilar*[1] and *Spinelli.*[2] In its place we reaffirm the totality of the circumstances analysis that traditionally has informed probable cause determinations.... The task of the issuing magistrate is simply to make a practical, common-sense decision whether, given all the circumstances set forth in the affidavit before him, including the 'veracity' and 'basis of knowledge' of persons supplying hearsay information,

---

[1] "[T]he magistrate must be informed of some of the underlying circumstances from which the informant concluded that the [seizable items] were where he claimed they were, and...from which the officer concluded that the informant...was 'credible' or his information 'reliable.'" *Aguilar v. Texas,* 378 U.S. 108, 114 (1964).

[2] "In the absence of a statement detailing the manner in which the information was gathered, it is especially important that the [informant] describe the accused's criminal activity in sufficient detail that the magistrate may know that he is relying on something more substantial than a casual rumor...." *Spinelli v. United States,* 393 U.S. 410, 416 (1969).

there is a fair probability that contraband or evidence of a crime will be found in a particular place. And the duty of a reviewing court is simply to ensure that the magistrate had a 'substantial basis for...conclud[ing]' that probable cause existed." *Illinois v. Gates,* 462 U.S. 213, ____(1983).

2. "Moreover, the 'two-pronged test' directs analysis into two largely independent channels—the informant's 'veracity' or 'reliability' and his 'basis of knowledge'.... There are persuasive arguments against according these two elements such independent status. Instead they are better understood as relevant considerations in the totality of circumstances analysis that traditionally has guided probable cause determinations: a deficiency in one may be compensated for, in determining the overall reliability of a tip, by a strong showing as to the other, or by some other indicia of reliability." *Illinois v. Gates*, 462 U.S. 213, ____ (1983).

3. "It is enough, for purposes of probable cause, that 'corroboration through other sources of information reduced the chances of a reckless or prevaricating tale,' thus providing 'a substantial basis' for crediting the hearsay." *Illinois v. Gates,* 462 U.S. 213, ____ (1983).

4. "In *Gates,* we did not merely refine or qualify the 'two-pronged test.' We rejected it as hypertechnical and divorced from 'the factual and practical considerations of everyday life on which reasonable and prudent men, not legal technicians, act.'" *Massachusetts v. Upton,* 466 U.S.____,____(1984).

5. "Although an informant's 'veracity' and 'basis of knowledge' are no longer to be 'understood as entirely separate and independent requirements to be rigidly exacted...in every case,' they are still 'highly relevant' in determining

whether probable cause existed. . . . When information is received from an 'identified bystander or victim-eyewitness to a crime,' we have held that such a non-professional informant's reliability need not be established in the officer's affidavit. The rationale for the victim or bystander exception is that the statements of such eyewitnesses will presumably be based on their own observations and thus are not likely to reflect 'idle rumor or irresponsible conjecture.' . . .' "[W]hen an average citizen tenders information to the police, the police should be permitted to assume that they are dealing with a credible person *in the absence of special circumstances suggesting that such might not be the case.*' " *United States v. Phillips,* 727 F.2d 392, 395, 397 (5th Cir. 1984).

G.   Staleness: An affidavit for a search warrant must present timely information, and the warrant must be promptly executed.

1.   "While the statute does not fix the time within which proof of probable cause must be taken by the judge or commissioner, it is manifest that the proof must be of facts so closely related to the time of the issue of the warrant as to justify a finding of probable cause at that time. Whether the proof meets this test must be determined by the circumstances of each case. It is in the light of the requirement that probable cause must properly appear when the warrant issues that we must read the provision which in explicit terms makes a warrant void unless executed within ten days after its date. That period marks the permitted duration of the proceeding in which the warrant is issued. There is no provision which authorizes the commissioner to extend its life or to revive it." *Sgro v. United States,* 287 U.S. 206, 210-11 (1932).

2. "It remains a fundamental principal of search and seizure law that information furnished in an application for a search warrant must be timely, and that probable cause must be found to exist 'at the time the warrant issues'.... A warrant application based upon stale information of previous misconduct is insufficient, because it fails to create probable cause that similar or other improper conduct is continuing to occur.... No mechanical test exists for determining when information becomes fatally stale; rather, 'staleness is an issue which must be decided on the peculiar facts of each case.'" *United States v. Bascaro,* 742 F.2d 1335, 1345 (11th Cir. 1984).

3. "Unreasonable delay in the execution of a warrant that results in the lapse of probable cause will invalidate a warrant.... These limitations exist to ensure 'the speediest possible execution of search warrants,'...and to lessen the possibility that the facts underlying the warrant may change.... The restrictions, however, not only ensure that probable cause continues to exist, but also that it is the neutral magistrate, not the executing officers, who determines whether probable cause continues to exist." *United States v. Marin-Buitrago,* 734 F.2d 889, 894 (2d Cir. 1984).

4. "Cases in which staleness becomes an issue arise in two different contexts. First, the facts alleged in the warrant may have been sufficient to establish probable cause when the warrant was issued, but the government's delay in executing the warrant possibly tainted the search. Second, the warrant itself may be suspect because the information on which it rested was arguably too old to furnish 'present' probable cause.... When, as here, however, the criminal activity alleged in the warrant is not ongoing in nature, nor the evidence sought intrinsically likely to remain at the location where it was originally observed, indicia external to the evidence itself should demonstrate that probable cause

has not lapsed." *United States v. McCall,* 740 F.2d 1331, 1336, 1337 (4th Cir. 1984).

5. "In general, the basic criterion as to the duration of probable cause is the inherent nature of the crime. The Circuits hold that where an affidavit recites a mere isolated violation then it is not unreasonable to believe that probable cause quickly dwindles with the passage of time. On the other hand, if an affidavit recites activity indicating protracted or continuous conduct, time is of less significance." *Bastida v. Henderson,* 487 F.2d 860, 864 (5th Cir. 1973).

H. Execution: The method of entry to execute a warrant must be lawful.

1. "[T]he method of entering the home may offend federal constitutional standards of reasonableness and therefore vitiate the legality of an accompanying search." *Ker v. California,* 374 U.S. 23, 38 (1963).

2. "[T]he Government claims no extraordinary circumstances—such as imminent destruction of vital evidence, or the need to rescue a victim in peril—...which excused the officer's failure truthfully to state his mission before he broke in." *Wong Sun v. United States,* 371 U.S. 471, 484 (1963).

3. "The requirement of prior notice of authority and purpose before forcing entry into a home is deeply rooted in our heritage and should not be given grudging application. Congress, codifying a tradition embedded in Anglo-American law, has declared in [18 U.S.C.] §3109 the reverence of the law for the individual's right of privacy in

his house. Every householder, the good and the bad, the guilty and the innocent, is entitled to the protection designed to secure the common interest against unlawful invasion of the house. The petitioner could not be lawfully arrested in his home by officers breaking in without first giving him notice of their authority and purpose." *Miller v. United States,* 357 U.S. 301, 313 (1958).

4. "An unannounced intrusion into a dwelling—what [18 U.S.C.] §3109 basically proscribes—is no less an unannounced intrusion whether officers break down a door, force open a chain lock on a partially open door, open a locked door by use of a passkey, or, as here, open a closed but unlocked door. The protection afforded by, and the values inherent in, §3109 must be 'governed by something more than the fortuitous circumstance of an unlocked door.'" *Sabbath v. United States,* 391 U.S. 585, 590 (1968).

5. "[L]aw officers constitutionally may break and enter to execute a search warrant where such entry is the only means by which the warrant effectively may be executed." *Dalia v. United States,* 441 U.S. 238, 247 (1979).

6. "We think that a person's right to privacy in his home (and the limitation of authority to a searching police officer) is governed by something more than the fortuitous circumstance of an unlocked door, and that the word 'break,' as used in 18 U.S.C. §3109, means 'enter without permission.' We think that a 'peaceful' entry which does not violate the provisions of §3109 must be a permissive one, and not merely one which does not result in a breaking of parts of the house." *Keiningham v. United States,* 287 F.2d 126, 130 (D.C. Cir. 1960).

7. "The interval of time an officer must wait between announcement and entry depends on the circumstances of each case.... When police have properly knocked and announced their identity and purpose, mild exigency is sufficient to justify simultaneous entry when entry can be accomplished without physical destruction of property. Mild exigency may exist where there is a likelihood that the occupants will try to escape, resist, or destroy evidence. More specific inferences of exigency are necessary if entry may be obtained only by the physical destruction of property; an explicit refusal of admittance or lapse of a significant amount of time is necessary if the officers have no facts indicating exigency." *United States v. McConney,* 728 F.2d 1195, 1206 (9th Cir. 1984), U.S. appeal pending.

8. "The statutory language...excuses preliminary notice 'when [entry is] necessary to liberate [the officer] or person aiding him in the execution of the warrant.' In addition...the Supreme Court has apparently approved three other exceptions: '(1) Where the persons within already know of the officers' authority and purpose, or (2) where the officers are justified in the belief that persons within are in imminent peril of bodily harm, or (3) where those within, made aware of the presence of someone outside (because, for example, there has been a knock at the door) are then engaged in activity which justifies the officers in the belief that an escape or the destruction of evidence is being attempted....' [Also] 'a police officer's reasonable belief that announcement might place him or his associates in physical peril' would excuse compliance with the statute." *United States v. Nolan,* 718 F.2d 589, 596 (3d Cir. 1983).

I. Standard of Review: The decision of the magistrate to issue a warrant must be examined with great

deference to see if there was a substantial basis for the finding of probable cause.

1. "[A]ffidavits for search warrants...must be tested and interpreted by magistrates and courts in a commonsense and realistic fashion.... A grudging or negative attitude by reviewing courts toward warrants will tend to discourage police officers from submitting their evidence to a judicial officer before acting. [W]hen a magistrate has found probable cause, the courts should not invalidate the warrant by interpreting the affidavit in a hypertechnical, rather than a commonsense, manner. Although in a particular case it may not be easy to determine when an affidavit demonstrates the existence of probable cause, the resolution of doubtful or marginal cases in this area should be largely determined by the preference to be accorded to warrants." *United States v. Ventresca,* 380 U.S. 102, 108-09 (1965).

2. "[A]fter-the-fact scrutiny by courts of the sufficiency of an affidavit should not take the form of *de novo* review. A magistrate's 'determination of probable cause should be paid great deference by reviewing courts.'... [S]o long as a magistrate had a 'substantial basis for...conclud[ing]' that a search would uncover evidence of wrongdoing, the Fourth Amendment requires no more." *Illinois v. Gates,* 462 U.S. 213,____(1983).

3. "[A] reviewing court is not to conduct a *de novo* determination of probable cause, but only to determine whether there is substantial evidence in the record supporting the magistrate's decision to issue the warrant." *Massachusetts v. Upton,* 466 U.S.____,____ (1984).

4. "Deference to the magistrate, however, is not boundless. It is clear, first, that the deference accorded to a

magistrate's finding of probable cause does not preclude inquiry into the knowing or reckless falsity of the affidavit on which that determination was based." *United States v. Leon,* 468 U.S.____,____(1984).

5. "Even if the warrant application was supported by more than a 'bare bones' affidavit, a reviewing court may properly conclude that, notwithstanding the deference that magistrates deserve, the warrant was invalid because the magistrate's probable-cause determination reflected an improper analysis of the totality of the circumstances...or because the form of the warrant was improper in some respect." *United States v. Leon,* 468 U.S.____,____(1984).

6. "While a reviewing court should 'not serve merely as a rubber stamp for the police,' it is firmly established that substantial deference should be accorded judicial determinations of probable cause.... '[I]n a close case any doubts should be resolved in favor of upholding the warrant....' It is against this backdrop of substantial deference to judicial findings of probable cause that we must view the district court's holding." *United States v. Zucco,* 694 F.2d 44, 46 (2d Cir. 1982).

7. "[C]ourts 'evince a strong preference for searches made pursuant to warrant, and, in some instances, may sustain them where warrantless searches based on a police officer's evaluation of probable cause might fail.'" *United States v. Doty,* 714 F.2d 761, 763 (8th Cir. 1983).

8. "Once a magistrate has made a determination on the issue of probable cause, our analysis shifts to the function of the reviewing court. Its after-the-fact examination of the papers is not to be *de novo* review. It should start with the proposition that the magistrate's finding of probable cause is entitled to substantial deference. In fact, a search based

upon a magistrate's determination will be upheld by a reviewing court on less persuasive evidence that would have justified a police officer acting on his own. Further, the magistrate's finding of probable cause is itself a substantial factor tending to uphold the validity of this warrant. This is particularly true in close cases where doubts should be resolved in favor of upholding the warrant. Having viewed the papers in light of these precepts and having accorded great deference to the magistrate's finding of probable cause, it remains for the reviewing court to decide whether the magistrate performed his neutral and detached function on the facts before him, and did not merely serve as a rubber stamp for conclusions drawn by the police." *United States v. Travisano,* 724 F.2d 341, 345 (2d Cir. 1983).

9. "To promote neutral and objective determination of the necessity to invade people's privacy, law enforcement officials should be encouraged to seek warrants. . . . One of the best ways to foster increased use of warrants is to give law enforcement officials the assurance that when a warrant is obtained in a close case, its validity will be upheld. . . ." *United States v. Lewis,* 392 F.2d 377, 379 (2d Cir.), *cert. denied,* 393 U.S. 891 (1968).

J. False Affidavits: The defendant is entitled to a hearing on specific allegations of deliberate or reckless material false statements in the affidavits upon which a search warrant was issued.

1. "[W]here the defendant makes a substantial preliminary showing that a false statement knowingly and intentionally, or with reckless disregard for the truth, was included by the affiant in the warrant affidavit, and if the allegedly false statement is necessary to the finding of

probable cause, the Fourth Amendment requires that a hearing be held at the defendant's request...." *Franks v. Delaware,* 438 U.S. 154, 155-56 (1978).

2. " '[W]hen the Fourth Amendment demands a factual showing sufficient to comprise "probable cause," the obvious assumption is that there will be a *truthful* showing' ... This does not mean 'truthful' in the sense that every fact recited in the warrant affidavit is necessarily correct, for probable cause may be founded upon hearsay and upon information received from informants, as well as upon information within the affiant's own knowledge that sometimes must be garnered hastily. But surely it is to be 'truthful' in the sense that the information put forth is believed or appropriately accepted by the affiant as true." *Franks v. Delaware,* 438 U.S. 154, 164-65 (1978).

3. "There is, of course, a presumption of validity with respect to the affidavit supporting the search warrant. To mandate an evidentiary hearing, the challenger's attack must be more than conclusory and must be supported by more than a mere desire to cross-examine. There must be allegations of deliberate falsehood or of reckless disregard for the truth, and those allegations must be accompanied by an offer of proof. They should point out specifically the portion of the warrant affidavit that is claimed to be false; and they should be accompanied by a statement of supporting reasons. Affidavits or sworn or otherwise reliable statements of witnesses should be furnished, or their absence satisfactorily explained. Allegations of negligence or innocent mistake are insufficient. The deliberate falsity or reckless disregard whose impeachment is permitted today is only that of the affiant, not of any nongovernmental informant. Finally, if these requirements are met, and if, when material that is the subject of the alleged falsity or reckless disregard is set to one side, there remains

sufficient content in the warrant affidavit to support a finding of probable cause, no hearing is required. On the other hand, if the remaining content is insufficient, the defendant is entitled, under the Fourth and Fourteenth Amendments, to his hearing. Whether he will prevail at that hearing is, of course, another issue." *Franks v. Delaware,* 438 U.S. 154, 171-72 (1978).

4. "Suppression...remains an appropriate remedy if the magistrate or judge in issuing a warrant was misled by information in an affidavit that the affiant knew was false or would have known was false except for his reckless disregard of the truth." *United States v. Leon,* 468 U.S.____,____(1984).

5. "By failing properly to identify their sources of information the affiants...made it impossible for the magistrate to evaluate the existence of probable cause. *Franks* teaches that when, as in this case, that failure is intentional the warrant must be invalidated. The fact that probable cause did exist and could have been established by a truthful affidavit does not cure the error.... While under *Franks* a warrant based upon a false affidavit may be upheld if the falsity was not material, the government in using such an affidavit runs the risk that a reviewing court may subsequently determine ' "that a truthful answer would have been of sufficient probative importance to the inquiry so that, as a minimum, further fruitful investigation would have occurred." ' " *United States v. Davis,* 714 F.2d 896, 899, 900 (9th Cir. 1983).

6. "We acknowledge that the rationale of *Franks* applies to omissions and that several courts have permitted litigants to challenge affidavits on the ground that facts were omitted.... [T]he omitted fact must be material—that is, if the fact were included, the affidavit would not support

a finding of probable cause." *United States v. Williams*, 737 F.2d 594, 604 (7th Cir. 1984).

7. "This court has embraced the doctrine of severance, which allows us to strike from a warrant those portions that are invalid and preserve those portions that satisfy the fourth amendment. Only those articles seized pursuant to the invalid portions need be suppressed." *United States v. Gamez-Soto*, 723 F.2d 649, 654 (9th Cir.), *cert. denied,* ____U.S.____(1984).

K.   Remedy: Where an officer reasonably relies on a warrant which is subsequently determined to be invalid, the evidence seized normally will not be suppressed.

1.   "[T]he Fourth Amendment exclusionary rule should be modified so as not to bar the use in the prosecution's case-in-chief of evidence obtained by officers acting in reasonable reliance on a search warrant issued by a detached and neutral magistrate but ultimately found to be unsupported by probable cause." *United States v. Leon*, 468 U.S.____,____(1984).

2.   "[T]he exclusionary rule is designed to deter police misconduct rather than to punish the errors of judges and magistrates. . . . [T]here exists no evidence suggesting that judges and magistrates are inclined to ignore or subvert the Fourth Amendment or that lawlessness among these actors requires application of the extreme sanction of exclusion." *United States v. Leon*, 468 U.S.____,____ (1984).

3. "In the absence of an allegation that the magistrate abandoned his detached and neutral role, suppression is appropriate only if the officers were dishonest or reckless in preparing their affidavit or could not have harbored an objectively reasonable belief in the existence of probable cause." *United States v. Leon,* 468 U.S.____,____(1984).

4. "[A] warrant may be so facially deficient—i.e., in failing to particularize the place to be searched or the things to be seized—that the executing officers cannot reasonably presume it to be valid." *United States v. Leon,* 468 U.S.____,____(1984).

5. "The exception. . .will also not apply in cases where the issuing magistrate wholly abandoned his judicial role in the manner condemned in *Lo-Ji Sales*. . .; in such circumstances, no reasonably well-trained officer should rely on the warrant. Nor would an officer manifest objective good faith in relying on a warrant based on an affidavit 'so lacking in indicia of probable cause as to render official belief in its existence entirely unreasonable.'" *United States v. Leon,* 468 U.S.____,____(1984).

Chapter 6

Warrantless Searches

A. Presumption: A warrantless search is presumed to be unreasonable.

1. "It is a first principle of Fourth Amendment jurisprudence that the police may not conduct a search unless they first convince a neutral magistrate that there is probable cause to do so." *New York v. Belton*, 453 U.S. 454, 457 (1981).

2. "[S]earches conducted outside the judicial process, without prior approval by judge or magistrate, are *per se* unreasonable under the Fourth Amendment—subject only to a few specifically established and well delineated exceptions." *Katz v. United States*, 389 U.S. 347, 357 (1967).

3. "The search . . . without a warrant . . . can survive constitutional inhibition only upon a showing that the surrounding facts brought it within one of the exceptions to the rule that a search must rest upon a search warrant." *Stoner v. California*, 376 U.S. 483, 486 (1964).

4. "Any assumption that evidence sufficient to support a magistrate's disinterested determination to issue a search warrant will justify the officers in making a search without a warrant would reduce the [Fourth] Amendment to a nullity and leave the people's homes secure only in the discretion of police officers." *Johnson v. United States*, 333 U.S. 10, 14 (1948).

5. "[T]here is no more basic constitutional rule in the Fourth Amendment area than that which makes a warrantless search *unreasonable* except in a few 'jealously and carefully drawn' exceptional circumstances." *United States v. Anderson*, 533 F.2d 1210, 1216 (D.C. Cir. 1976).

6. "Although the homicide investigators in this case may well have had probable cause to search the premises, it is undisputed that they did not obtain a warrant. Therefore, for the search to be valid, it must fall within one of the narrow and specifically delineated exceptions to the warrant requirement. In *Mincey v. Arizona*, we unanimously rejected the contention that one of the exceptions to the warrant clause is a 'murder scene exception.' Although we noted that police may make warrantless entries on premises where 'they reasonably believe that a person within is in need of immediate aid,' and that 'they may make a prompt warrantless search of the area to see if there are other victims or if a killer is still on the premises,' we held that 'the "murder scene exception"...is inconsistent with the Fourth and Fourteenth Amendments.'" *Thompson v. Louisiana*, ____U.S. ____, ____(1984).

B.   Burden of Proof: The prosecution must establish the validity of a warrantless search.

1. "We cannot be true to that constitutional requirement and excuse the absence of a search warrant without a showing by those who seek exemption from the constitutional mandate that the exigencies of the situation made that course imperative." *McDonald v. United States*, 335 U.S. 451, 456 (1948).

2. "[T]he burden is on those seeking the exemption to show the need for it." *United States v. Jeffers*, 342 U.S. 48, 51 (1951).

3. "The government bears a heavy burden when it seeks to justify warrantless arrests and searches." *United States v. Coker*, 599 F.2d 950, 950-51 (10th Cir. 1979).

4. "[T]he burden is on those seeking an exemption [to the requirement that a search warrant must be obtained] to show the need for the exemption. . . . [T]he general requirement that a search warrant be obtained is not to be lightly dispensed with." *United States v. Baca*, 417 F.2d 103, 106 (10th Cir. 1969), *cert. denied,* 404 U.S. 979 (1971).

C. Exceptions: Many exceptions to the warrant requirement have been recognized. Their elements are set forth in subsequent chapters.

1. "Since warrantless searches of a home are impermissible absent consent or exigent circumstances, we conclude that the instant search violated the Fourth Amendment." *Steagald v. United States*, 451 U.S. 204, 216 (1981).

2. "[A] few 'jealously and carefully drawn' exceptions provide for those cases where the societal costs of obtaining a warrant, such as danger to law officers or the risk of loss or destruction of evidence, outweigh the reasons for prior recourse to a neutral magistrate." *Arkansas v. Sanders*, 442 U.S. 753, 759 (1979).

3. "[O]ur past decisions make clear that only in 'a few specifically established and well-delineated' situations

...may a warrantless search of a dwelling withstand constitutional scrutiny, even though the authorities have probable cause to conduct it.... There is no suggestion that anyone consented to the search.... The officers were not responding to an emergency.... They were not in hot pursuit of a fleeing felon.... The goods ultimately seized were not in the process of destruction.... Nor were they about to be removed from the jurisdiction...." *Vale v. Louisiana*, 399 U.S. 30, 34-35 (1970).

Chapter 7

Searches Incident to Arrest

A. Scope: A search incident to a lawful arrest is permissible but must be limited in scope.

1. "[I]mmediately upon arrest an officer may lawfully search the person of an arrestee...; he may also search the area within the arrestee's immediate control...." *Illinois v. Lafayette,* 462 U.S. 640, _____ (1983).

2. "When an arrest is made, it is reasonable for the arresting officer to search the person arrested in order to remove any weapons that the latter might seek to use in order to resist arrest or effect his escape. Otherwise, the officer's safety might well be endangered, and the arrest itself frustrated. In addition, it is entirely reasonable for the arresting officer to search for and seize any evidence on the arrestee's person in order to prevent its concealment or destruction. And the area into which an arrestee might reach in order to grab a weapon or evidentiary items must, of course, be governed by a like rule. A gun on a table or in a drawer in front of one who is arrested can be as dangerous to the arresting officer as one concealed in the clothing of the person arrested. There is ample justification, therefore, for a search of the arrestee's person and the area 'within his immediate control'—construing that phrase to mean the area from within which he might gain possession of a weapon or destructible evidence." *Chimel v. California*, 395 U.S. 752, 762-63 (1969).

3.   "The authority to search the person incident to a lawful custodial arrest, while based upon the need to disarm and to discover evidence, does not depend on what a court may later decide was the probability in a particular arrest situation that weapons or evidence would in fact be found upon the person of the suspect. A custodial arrest of a suspect based on probable cause is a reasonable intrusion under the Fourth Amendment; that intrusion being lawful, a search incident to the arrest requires no additional justification." *United States v. Robinson*, 414 U.S. 218, 235 (1973).

4.   "[C]ontemporaneous searches [are] justified...by the need to seize weapons and other things which might be used to assault an officer or effect an escape, as well as by the need to prevent the destruction of evidence of the crime—things which might easily happen where the weapon or evidence is on the accused's person or under his immediate control." *Preston v. United States*, 376 U.S. 364, 367 (1964).

5.   "[I]t is not 'unreasonable' under the Fourth Amendment for a police officer, as a matter of routine, to monitor the movements of an arrested person, as his judgment dictates, following the arrest. The officer's need to ensure his own safety—as well as the integrity of the arrest—is compelling. Such surveillance is not an impermissible invasion of the privacy or personal liberty of an individual who has been arrested.... It is of no legal significance whether the officer was in the room, on the threshold, or in the hallway, since he had a right to be in any of these places as an incident of a valid arrest." *Washington v. Chrisman*, 455 U.S. 1, 7, 8 (1982).

6.   "[W]hen a policeman has made a lawful custodial arrest of the occupant of an automobile, he may, as a contemporaneous incident of that arrest, search the pas-

senger compartment of that automobile. It follows from this conclusion that the police may also examine the contents of any containers found within the passenger compartment, for if the passenger compartment is within reach of the arrestee, so also will containers in it be within his reach.... Such a container may, of course, be searched whether it is open or closed, since the justification for the search is not that the arrestee has no privacy interest in the container, but that the lawful custodial arrest justifies the infringement of any privacy interest the arrestee may have." *New York v. Belton*, 453 U.S. 454, 460-61 (1981).

7. "[A] search incident to arrest can be undertaken without a warrant to prevent an arrested person from seizing a weapon or destroying evidence within his 'grabbing area,' but the availability and scope of such a search cannot be expanded beyond the reasons for allowing it." *United States v. Fleming,* 677 F.2d 602, 606 (7th Cir. 1982).

8. "We question...whether law enforcement officers should be allowed to maneuver an arrestee close to personal belongings in order to search all items thus brought within the arrestee's immediate control.... 'The police can not circumvent the Fourth Amendment's warrant requirement by arresting a person and then bringing that person into contact with his possessions which are otherwise unrelated to the arrest.'" *United States v. Hill,* 730 F.2d 1163, 1167 (8th Cir. 1984).

B. Nature: A search incident to a lawful arrest must be contemporaneous in time and place.

1. "[A] search 'can be incident to an arrest only if it is substantially contemporaneous with the arrest.'" *Shipley v. California*, 395 U.S. 818, 819 (1969).

2.   "Once petitioner admitted ownership of the sizable quantity of drugs...the police clearly had probable cause to place the petitioner under arrest. Where the formal arrest followed quickly on the heels of the challenged search of petitioner's person, we do not believe it particularly important that the search preceded the arrest rather than vice versa." *Rawlings v. Kentucky*, 448 U.S. 98, 111 (1980).

3.   "[I]t is axiomatic that an incident search may not precede an arrest and serve as part of its justification." *Sibron v. United States*, 392 U.S. 40, 63 (1968).

4.   "Once an accused is under arrest and in custody, then a search made at another place, without a warrant, is simply not incident to the arrest." *Preston v. United States*, 376 U.S. 364, 367 (1964).

5.   "A search is valid as incident to an arrest even if it is conducted before the actual arrest, provided that (1) the arrest and the search are substantially contemporaneous, and (2) probable cause to arrest existed before the search.... [A] search incident to an arrest may not precede the arrest and yet serve as part of its justification." *United States v. Ilazi*, 730 F.2d 1120, 1126, 1127 (8th Cir. 1984).

6.   "[I]n order for a search incident to arrest to be reasonable, it must be contemporaneous both in time and in place with the arrest. Any evidence found in a search which does not meet this requirement is inadmissible." *Welch v. United States*, 411 F.2d 66, 68 (10th Cir. 1969).

7.   "[T]o come within this exception to the necessity for a warrant the seizure must be contemporaneous with the arrest and not remote from it either in time or place." *Price v. United States*, 348 F.2d 68, 69 (D.C. Cir.), *cert. denied*, 382 U.S. 888 (1965).

C. Booking Searches: A jailhouse search of an arrest-ed person's possessions is sometimes justified as a delayed search incident to arrest.

1. "An arrested person is not invariably taken to a police station or confined; if an arrestee is taken to the police station, that is no more than a continuation of the custody inherent in the arrest status. Nonetheless, the factors justifying a search of the person and personal effects of an arrestee upon reaching a police station but prior to being placed in confinement are somewhat different from the factors justifying an immediate search at the time and place of arrest." *Illinois v. Lafayette,* 462 U.S. 640, ____ (1983).

2. "The property. . .was subject to search at the place of arrest. We do not think it significantly different, when the accused decides to take the property with him, for the search of it to occur instead at the first place of detention when the accused arrives there, especially as the search of property carried by an accused to the place of detention has additional justifications, similar to those which justify a search of the person of one who is arrested." *Abel v. United States*, 362 U.S. 217, 239 (1960).

3. "[O]nce the accused is lawfully arrested and is in custody, the effects in his possession at the place of detention that were subject to search at the time and place of his arrest may lawfully be searched and seized without a warrant even though a substantial period of time has elapsed between the arrest and subsequent administrative processing, on the one hand, and the taking of the property for use as evidence, on the other. This is true where the clothing or effects are immediately seized upon arrival at the jail, held under the defendant's name in the 'property room' of the jail, and at a later time searched and taken for

use at the subsequent criminal trial." *United States v. Edwards*, 415 U.S. 800, 807 (1974).

4.   "[S]earches of an individual and his wallet or other personal property at this stage of the arrest [incarceration] have been upheld both as incident to a lawful arrest when conducted shortly afterward at the jail or place of detention and for the purpose of discovering concealed weapons. Likewise, such search has been upheld as being part of the necessary inventory of an accused's personal property both to preserve the accused's belongings while he is incarcerated and to safeguard the police from a later groundless claim that some item has not been returned to him." *United States v. Gardner*, 480 F.2d 929, 931 (10th Cir.), *cert. denied*, 414 U.S. 977 (1973).

Chapter 8

Exigent Circumstances

A. Justification: A warrantless search is permitted when both probable cause to believe that a serious crime has been committed and exigent circumstances exist.

1. "[T]here are some exceptions to the warrant requirement. These have been established where it was concluded that the public interest required some flexibility in the application of the general rule that a valid warrant is a prerequisite for a search [and some arrests].... Thus, a few 'jealously and carefully drawn' exceptions provide for those cases where the societal costs of obtaining a warrant, such as danger to law officers or the risk of loss or destruction of evidence, outweigh the reasons for prior recourse to a neutral magistrate." *Arkansas v. Sanders*, 442 U.S. 753, 759 (1979).

2. "The Fourth Amendment does not require police officers to delay in the course of an investigation if to do so would gravely endanger their lives or the lives of others." *Warden v. Hayden*, 387 U.S. 294, 298-99 (1967).

3. " '[A] search or seizure carried out on a suspect's premises without a warrant is *per se* unreasonable, unless the police can show...the presence of "exigent circumstances...." ' [T]he court decided in *Payton v. New York* that warrantless felony arrests in the home are prohibited by the Fourth Amendment, absent probable cause and exigent circumstances.... Before agents of the govern-

ment may invade the sanctity of the home, the burden is on the government to demonstrate exigent circumstances that overcome the presumption of unreasonableness that attaches to all warrantless home entries." *Welsh v. Wisconsin,* 466 U.S.____,____(1984).

4. "The ultimate test is whether there is such a compelling necessity for immediate action as will not brook the delay of obtaining a warrant." *United States v. Adams,* 621 F.2d 41, 44 (1st Cir. 1980).

5. "[A]n important factor to be considered when determining whether any exigency exists is the gravity of the underlying offense for which the arrest is being made. Moreover, although no exigency is created simply because there is probable cause to believe that a serious crime has been committed, application of the exigent-circumstances exception in the context of a home entry should rarely be sanctioned when there is probable cause to believe that only a minor offense, such as the kind at issue in this case, has been committed." *Welsh v. Wisconsin,* 466 U.S.____, ____(1984).

6. "[I]n determining whether exigent circumstances justify an exception to the general rule requiring a warrant, the burden rests on the government to show that the warrantless entry was 'imperative....' [T]his standard is not satisfied unless the government demonstrates that a warrant could not have been obtained in time even by telephone under the procedure authorized by Fed. R. Crim. P. 41(c)(2)." *United States v. Manfredi,* 722 F.2d 519, 522 (9th Cir. 1983).

7. "[A]n officer entering a home pursuant to the exigent circumstances exception may not search the premises beyond the scope justified by the exigency without obtain-

ing a warrant." *United States v. Parr,* 716 F.2d 796, 813 (11th Cir. 1983).

B. Definition: Hot pursuit, a fleeing suspect, destruction of evidence, or other situations in which speed is essential are examples of exigent circumstances.

1. "The police were informed that an armed robbery had taken place, and that the suspect had entered [the house] less than five minutes before they reached it. They acted reasonably when they entered the house and began to search for a man of the description they had been given and for weapons which he had used in the robbery or might use against them.... Speed here was essential, and only a thorough search of the house for persons and weapons could have insured that [the suspect] was the only man present and that the police had control of all weapons which could be used against them or to effect an escape." *Warden v. Hayden,* 387 U.S. 294, 298-99 (1967).

2. "[The police] saw [the suspect] standing in the doorway of the house with a brown paper bag in her hand. They pulled up to within 15 feet of [the suspect] and got out of their van, shouting 'police' and displaying their identification. As the officers approahced, [the suspect] retreated into the vestibule of her house.... The...question is whether her act of retreating into her house could thwart an otherwise proper arrest. We hold that it could not." *United States v. Santana,* 427 U.S. 38, 40 (1976).

3. "Except for the fact that the offense under investigation was a homicide, there were no exigent circumstances in this case.... There was no indication that evidence would be lost, destroyed, or removed during the time

required to obtain a search warrant. Indeed, the police guard at the apartment minimized that possibility. And there is no suggestion that a search warrant could not easily and conveniently have been obtained. We decline to hold that the seriousness of the offense under investigation itself creates exigent circumstances of the kind that under the Fourth Amendment justify a warrantless search." *Mincey v. Arizona*, 437 U.S. 385, 394 (1978).

4. "The most common examples of exigent circumstances are the hot-pursuit, fleeing-suspect, and destruction-of-evidence cases.... [T]he following factors [are] relevant in a fleeing-suspect case: (1) the gravity of the offense committed; (2) the belief that the suspect was armed; and (3) the likelihood that the suspect would escape in the absence of swift police action." *United States v. Williams,* 612 F.2d 735, 739 (3d Cir. 1979), *cert. denied,* 445 U.S. 934 (1980).

5. "When officers have arrested a person inside his residence, the exigent circumstances exception permits a protective search of part or all of the residence when the officers reasonably believe that there might be other persons on the premises who could pose some danger to them." *United States v. Gardner,* 627 F.2d 906, 909-10 (9th Cir. 1980).

6. "That an officer's life or the lives of those around him might be in danger has been recognized by the United States Supreme Court as an exigent circumstance allowing a pat-down search for weapons of a person reasonably believed to pose such a danger. A sweep search or security search *may* be justified for similar reasons. However, the suspicion of danger must be clear and reasonable in light of all surrounding circumstances. Officers of the law are not given free reign to conduct sweep searches on the

pretense that a dangerous situation might be imminent." *United States v. Tabor,* 722 F.2d 596, 598 (10th Cir. 1983).

7. "The indicia of danger in this case, the movement at the window and the noise at the back door, are likely to occur in any occupied dwelling. These noises do not constitute a physical threat. Therefore, we hold that the government has failed to demonstrate exigent circumstances which would justify a warrantless search." *United States v. Kinney,* 638 F.2d 941, 944-45 (6th Cir.), *cert. denied,* 452 U.S. 918 (1981).

8. "[W]e think [the officer's] entry was justified as an entry in hot pursuit of [the suspect]. The fourth man had vanished just moments before; it was only reasonable to believe he was in the house; and speed was essential." *United States v. Haynie,* 637 F.2d 227, 236 (4th Cir. 1980), *cert. denied,* 451 U.S. 972 (1981).

9. "For destruction of evidence to constitute exigency, evidence must be present that could be destroyed. The mere suspicion that evidence may be present does not justify entry by the police; rather, there must be a 'finding of probable cause coupled with exigent circumstances.' Thus, to establish exigent circumstances due to the possible destruction of evidence, the state must demonstrate probable cause to suspect that evidence was present at [co-defendant's] residence." *United States v. Impink,* 728 F.2d 1228, 1231 (9th Cir. 1984).

10. "The Court has noted that 'imminent destruction, removal, or concealment of the [evidence] to be seized' may be one type of exigent circumstance which would justify warrantless entry into a dwelling. When such an exigency is found, however, the least restrictive intrusion is to be adopted, or the whole constitutional requirement for

obtaining a warrant would be defeated. When it is known that no one is presently on the premises, they may be secured merely by guarding the entrances. When persons are present and such persons may reasonably be feared to pose a substantial threat to destroy evidence, more intrusive action may be proper. Even then, the police might be well advised to give the occupants a choice of exiting the premises. This might be accompanied by 'a very quick and limited pass through the premises to check for third persons who may destroy evidence.'" *United States v. Palumbo,* 742 F.2d 656, 658-59 (1st Cir. 1984).

11. "[A] warrantless search may not be justified on the basis of exigent circumstances which are created by the government itself.... ' "[S]light delay or the inconvenience of presenting facts to a magistrate are not sufficient circumstances to by-pass the warrant requirement." '... The important point...is that the exigency, while perhaps not *unexpected,* had not been *created* by the government." *United States v. Hultgren,* 713 F.2d 79, 86, 88 (5th Cir. 1983).

12. "That the officers might have obtained a warrant before going to the hotel is not fatal to the finding that exigent circumstances justified their entry. The officers were conducting an ongoing investigation, and were not required to seek a warrant as soon as they had probable cause to suspect a conspiracy to distribute cocaine. Rather, they could legitimately wait in order to gather additional evidence of conspiracy and to establish probable cause for the possession offense. That the exigency might have been foreseeable does not invalidate the entry and arrest. The important point is that the exigency, while perhaps not unexpected, was not created by the officers." *United States v. Palumbo,* 735 F.2d 1095, 1097 (8th Cir. 1984).

Chapter 9

Stop and Frisk

A. Nature of Stop: A forcible stop of an individual constitutes a seizure, thus the Fourth Amendment is implicated.

1. "It must be recognized that whenever a police officer accosts an individual and restrains his freedom to walk away, he has 'seized' that person." *Terry v. Ohio*, 392 U.S. 1, 16 (1968).

2. "[D]etention of the respondent against his will constituted a seizure of his person, and the Fourth Amendment guarantee of freedom from 'unreasonable searches and seizures' is clearly implicated." *Cupp v. Murphy*, 412 U.S. 291, 294 (1973).

3. "Obviously, not all personal intercourse between policemen and citizens involves 'seizures' of persons. Only when the officer, by means of physical force or show of authority, has in some way restrained the liberty of a citizen may we conclude that a 'seizure' has occurred." *Terry v. Ohio*, 392 U.S. 1, 19 n.16 (1968).

4. "If there is no detention—no seizure within the meaning of the Fourth Amendment—then no constitutional rights have been infringed." *Florida v. Royer*, 460 U.S. 491, 498 (1983).

5. "We conclude that a person has been 'seized' within the meaning of the Fourth Amendment only if, in view of all

the circumstances surrounding the incident, a reasonable person would have believed that he was not free to leave. Examples of circumstances that might indicate a seizure, even where the person did not attempt to leave, would be the threatening presence of several officers, the display of a weapon by an officer, some physical touching of the person of the citizen, or the use of language or tone of voice indicating that compliance with the officer's request might be compelled.... In the absence of some such evidence, otherwise inoffensive contact between a member of the public and the police cannot, as a matter of law, amount to a seizure of that person." *United States v. Mendenhall*, 446 U.S. 544, 554-55 (1980).

6. "We must balance the nature and quality of the intrusion of the individual's Fourth Amendment interests against the importance of the governmental interests alleged to justify the intrusion. When the nature and extent of the detention are minimally intrusive of the individual's Fourth Amendment interests, the opposing law enforcement interests can support a seizure based on less than probable cause." *United States v. Place,* 462 U.S. 696, ____ (1983).

7. "In *Terry* the Supreme Court rejected both the notion that the fourth amendment does not regulate police-citizen encounters falling short of arrests, and the notion that it prohibits encounters based on less than probable cause for arrest. Instead, the court held that, although some police-citizen encounters do not implicate fourth amendment concerns at all, more intrusive encounters short of arrests must be justified by reasonable suspicion proportional to the degree of the intrusion. That suspicion cannot be inchoate, but must be based on 'specific and articulable facts...together with rational inferences from those facts' in order to establish a basis for review of the police

actions." *United States v. Berryman,* 717 F.2d 651, 653 (1st Cir. 1983), *cert. denied,* ____U.S.____(1984).

8. "*Terry*-type investigative stops are the result of a balance between governmental interests in law enforcement and the individual's Fourth Amendment right to be free from unreasonable searches and seizures. It is only when law enforcement interests are particularly strong and the proposed contact between police and citizen is of a limited nature that the Court has allowed *Terry*-type stops on less than probable cause." *United States v. Mosquera-Ramirez,* 729 F.2d 1352, 1355-56 (11th Cir. 1984).

B. Grounds for Stop: To lawfully stop an individual, the police officer must have a reasonable suspicion that the person stopped is involved in criminal activity.

1. "[A] police officer may in appropriate circumstances and in an appropriate manner approach a person for purposes of investigating possible criminal behavior even though there is no probable cause to make an arrest." *Terry v. Ohio,* 392 U.S. 1, 22 (1968).

2. "[T]he Court...acknowledge[s] the authority of the police to make a *forcible stop* of a person when the officer has reasonable, articulable suspicion that the person has been, is, or is about to be engaged in criminal activity." *United States v. Place,* 462 U.S. 696,____(1983).

3. "[A person] may not be detained even momentarily without reasonable, objective grounds for doing so; and his refusal to listen or answer does not, without more, furnish those grounds. [N]ot all seizures of the person must be justified by probable cause to arrest for a crime....

[C]ertain seizures are justifiable under the Fourth Amendment if there is articulable suspicion that a person has committed or is about to commit a crime." *Florida v. Royer*, 460 U.S. 491, 498 (1983).

4. "[A]ny curtailment of a person's liberty by the police must be supported at least by a reasonable and articulable suspicion that the person seized is engaged in criminal activity." *Reid v. Georgia*, 448 U.S. 438, 440 (1980).

5. "The idea that an assessment of the whole picture must yield a particularized suspicion contains two elements, each of which must be present before a stop is permissible. First, the assessment must be based upon all the circumstances. The analysis proceeds with various objective observations, information from police reports, if such are available, and consideration of the modes or patterns of operation of certain kinds of lawbreakers.... The process does not deal with hard certainties, but with probabilities.... Finally, the evidence thus collected must be seen and weighed not in terms of library analysis by scholars, but as understood by those versed in the field of law enforcement. The second element contained in the idea that an assessment of the whole picture must yield a particularized suspicion is the concept that the process just described must raise a suspicion that the particular individual being stopped is engaged in wrongdoing." *United States v. Cortez*, 449 U.S. 411, 418 (1981).

6. "[E]ven assuming that purpose [to prevent crime] is served to some degree by stopping and demanding identification from an individual without any specific basis for believing he is involved in criminal activity, the guarantees of the Fourth Amendment do not allow it. When such a stop is not based on objective criteria, the risk of arbitrary

and abusive police practices exceeds tolerable limits."
Brown v. Texas, 443 U.S. 47, 52, (1979).

7. "[T]he police are not automatically shorn of authority to
stop a suspect in the absence of probable cause merely
because the criminal has completed his crime and escaped
from the scene.... The factors in the balance may be
somewhat different when a stop to investigate past criminal
activity is involved rather than a stop to investigate ongoing
criminal conduct.... Particularly in the context of felonies
or crimes involving a threat to public safety, it is in the
public interest that the crime be solved and the suspect
detained as promptly as possible. The law enforcement
interests at stake in these circumstances outweigh the
individual's interest to be free of a stop and detention that
is no more extensive than permissible in the investigation
of imminent or ongoing crimes." *United States v. Hensley*,
_____U.S. _____, _____(1985).

8. "[I]f police have a reasonable suspicion, grounded in
specific and articulable facts, that a person they encounter
was involved in or is wanted in connection with a completed felony, then a *Terry* stop may be made to investigate
that suspicion.... Assuming the police make a *Terry* stop in
objective reliance on a flyer or bulletin, we hold that the
evidence uncovered in the course of the stop is admissible
if the police who *issued* the flyer or bulletin possessed a
reasonable suspicion justifying a stop, and if the stop that
in fact occurred was not significantly more intrusive than
would have been permitted the issuing department."
United States v. Hensley, _____ U.S._____, _____(1985).

9. "[R]estrictions on a person's freedom of movement
may be imposed to maintain the status quo while making
an initial inquiry provided the force displayed is not

excessive under the circumstances." *United States v. Maybusher,* 735 F.2d 366, 372 (9th Cir. 1984).

10. "[T]he degree of intrusiveness of stops that do not rise to the level of arrests may vary, and in order to be lawful in a given case it must be proportional to the degree of suspicion that prompted the intrusion. When little or no suspicion exists, therefore, very little intrusion is tolerable." *United States v. Berryman,* 717 F.2d 651, 657 (1st Cir. 1983), *cert. denied,* ____U.S.____(1984).

11. "The legality of an investigatory stop depends on (1) the nature and extent of the government's need for the stop, which must be judged according to the importance of its law enforcement interests under the circumstances, and (2) the reasonableness of the stop, which depends mainly on the degree of police intrusion on the defendants' freedom of movement.... The longer and more intrusive the stop, the stronger must be the justification for it." *United States v. Pelusio,* 725 F.2d 161, 165 (2d Cir. 1983).

C. Grounds for Frisk: To lawfully frisk an individual, the police officer must have a reasonable belief that the person stopped is armed and dangerous.

1. "[A] law enforcement officer, for his own protection and safety, may conduct a patdown to find weapons that he reasonably believes or suspects are then in the possession of the person he has accosted." *Ybarra v. Illinois,* 444 U.S. 85, 93 (1979).

2. "The officer need not be absolutely certain that the individual is armed; the issue is whether a reasonably prudent man in the circumstances would be warranted in

the belief that his safety or that of others was in danger."
Terry v. Ohio, 392 U.S. 1, 27 (1968).

3. "The police officer is not entitled to seize and search every person whom he sees on the street or of whom he makes inquiries. Before he places a hand on the person of a citizen in search of anything, he must have constitutionally adequate, reasonable grounds for doing so. In the case of the self-protective search for weapons, he must be able to point to particular facts from which he reasonably inferred that the individual was armed and dangerous." *Sibron v. New York*, 392 U.S. 40, 64 (1968).

4. "The 'narrow scope' of the *Terry* exception does not permit a frisk for weapons on less than reasonable belief or suspicion directed at the person to be frisked, even though that person happens to be on premises where an authorized narcotics search is taking place." *Ybarra v. Illinois*, 444 U.S. 85, 94 (1979).

5. "[O]ur review of the record reveals no facts...from which we can reasonably infer that [defendant] was armed and dangerous. We do not think the testimony that '[a]ny time we [the officers] stop a car we are in danger' is adequate for the jury, trial court, or ourselves to reasonably infer that the officers were in danger." *United States v. Humphrey*, 409 F.2d 1055, 1058 (10th Cir. 1969).

D. Arrests: An investigatory stop which is overly intrusive may be viewed as an arrest requiring probable cause.

1. "Detentions may be 'investigative' yet violative of the Fourth Amendment absent probable cause. In the name of

investigating a person who is no more than suspected of criminal activity, the police may not carry out a full search of the person or of his automobile or other effects. Nor may the police seek to verify their suspicions by means that approach the conditions of arrest." *Florida v. Royer,* 460 U.S. 491, 499 (1983).

2.   "This Court utilizes a four factor test to determine when an interrogation rises to the level of an arrest requiring probable cause. These factors are: '(1) whether probable cause to arrest has arisen, (2) whether the subjective intent of the officer conducting the interrogation was to hold the defendant, (3) whether the subjective belief of the defendant was that his freedom was significantly restricted, and (4) whether the investigation had focused on the defendant at the time of the interrogation.'... [Also,] [e]xcept in the context of border searches, successive stops of an individual based on the same information strongly indicate a finding that an arrest has taken place." *United States v. Morin,* 665 F.2d 765, 769 (5th Cir. 1982).

3.   "That the three were moved from one spot of temporary detention to another did not vitiate the investigatory nature of the stop. The Supreme Court has held that relocation is permissible for reasons of security and safety.... Relocation may be permissible for other reasons as well (e.g., comfort or convenience).... The ultimate question is not why the detainees were moved, but whether the move made the stop more intrusive. We note that the transfer here was not to a more institutional setting, such as a police station or interrogation room, but to a residential dwelling unit. Such a transfer is unlikely to raise the intrusiveness of the stop to the level of an arrest." *United States v. Vanichromanee,* 742 F.2d 340, 345 (7th Cir. 1984).

4. "[S]uccessive stops of an individual based on the same information strongly indicate a finding that an arrest has taken place.... [W]e do not believe this stop exceeded permissible bounds *merely* because it was a second stop— even though, as a second stop, it was inherently more intrusive and coercive than the first. To so hold would preclude law enforcement officials from stopping a suspect a second time whenever the first stop did not provide probable cause, even though it tended to confirm their suspicions of illegal activity. We believe that to adopt a per se rule prohibiting successive investigatory stops would unduly hinder efforts to interdict illegal drug traffic." *United States v. Ilazi,* 730 F.2d 1120, 1125, 1126 (8th Cir. 1984).

5. "A law enforcement officer may make an investigative stop of a suspicious individual to maintain the status quo while obtaining more information even though the officer lacks probable cause to arrest the individual.... Such a stop requires only 'founded suspicion'.... The investigative stop did not become an arrest when the deputy pointed his gun at defendant and ordered her to 'prone out.' 'A valid stop is not transformed into an arrest merely because law enforcement agents momentarily restrict a person's freedom of movement.'" *United States v. Jacobs,* 715 F.2d 1343, 1345 (9th Cir. 1983).

E. Nature of Frisk: The search for weapons must be only a limited intrusion.

1. "[The pat-down seeking concealed weapons] must...be confined in scope to an intrusion reasonably designed to discover guns, knives, clubs, or other hidden instruments for the assault of the police officer." *Terry v. Ohio,* 392 U.S. 1, 29 (1968).

2. "Nothing in *Terry* can be understood to allow a generalized 'cursory search for weapons' or, indeed, any search whatever for anything but weapons." *Ybarra v. Illinois*, 444 U.S. 85, 93-94 (1979).

3. "The purpose of this limited search is not to discover evidence of crime, but to allow the officer to pursue his investigation without fear of violence, and thus the frisk for weapons must be equally necessary and reasonable. . . ." *Adams v. Williams*, 407 U.S. 143, 146 (1972).

4. "[The officer] was looking for narcotics and he found them. The search was not reasonably limited in scope to the accomplishment of the only goal which might conceivably have justified its inception—the protection of the officer by disarming a potentially dangerous man." *Sibron v. New York*, 392 U.S. 40, 65 (1968).

5. "[W]hen a policeman is entitled to forcibly 'stop' a person. . .and has reason to believe that the person is armed and dangerous, he may conduct a limited pat-down search for weapons to protect himself while conducting the inquiry." *United States v. Davis*, 482 F.2d 893, 906 (9th Cir. 1973).

6. "[T]he use of handcuffs, if reasonably necessary, while substantially aggravating the intrusiveness of an investigatory stop, do[es] not necessarily convert a *Terry* stop into an arrest necessitating probable cause. Likewise, requiring the suspect to lie down while a frisk is performed, if reasonably necessary, does not transform a *Terry* stop into an arrest." *United States v. Taylor,* 716 F.2d 701, 709 (9th Cir. 1983).

7. "[T]he lifting by the officer of [the suspect's] shirt was not, under the circumstances, overly intrusive. . . . In the

instant case the officer's investigation was wholly confined to the area of the bulge in question and was a direct and specific inquiry. As such it did not transcend the permissible bounds established by *Terry." United States v. Hill*, 545 F.2d 1191, 1193 (9th Cir. 1976).

F.   Search After Frisk: Feeling an object which might be a weapon will justify a more extensive intrusion to seize the weapon.

1.   "[The officer] confined his search strictly to what was minimally necessary to learn whether the men were armed and to disarm them once he discovered the weapons. He did not conduct a general exploratory search for whatever evidence of criminal activity he might find.... Such a search is a reasonable search under the Fourth Amendment...." *Terry v. Ohio*, 392 U.S. 1, 30-31 (1968).

2.   "While...a 'pat-down' involve[s] only the patting of external clothing in the vicinity of the pockets, belts or shoulders where a weapon such as a gun might be secreted, in any given case the right to pat-down carries with it authorization for a full frisk since presumably, if we are authorizing anything, we are authorizing what is necessary to get the job done." *United States v. Albarado*, 495 F.2d 799, 807 (2d Cir. 1974).

3.   "[T]he search of [the suspect's] breast pocket which produced ten matchboxes which in turn contained narcotics exceeded the outer limits of a weapons search." *United States v. Peep*, 490 F.2d 903, 906 (8th Cir. 1974).

4.   "Even if such a 'pat-down' could have been justified by fear that one who allegedly tried to use a stolen credit card

might be armed, [the officer's] reaching into [the suspect's] pockets and extracting the credit card went beyond the permissible scope of a non-arrest 'pat-down' for weapons." *United States v. Wilson*, 479 F.2d 936, 939 (7th Cir. 1973).

G. Protective Searches of Vehicles: When police have lawfully stopped a vehicle and have a reasonable suspicion that it contains weapons that may be dangerous to the officers, they may conduct a protective search of the passenger compartment.

1. "In *Terry v. Ohio*, 392 U.S. 1 (1968), we upheld the validity of a protective search for weapons in the absence of probable cause to arrest because it is unreasonable to deny a police officer the right 'to neutralize the threat of physical harm'...when he possesses an articulable suspicion that an individual is armed and dangerous. We did not, however, expressly address whether such a protective search for weapons could extend to an area beyond the person in the absence of probable cause to arrest. . . . [T]he police searched the passenger compartment because they had reason to believe that the vehicle contained weapons potentially dangerous to the officers. We hold that the protective search of the passenger compartment was reasonable under the principles articulated in *Terry* and other decisions of this Court." *Michigan v. Long,* 463 U.S.____,____(1983).

2. "Our past cases indicate then that protection of police and others can justify protective searches when police have a reasonable belief that the suspect poses a danger, that roadside encounters between police and suspects are especially hazardous, and that danger may arise from the possible presence of weapons in the area surrounding a

suspect. These principles compel our conclusion that the search of the passenger compartment of an automobile, limited to those areas in which a weapon may be placed or hidden, is permissible if the police officer possesses a reasonable belief based on 'specific and articulable facts which, taken together with the rational inferences from those facts, reasonably warrant' the officers in believing that the suspect is dangerous and the suspect may gain immediate control of weapons." *Michigan v. Long,* 463 U.S.____,____(1983).

3. "Therefore, the balancing required by *Terry* clearly weighs in favor of allowing the police to conduct an area search of the passenger compartment to uncover weapons, as long as they possess an articulable and objectively reasonable belief that the suspect is potentially dangerous." *Michigan v. Long,* 463 U.S.____,____(1983).

4. "If, while conducting a legitimate *Terry* search of the interior of the automobile, the officer should, as here, discover contraband other than weapons, he clearly cannot be required to ignore the contraband, and the Fourth Amendment does not require its suppression in such circumstances." *Michigan v. Long,* 463 U.S.____,____ (1983).

Chapter 10

Vehicle Stops

A. Significance of Stop: A "seizure" occurs whenever a vehicle is stopped, and therefore the Fourth Amendment applies.

1. "The Fourth and Fourteenth Amendments are implicated in this case because stopping an automobile and detaining its occupants constitute a 'seizure' within the meaning of those Amendments, even though the purpose of the stop is limited and the resulting detention quite brief." *Delaware v. Prouse*, 440 U.S. 648, 653 (1979).

2. "The Fourth Amendment applies to seizures of the person, including brief investigatory stop such as the stop of the vehicle here." *United States v. Cortez*, 449 U.S. 411, 417 (1981).

3. "It is agreed that checkpoint stops are 'seizures' within the meaning of the Fourth Amendment." *United States v. Martinez-Fuerte*, 428 U.S. 543, 556 (1976).

4. "The stop of a moving vehicle—even if the period of detention is brief—involves a 'seizure' within the meaning of the Fourth Amendment." *United States v. Montgomery* , 561 F.2d 875, 878 (D.C. Cir. 1977).

B. Grounds for Stop: There must be reasonable suspicion to justify an investigatory stop of an individual vehicle.

1. "The marginal contribution to roadway safety possibly resulting from a system of spot checks cannot justify subjecting every occupant of every vehicle on the roads to a seizure—limited in magnitude compared to other intrusions but nonetheless constitutionally cognizable—at the unbridled discretion of law enforcement officials. To insist neither upon an appropriate factual basis for suspicion directed at a particular automobile nor upon some other substantial and objective standard or rule to govern the exercise of discretion 'would invite intrusions upon constitutionally guaranteed rights based on nothing more substantial than inarticulate hunches. . . .' [E]xcept in those situations in which there is at least articulable and reasonable suspicion that a motorist is unlicensed or that an automobile is not registered, or that either the vehicle or an occupant is otherwise subject to seizure for violation of law, stopping an automobile and detaining the driver in order to check his driver's license and the registration of the automobile are unreasonable under the Fourth Amendment." *Delaware v. Prouse*, 440 U.S. 648, 661, 663 (1979).

2. "Based upon that whole picture the detaining officers must have a particularized and objective basis for suspecting the particular person stopped of criminal activity. . . . First, the assessment must be based upon all of the circumstances. The analysis proceeds with various objective observations, information from police reports, if such are available, and consideration of the modes or patterns of operation of certain kinds of lawbreakers. . . . The second element contained in the idea that an assessment of the whole picture must yield a particularized suspicion is the concept that the process just described must raise a

suspicion that the particular individual being stopped is engaged in wrongdoing." *United States v. Cortez*, 449 U.S. 411, 417-18 (1981).

3.   "[T]he police do not have an unrestricted right to stop people, either pedestrians or drivers. The 'good faith' of the police is not enough, nor is an inarticulate hunch. They must have an articulable suspicion of wrongdoing, done or in prospect." *United States v. Montgomery*, 561 F.2d 875, 887 (D.C. Cir. 1977).

C.   Vehicle Roadblocks: Vehicles may also be stopped at general roadblocks which serve legitimate government purposes.

1.   "This holding does not preclude the...States from developing methods for spot checks that involve less intrusion or that do not involve the unconstrained exercise of discretion. Questioning of all oncoming traffic at roadblock-type stops is one possible alternative." *Delaware v. Prouse*, 440 U.S. 648, 663 (1979).

2.   "[S]tops for brief questioning routinely conducted at permanent checkpoints are consistent with the Fourth Amendment and need not be authorized by warrant." *United States v. Martinez-Fuerte*, 428 U.S. 543, 566 (1976).

3.   "The purpose of the roadblock, *i.e.*, to check drivers' licenses and car registrations, was a legitimate one. If, in the process of so doing, the officers saw evidence of other crimes, they had the right to take reasonable investigative steps and were not required to close their eyes." *United States v. Prichard*, 645 F.2d 854, 857 (10th Cir.), *cert. denied*, 454 U.S. 832 (1981).

D. Initial Intrusion: The police may take reasonable actions to protect themselves after a lawful stop of a motor vehicle.

1. "Certainly it would be unreasonable to require that police officers take unnecessary risks in the performance of their duties." *Terry v. Ohio*, 392 U.S. 1, 23 (1968).

2. "[O]nce a motor vehicle has been lawfully detained for a traffic violation, the police officers may order the driver to get out of the vehicle without violating the Fourth Amendment's proscription of unreasonable searches and seizures." *Pennsylvania v. Mimms*, 434 U.S. 106, 111 n.6 (1977).

3. "What is at most a mere inconvenience cannot prevail when balanced against legitimate concerns for the officer's safety." *Pennsylvania v. Mimms*, 434 U.S. 106, 111 (1977).

E. Further Intrusion: If the police officer has a reasonable belief that the person stopped is presently armed and dangerous, he or she may conduct a limited protective frisk.

1. "[T]he officer [was] justified in conducting a limited search for weapons once he had resonably concluded that the person whom he had legitimately stopped might be armed and presently dangerous." *Pennsylvania v. Mimms*, 434 U.S. 106, 111-12 (1977).

2. "[The pat-down seeking concealed weapons] must ... be confined in scope to an intrusion reasonably designed to discover guns, knives, clubs, or other hidden instruments

for the assault of the police officer." *Terry v. Ohio*, 392 U.S. 1, 29 (1968).

3. "When Williams rolled down his window, rather than complying with the policeman's request to step out of the car so that his movements could more easily be seen, the revolver allegedly at Williams' waist became an even greater threat. Under these circumstances the policeman's action in reaching to the spot where the gun was thought to be hidden constituted a limited intrusion designed to insure his safety, and we conclude that it was reasonable." *Adams v. Williams*, 407 U.S. 143, 148 (1972).

4. "So long as the officer is entitled to make a forcible stop, and has reason to believe that the suspect is armed and dangerous, he may conduct a weapons search limited in scope to this protective purpose." *United States v. Cupps*, 503 F.2d 277, 281 (6th Cir. 1974).

F. Protective Searches of Vehicles: When police have lawfully stopped a vehicle and have a reasonable suspicion that it contains weapons that may be dangerous to the officers, they may conduct a protective search of the passenger compartment.

1. "In *Terry v. Ohio*, 392 U.S. 1 (1968), we upheld the validity of a protective search for weapons in the absence of probable cause to arrest because it is unreasonable to deny a police officer the right 'to neutralize the threat of physical harm'...when he possesses an articulable suspicion that an individual is armed and dangerous. We did not, however, expressly address whether such a protective search for weapons could extend to an area beyond the person in the absence of probable cause to arrest.... [T]he

police searched the passenger compartment because they had reason to believe that the vehicle contained weapons potentially dangerous to the officers. We hold that the protective search of the passenger compartment was reasonable under the principles articulated in *Terry* and other decisions of this Court." *Michigan v. Long,* 463 U.S.____, ____(1983).

2. "Our past cases indicate then that protection of police and others can justify protective searches when police have a reasonable belief that the suspect poses a danger, that roadside encounters between police and suspects are especially hazardous, and that danger may arise from the possible presence of weapons in the area surrounding a suspect. These principles compel our conclusion that the search of the passenger compartment of an automobile, limited to those areas in which a weapon may be placed or hidden, is permissible if the police officer possesses a reasonable belief based on 'specific and articulable facts which, taken together with the rational inferences from those facts, reasonably warrant' the officers in believing that the suspect is dangerous and the suspect may gain immediate control of weapons." *Michigan v. Long,* 463 U.S.____,____(1983).

3. "Therefore, the balancing required by *Terry* clearly weighs in favor of allowing the police to conduct an area search of the passenger compartment to uncover weapons, as long as they possess an articulable and objectively reasonable belief that the suspect is potentially dangerous." *Michigan v. Long,* 463 U.S.____,____(1983).

4. "If, while conducting a legitimate *Terry* search of the interior of the automobile, the officer should, as here, discover contraband other than weapons, he clearly cannot be required to ignore the contraband, and the Fourth

Amendment does not require its suppression in such circumstances." *Michigan v. Long,* 463 U.S.____,____ (1983).

G. Vehicle Searches Incident to Arrest: If a person is arrested after a vehicle stop, accessible portions of the vehicle may be searched incident to the arrest.

1. "[W]hen a policeman has made a lawful custodial arrest of the occupant of an automobile, he may, as a contemporaneous incident of that arrest, search the passenger compartment of that automobile. It follows from this conclusion that the police may also examine the contents of any containers found within the passenger compartment, for if the passenger compartment is within reach of the arrestee, so also will containers in it be within his reach. . . . Such a container may, of course, be searched whether it is open or closed, since the justification for the search is not that the arrestee has no privacy interest in the container, but that the lawful custodial arrest justifies the infringement of any privacy interest the arrestee may have." *New York v. Belton,* 453 U.S. 454, 460-61 (1981).

2. "[A]n officer at the time of a lawful custodial arrest may, without a warrant, make a 'full' search of the person of the accused, a limited area within the control of the person arrested, and of an automobile in his possession. . . ." *United States v. Roe,* 495 F.2d 600, 603 (10th Cir.), *cert. denied,* 419 U.S. 858 (1974).

Chapter 11

Vehicle Searches

A.   Expectation of Privacy: A person has less expectation of privacy in a vehicle than in a residence or luggage.

1.   "The automobile exception...is...supported by 'the diminished expectation of privacy which surrounds the automobile' and which arises from the facts that a car is used for transportation and not as a residence or a repository of personal effects, that a car's occupants and contents travel in plain view, and that automobiles are necessarily highly regulated by government." *Robbins v. California,* 453 U.S. 420, 424 (1981).

2.   "[T]he configuration, use, and regulation of automobiles often may dilute the reasonable expectation of privacy that exists with respect to differently situated property." *Arkansas v. Sanders,* 442 U.S. 753, 761 (1979).

3.   "A person travelling in an automobile on public thoroughfares has no reasonable expectation of privacy in his movements from one place to another." *United States v. Knotts,* 460 U.S.276, 281 (1983).

4.   "[A]n automobile may be searched without a warrant in circumstances that would not justify the search without a warrant of a house or an office, provided that there is probable cause to believe that the motor vehicle contains articles that the officers are entitled to seize." *United*

States v. Young, 567 F.2d 799, 802 (8th Cir. 1977), *cert. denied,* 434 U.S. 1079 (1978).

5. "[A]s a result of the extensive regulation of motor vehicles, drivers and traffic, automobiles frequently come into contact with police officers in both criminal and non-criminal contexts. These factors result in an expansion of the intrusions police officers may justifiably make without invading individual privacy with regard to automobiles." *United States v. One 1977 Mercedes Benz,* 708 F.2d 444, 448 (9th Cir. 1983).

6. "[U]nder the facts known to the officers at the time of the search, the motor homes were being used as automobiles, or trucks, and...the standard of reasonableness that applies to such vehicles applies here. The use of a vehicle, not its shape, should control the standard that applies." *United States v. Holland,* 740 F.2d 878, 880 (11th Cir. 1984).

B. Exigent Circumstances: The mobility of motor vehicles often constitutes exigent circumstances authorizing a warrantless search.

1. "[S]ince its earliest days Congress had recognized the impracticability of securing a warrant in cases involving the transportation of contraband goods.... Given the nature of an automobile in transit, the Court recognized that an immediate intrusion is necessary if police officers are to secure the illicit substance. In this class of cases, the Court held that a warrantless search of an automobile is not unreasonable." *United States v. Ross,* 456 U.S. 798, 806-07 (1982).

2.   "The willingness of courts to excuse the absence of a warrant where spontaneous searches are required of a vehicle on the road has led to what is called the 'automobile exception' to the warrant requirement, although the exception does not invariably apply whenever automobiles are searched." *Arkansas v. Sanders,* 442 U.S. 753, 760 n.7 (1979).

3.   "Exigent circumstances with regard to vehicles are not limited to situations where probable cause is unforeseeable and arises only at the time of arrest.... The exigency may arise at any time, and the fact that the police might have obtained a warrant earlier does not negate the possibility of a current situation's necessitating prompt police action." *Cardwell v. Lewis,* 417 U.S. 583, 595-96 (1974).

4.   "[T]he circumstances that furnish probable cause to search a particular auto for particular articles are most often unforeseeable; moreover, the opportunity to search is fleeting since a car is readily moveable.... [T]he occupants are alerted, and the car's contents may never be found again if a warrant must be obtained." *Chambers v. Maroney,* 399 U.S. 42, 50-51 (1970).

5.   "The word 'automobile' is not a talisman in whose presence the Fourth Amendment fades away and disappears. And surely there is nothing in this case to invoke the meaning and purpose of the rule of *Carroll v. United States*—no alerted criminal bent on flight, no fleeting opportunity on an open highway after a hazardous chase, no contraband or stolen goods or weapons, no confederates waiting to move the evidence, not even the inconvenience of a special police detail to guard the immobilized automobile." *Coolidge v. New Hampshire,* 403 U.S. 443, 461-62 (1971).

6. "[A] car traveling on the public highway affords less privacy than the home, but...one's expectation of privacy in a vehicle is enhanced when the car is nestled in the driveway. Still, the danger posed by the inherent mobility of an automobile must outweigh whatever enhanced privacy interest exists when the car is parked at home if it appears the car is about to take flight." *United States v. Shepherd,* 714 F.2d 316, 319-20 (4th Cir. 1983), *cert. denied,* _____ U.S. ____(1984).

7. "[A] warrantless seizure of a parked car is lawful under the automobile exception only where specific exigent circumstances justify an immediate seizure." *United States v. Spetz,* 721 F.2d 1457, 1472 (9th Cir. 1983).

8. "Although a parked airplane whose occupants are removed is arguably less mobile than a similarly situated automobile—given the relatively few persons capable of piloting an airplane—an airplane is even more mobile in terms of its ability to cover great distances in a short time and its capacity to move without being restricted to discrete roadways. In terms of mobility, then, airplanes are logically encompassed within the *Chambers* doctrine." *United States v. Nigro,* 727 F.2d 100, 107 (6th Cir. 1984).

C. Standard: To search a vehicle under exigent circumstances the police must have probable cause to believe that it contains seizable items.

1. "[I]f the search and seizure without a warrant are made upon probable cause, that is, upon a belief, reasonably arising out of circumstances known to the seizing officer, that an automobile or other vehicle contains that which by

law is subject to seizure...the search and seizure are valid." *Carroll v. United States,* 267 U.S. 132, 149 (1925).

2. "[T]he exception to the warrant requirement established in *Carroll...*applies only to searches of vehicles that are supported by probable cause. In this class of cases, a search is not unreasonable if based on facts that would justify the issuance of a warrant, even though a warrant has not actually been obtained." *United States v. Ross,* 456 U.S. 798, 809 (1982).

3. "One of the circumstances in which the Constitution does not require a search warrant is when the police stop an automobile on the street or highway because they have probable cause to believe it contains contraband or evidence of a crime." *Arkansas v. Sanders,* 442 U.S. 753, 760 (1979).

4. "We have held that probable cause to search an automobile exists when 'trustworthy facts and circumstances within the officer's personal knowledge would cause a reasonably prudent man to believe that the vehicle contained contraband.' When determining whether probable cause exists, we consider the 'sum total of layers of information and the synthesis of what the police have heard, what they know, and what they observe as trained officers.'" *United States v. Melendez-Gonzalez,* 727 F.2d 407, 413 (5th Cir. 1984).

D. Time and Place of Search: If probable cause and exigent circumstances existed originally, the police may search the vehicle at a later time without securing a warrant.

1. "[I]f an immediate search on the street is permissible without a warrant, a search soon thereafter at the police

station is permissible if the vehicle is impounded." *United States v. Ross,* 456 U.S. 798, 807 n.9 (1982).

2. "[P]olice officers with probable cause to search an automobile at the scene where it was stopped could constitutionally do so later at the station house without first obtaining a warrant.... '[T]he probable-cause factor' that developed at the scene 'still obtained at the station house.'" *Texas v. White,* 423 U.S. 67, 68 (1975).

3. "[W]here the police may stop and search an automobile under *Carroll,* they may also seize it and search it later at the police station." *Coolidge v. New Hampshire,* 403 U.S. 443, 463 (1971).

4. "If a warrantless search of a vehicle is permissible at the time of seizure, a search does not become improper because the vehicle is moved before the search is conducted." *United States v. Capo,* 693 F.2d 1330, 1337 (11th Cir. 1982), *cert. denied,* 460 U.S. 1092 (1983).

E.   Containers in Vehicles: A vehicle search based on probable cause and exigent circumstances may encompass any container in which the contraband might be hidden.

1. "If probable cause justifies the search of a lawfully stopped vehicle, it justifies the search of every part of the vehicle and its contents that may conceal the object of the search." *United States v. Ross,* 456 U.S. 798, 825 (1982).

2. "The scope of a warrantless [automobile] search based on probable cause is no narrower—and no broader—than the scope of a search authorized by a warrant supported by probable cause. Only the prior approval of the magistrate is waived; the search otherwise is as the magistrate could authorize. The scope of a warrantless search of an automobile thus is not defined by the nature of the container in which the contraband is secreted. Rather, it is defined by the object of the search and the places in which there is probable cause to believe that it may be found. Just as probable cause to believe that a stolen lawnmower may be found in a garage will not support a warrant to search an upstairs bedroom, probable cause to believe that undocumented aliens are being transported in a van will not justify a warrantless search of a suitcase." *United States v. Ross,* 456 U.S. 798, 823-24 (1982).

3. "Because the Customs officers had probable cause to believe that the pickup trucks contained contraband, any expectation of privacy in the vehicles or their contents was subject to the authority of the officers to conduct a warrantless search.... The warrantless search of the packages was not unreasonable merely because the Customs officers returned to Tucson and placed the packages in a DEA warehouse rather than immediately opening them.... Inasmuch as the Government was entitled to seize the packages and could have searched them immediately without a warrant, we conclude that the warrantless search three days after the packages were placed in the DEA warehouse was reasonable and consistent with our precedent involving searches of impounded vehicles." *United States v. Johns,* _____U.S._____, _____ (1985).

4. "[I]f the police officers have probable cause to search a vehicle, they may conduct a warrantless search of every

part of the vehicle and its contents, including closed containers, that might conceal the object of the search." *United States v. Martin,* 690 F.2d 416, 420-21 (4th Cir. 1982).

F.   Arrest of Occupant: If a person is arrested after a vehicle stop, the passenger compartment of the vehicle may be searched incident to the arrest.

1.   "[W]hen a policeman has made a lawful custodial arrest of the occupant of an automobile, he may, as a contemporaneous incident of that arrest, search the passenger compartment of that automobile. It follows from this conclusion that the police may also examine the contents of any containers found within the passenger compartment, for if the passenger compartment is within reach of the arrestee, so also will containers in it be within his reach. ... Such a container may, of course, be searched whether it is open or closed, since the justification for the search is not that the arrestee has no privacy interest in the container, but that the lawful custodial arrest justifies the infringement of any privacy interest the arrestee may have." *New York v. Belton,* 453 U.S. 454, 460-61 (1981).

2.   "*Belton* 'establish[ed] the workable rule' that objects located inside a car's passenger compartment are 'within the arrestee's immediate control'. ... [T]he *Belton* Court squarely rejected the 'fallacious theory' that a warrantless search is ruled out once a police officer seizes an article from the arrestee, thus gaining 'exclusive control' over it prior to the search." *United States v. Brown,* 671 F.2d 585, 587 (D.C. Cir. 1982).

3. "[A] search of the passenger compartment of a car incident to a lawful, custodial arrest of an occupant of the car is reasonable, because articles within this part of a car are 'generally, if not inevitably, within the area into which an arrestee might reach in order to grab a weapon or evidentiary item.'" *United States v. Montclavo-Cruz,* 662 F.2d 1285, 1287-88 (9th Cir. 1981).

4. "[A]n officer at the time of a lawful custodial arrest may, without a warrant, make a 'full' search of the person of the accused, a limited area within the control of the person arrested, and of an automobile in his possession...." *United States v. Roe,* 495 F.2d 600, 603 (10th Cir.), *cert. denied,* 419 U.S. 858 (1974).

5. "Any extension beyond the exact limits set by *Belton* (objects within the passenger compartment of the vehicle) would open a new set of temporal and spacial uncertainties, as well as increase the likelihood of unjustified invasion of the privacy of individuals." *United States v. Vaughn,* 718 F.2d 332, 333-34 (9th Cir. 1983).

G. Protective Searches of Vehicles: When police have lawfully stopped a vehicle and have a reasonable suspicion that it contains weapons that may be dangerous to the officers, they may conduct a protective search of the passenger compartment.

1. "In *Terry v. Ohio,* 392 U.S. 1 (1968), we upheld the validity of a protective search for weapons in the absence of probable cause to arrest because it is unreasonable to deny a police officer the right 'to neutralize the threat of physical harm'...when he possesses an articulable suspicion that an individual is armed and dangerous. We did not,

however, expressly address whether such a protective search for weapons could extend to an area beyond the person in the absence of probable cause to arrest.... [T]he police searched the passenger compartment because they had reason to believe that the vehicle contained weapons potentially dangerous to the officers. We hold that the protective search of the passenger compartment was reasonable under the principles articulated in *Terry* and other decisions of this Court." *Michigan v. Long,* 463 U.S. ____, ____ (1983).

2. "Our past cases indicate then that protection of police and others can justify protective searches when police have a reasonable belief that the suspect poses a danger, that roadside encounters between police and suspects are especially hazardous, and that danger may arise from the possible presence of weapons in the area surrounding a suspect. These principles compel our conclusion that the search of the passenger compartment of an automobile, limited to those areas in which a weapon may be placed or hidden, is permissible if the police officer possesses a reasonable belief based on 'specific and articulable facts which, taken together with the rational inferences from those facts, reasonably warrant' the officers in believing that the suspect is dangerous and the suspect may gain immediate control of weapons." *Michigan v. Long,* 463 U.S. ____, ____ (1983).

3. "Therefore, the balancing required by *Terry* clearly weighs in favor of allowing the police to conduct an area search of the passenger compartment to uncover weapons, as long as they possess an articulable and objectively reasonable belief that the suspect is potentially dangerous." *Michigan v. Long,* 463 U.S. ____, ____ (1983).

4. "If, while conducting a legitimate *Terry* search of the interior of the automobile, the officer should, as here, discover contraband other than weapons, he clearly cannot be required to ignore the contraband, and the Fourth Amendment does not require its suppression in such circumstances." *Michigan v. Long,* 463 U.S. ____, ____ (1983).

Chapter 12

Container and Luggage Searches

A. Seizure: Reasonable suspicion that a container holds seizable items will justify a warrantless seizure of the container. The seizure must be limited in scope, and the facts which justify the seizure will not justify a search of the container.

1. "[T]he Government asks us to recognize the reasonableness under the Fourth Amendment of warrantless seizures of personal luggage from the custody of the owner on the basis of less than probable cause, for the purpose of pursuing a limited course of investigation, short of opening the luggage, that would quickly confirm or dispel the authorities' suspicion. Specifically, we are asked to apply the principles of *Terry v. Ohio* [392 U.S. 1 (1968)] to permit such seizures on the basis of reasonable, articulable suspicion, premised on objective facts, that the luggage contains contraband or evidence of a crime. In our view, such application is appropriate." *United States v. Place,* 462 U.S. 696,____(1983).

2. "Given the fact that seizures of property can vary in intrusiveness, some brief detentions of personal effects may be so minimally intrusive of Fourth Amendment interests that strong countervailing governmental interests will justify a seizure based only on specific articulable facts that the property contains contraband or evidence of a crime." *United States v. Place,* 462 U.S. 696,____(1983).

3. "[W]hen the police seize luggage from the suspect's custody, we think the limitations applicable to investigative detentions of the person should define the permissible scope of an investigative detention of the person's luggage on less than probable cause. Under this standard, it is clear that the police conduct here exceeded the permissible limits of a *Terry*-type investigative stop. The length of the detention of respondent's luggage alone precludes the conclusion that the seizure was reasonable in the absence of probable cause." *United States v. Place,* 462 U.S. 696,____(1983).

4. "[T]he Court must determine whether the detaining officer has a reasonable and articulable suspicion that the property he wishes to seize is connected with criminal activity. If there is reasonable suspicion, the Court must then ascertain whether the detention is reasonable, that is, (1) was it sufficiently limited in time, and (2) were the investigative means used 'the least intrusive means reasonably available.'" *United States v. Sanders,* 719 F.2d 882, 887 (6th Cir. 1983).

5. "[I]f the police possess reasonable suspicion to stop someone under *Terry,* they may also seize any luggage he may be carrying, for a brief, investigatory purpose. Even though such detention restricts the possessor's freedom of movement, the seizure is permissible if the police possess reasonable, articulable suspicion, in view of the totality of the circumstances, that the luggage contains contraband or evidence of a crime. *Place* requires the same test as *Terry:* a court must weigh the intrusiveness of a limited seizure of the individual against society's interest in detection and prevention of crime.... A court analyzing a fact situation under *Place* must determine (1) whether the seizure of luggage was based on reasonable suspicion and, if so, (2) whether the seizure was of such a duration

and so restricted the possessor's freedom of movement that, given the circumstances, the seizure may only be supported by probable cause." *United States v. Puglisi,* 723 F.2d 779, 785 (11th Cir. 1984).

B. Search: Searches of closed containers normally require a warrant based on probable cause.

1. "We do not agree that the Warrant Clause protects only dwellings and other specifically designated locales.... [T]he Fourth Amendment 'protects people, not places,'...more particularly, it protects people from unreasonable government intrusions into their legitimate expectations of privacy." *United States v. Chadwick,* 433 U.S. 1, 7 (1977).

2. "[T]he general principle [is] that closed packages and containers may not be searched without a warrant." *United States v. Ross,* 456 U.S. 798, 812 (1982).

3. "A lawful search of luggage generally may be performed only pursuant to a warrant.... [L]uggage is a common repository for one's personal effects, and therefore is inevitably associated with the expectation of privacy." *Arkansas v. Sanders,* 442 U.S. 753, 762 (1979).

4. "Where law enforcement authorities have probable cause to believe that a container holds contraband or evidence of a crime, but have not secured a warrant, the Court has interpreted the [Fourth] Amendment to permit seizure of the property, pending issuance of a warrant to examine its contents, if the exigencies of the circumstances demand it or some other recognized exception to

the warrant requirement is present." *United States v. Place,* 462 U.S. 696,____(1983).

5.   "[A] package that is carefully wrapped and sealed in an opaque casing is protected by an independent, legitimate expectation of privacy and, absent some independent exemption from the warrant requirement, may not be opened without a search warrant." *United States v. Martino,* 664 F.2d 860, 873 (2d Cir. 1981), *cert. denied,* 458 U.S. 1110 (1982).

6.   "A backpack would seem to be governed by the 'suitcase' rule, as a backpack, like a suitcase, is a 'repository for personal items when one wishes to transport them.'... We therefore conclude that the warrantless search of [Defendant's] backpack violated the Fourth Amendment." *United States v. Meier,* 602 F.2d 253, 255 (10th Cir. 1979).

C.   Automobiles: The automobile exception will justify a warrantless search of containers in automobiles if the contraband for which there is probable cause to search might be secreted in such containers.

1.   "If probable cause justifies the search of a lawfully stopped vehicle, it justifies the search of every part of the vehicle and its contents that may conceal the object of the search." *United States v. Ross,* 456 U.S. 798, 825 (1982).

2.   "The scope of a warrantless [automobile] search based on probable cause is no narrower—and no broader—than the scope of a search authorized by a warrant supported by probable cause. Only the prior approval of the magistrate is waived; the search otherwise is as the

magistrate could authorize. The scope of a warrantless search of an automobile thus is not defined by the nature of the container in which the contraband is secreted. Rather, it is defined by the object of the search and the places in which there is probable cause to believe that it may be found. Just as probable cause to believe that a stolen lawnmower may be found in a garage will not support a warrant to search an upstairs bedroom, probable cause to believe that undocumented aliens are being transported in a van will not justify a warrantless search of a suitcase." *United States v. Ross,* 456 U.S. 798, 823-24 (1982).

3.   "Because the Customs officers had probable cause to believe that the pickup trucks contained contraband, any expectation of privacy in the vehicles or their contents was subject to the authority of the officers to conduct a warrantless search.... The warrantless search of the packages was not unreasonable merely because the Customs officers returned to Tucson and placed the packages in a DEA warehouse rather than immediately opening them.... Inasmuch as the Government was entitled to seize the packages and could have searched them immediately without a warrant, we conclude that the warrantless search three days after the packages were placed in the DEA warehouse was reasonable and consistent with our precedent involving searches of impounded vehicles." *United States v. Johns,* _____U.S._____, _____ (1985).

4.   "[I]f police officers have probable cause to search a vehicle, they may conduct a warrantless search of every part of the vehicle and its contents, including closed containers, that might conceal the object of the search." *United States v. Martin,* 690 F.2d 416, 420-21 (4th Cir. 1982).

5. "Once the Customs agents had probable cause to search the vessel, that probable cause supported a search of every part of the vessel that might contain the object of the search, including containers or briefcases." *United States v. Gollwitzer,* 697 F.2d 1357, 1362 (11th Cir. 1983).

D. Other Exceptions: The search incident to arrest and plain view doctrines may obviate the need to secure a warrant to search containers.

1. "[T]he protection afforded by the [Fourth] Amendment varies in different settings. The luggage carried by a traveler entering the country may be searched at random by a customs officer; the luggage may be searched no matter how great the traveler's desire to conceal the contents may be. A container carried at the time of arrest often may be searched without a warrant and even without any specific suspicion concerning its contents." *United States v. Ross,* 456 U.S. 798, 823 (1982).

2. "[W]hen a policeman has made a lawful custodial arrest of the occupant of an automobile, he may, as a contemporaneous incident of that arrest, search the passenger compartment of that automobile. It follows from this conclusion that the police may also examine the contents of any containers found within the passenger compartment, for if the passenger compartment is within reach of the arrestee, so also will containers in it be within his reach. . . . Such a container may, of course, be searched whether it is open or closed, since the justification for the search is not that the arrestee has no privacy interest in the

container, but that the lawful custodial arrest justifies the infringement of any privacy interest the arrestee may have." *New York v. Belton,* 453 U.S. 454, 460-61 (1981).

3. "Not all containers and packages found by police during the course of a search will deserve the full protection of the Fourth Amendment. Thus, some containers (for example a kit of burglar tools or a gun case) by their very nature cannot support any reasonable expectation of privacy because their contents can be inferred from their outward appearance. Similarly, in some cases the contents of a package will be open to 'plain view,' thereby obviating the need for a warrant." *Arkansas v. Sanders,* 442 U.S. 753, 764-65 n.13 (1979).

4. "After the agents determined that they had probable cause to arrest [Defendants], the agents ordered them to leave their vehicle and searched their persons. The search was conducted within the immediate vicinity of the vehicle, and the floorboard of the car was within the area of Biggles's immediate control from which he might have gained a weapon or destructible evidence." *United States v. Sanders,* 631 F.2d 1309, 1313 (8th Cir. 1980), *cert. denied,* 449 U.S. 1137 (1981).

5. "The automobile and the attache case were within the area of [Defendant's] immediate control. The attache case was not isolated or hidden in some distant room of the house or securely locked in the trunk of the car. It was in plain view and readily accessible to [Defendant]. The possibility of it housing, not only the evidence found, but also a dangerous weapon was not remote." *United States v. Frick,* 490 F.2d 666, 669 (5th Cir. 1973), *cert. denied,* 419 U.S. 831 (1974).

E. Inventory: It is an open question whether closed containers may be opened under the rationale of inventory searches when a vehicle is impounded. Closed containers may be searched under the rationale of inventory searches when an arrestee is booked.

1. "At the stationhouse, it is entirely proper for police to remove and list or inventory property found on the person or in the possession of an arrested person who is to be jailed. A range of governmental interests support an inventory process.... A standardized procedure for making a list or inventory as soon as reasonable after reaching the stationhouse not only deters false claims but also inhibits theft or careless handling of articles taken from the arrested person. Arrested persons have also been known to injure themselves—or others—with belts, knives, drugs or other items on their person while being detained. Dangerous instrumentalities—such as razor blades, bombs, or weapons—can be concealed in innocent-looking articles taken from the arrestee's possession.... Finally, inspection of an arrestee's personal property may assist the police in ascertaining or verifying his identity.... Applying these principles, we hold that it is not 'unreasonable' for police, as part of the routine procedure incident to incarcerating an arrested person, to search any container or article in his possession, in accordance with established inventory procedures." *Illinois v. Lafayette,* 462 U.S. 640,____(1983).

2. " '*Opperman [v. South Dakota,* 428 U.S. 364 (1976)]* does not authorize the inspection of suitcases, boxes, or other containers which might themselves be sealed, removed, and secured without further intrusion.' [Nor does it say] that inspection of containers is *not* authorized in an inventory search, and arguably such containers, at least if

unlocked, should be as inspectable as the unlocked glove compartment in *Opperman,* which could also have been sealed.... [T]he question whether *Opperman* permits inspection of sealable containers as an incident to an inventory is an open and serious one." *United States v. Ochs,* 595 F.2d 1247, 1256 (2d Cir.), *cert. denied,* 444 U.S. 955 (1979).

3.   "[T]he [tightly sealed] knapsack [found in Defendant's car] should have been inventoried as a unit rather than opened and itemized.... [However] [i]f a container which is to be inventoried is not securely closed, so that the articles within could possibly fall out, it may be wiser for police to itemize the articles.... And, if police have some reason to believe a container which is to be inventoried holds instrumentalities which could be dangerous even when sitting idly in the police locker, the police may, and should, inventory the contents of the container." *United States v. Bloomfield,* 594 F.2d 1200, 1203 (8th Cir. 1979).

Chapter 13

Inventory Searches

A. Seizure of Vehicles: For an inventory of a vehicle to fall within the inventory exception to the Fourth Amendment, police custody of the vehicle must be lawful.

1. "In the interests of public safety and as part of what the Court has called 'community caretaking functions' …automobiles are frequently taken into police custody. Vehicle accidents present one such occasion. … Police will also frequently remove and impound automobiles which violate parking ordinances and which thereby jeopardize both the public safety and the efficient movement of vehicular traffic. The authority of police to seize and remove from the streets vehicles impeding traffic or threatening public safety and convenience is beyond challenge." *South Dakota v. Opperman,* 428 U.S. 364, 368-69 (1976).

2. "[T]he car was lawfully in police custody, and the police were responsible for protecting the car; while engaged in the performance of their duty to protect the car…they came across incriminating evidence." *Harris v. United States,* 390 U.S. 234, 237 (1968).

3. "Just as a search authorized by state law may be an unreasonable one under…[the Fourth] Amendment, so may a search not expressly authorized by state law be justified as a constitutionally reasonable one. While it is true…that 'lawful custody of an automobile does not of

itself dispense with constitutional requirements of searches thereafter made of it...the reason for and nature of the custody may constitutionally justify the search.' " *Cooper v. California,* 386 U.S. 58, 61 (1967).

4. "Inventory searches of automobiles which are being impounded under local municipal ordinance have generally been upheld as being reasonable and not in violation of the Fourth or Fourteenth Amendments." *United States v. Martin,* 556 F.2d 1143, 1145 (10th Cir. 1977).

5. "[W]hen officers lawfully impound a vehicle in the regular course of their duties, the Constitution allows them to search the vehicle if to do so accords with their routine procedures." *United States v. Edwards,* 554 F.2d 1331, 1337 (5th Cir. 1977), *cert. denied,* 439 U.S. 968 (1978).

B. Justification: The inventory search may be conducted only to protect the owner's property and to protect the police.

1. "When vehicles are impounded, local police departments generally follow a routine practice of securing and inventorying the automobiles' contents. These procedures developed in response to three distinct needs: [1] the protection of the owner's property...[2] the protection of the police against claims or disputes over lost or stolen property...and [3] the protection of the police from potential danger." *South Dakota v. Opperman,* 428 U.S. 364, 369 (1976).

2. "[O]nce a vehicle is seized and legitimately taken into police custody, the routine practice of securing and inventorying its contents is justified as serving three distinct

needs: '[T]he protection of the owner's property while it remains in police custody...; the protection of the police against claims or disputes over lost or stolen property...; and the protection of the police from potential danger.'" *United States v. Maier,* 691 F.2d 421, 423 (8th Cir. 1982), *cert. denied,* ____U.S.____(1984).

3.   "Thus, the justification for an inventory search 'does not rest on probable cause and...the absence of a warrant is immaterial to the reasonableness of the search.'" *United States v. Griffin,* 729 F.2d 475, 481 (7th Cir. 1984).

4.   " '[I]nventory searches must be limited to effectuation of the recognized purposes for which they are conducted and they may not be used as a pretext for intrusive investigatory searches that would otherwise be impermissible.' One of the strongest indications that an inventory check was indeed conducted for legitimate purposes is evidence that such a search is a standard practice for the particular law enforcement agency." *United States v. Laing,* 708 F.2d 1568, 1570 (11th Cir.), *cert. denied,* ____ U.S.____(1983).

5.   "One reason for an inventory search in connection with the impounding of a vehicle under local municipal ordinance is to protect the police against subsequent disputes over allegedly lost or stolen property." *United States v. Martin,* 566 F.2d 1143, 1145 (10th Cir. 1977).

C.   Nature of Search: The inventory search must be a routine part of standard police procedure rather than a pretext for an investigatory search.

1.   "[T]here is no suggestion whatever that this standard [inventory] procedure, essentially like that followed

throughout the country, was a pretext concealing an investigatory police motive." *South Dakota v. Opperman,* 428 U.S. 364, 376 (1976).

2. "The Court's previous recognition of the distinction between motor vehicles and dwelling places leads us to conclude that the type of caretaking 'search' conducted here of a vehicle that was neither in the custody nor on the premises of its owner, and that had been placed where it was by virtue of lawful police action, was not unreasonable solely because a warrant had not been obtained.... Where, as here, the trunk of an automobile, which the officer reasonably believed to contain a gun, was vulnerable to intrusion by vandals, we hold that the search was not 'unreasonable' within the meaning of the Fourth and Fourteenth Amendments." *Cady v. Dombrowski,* 413 U.S. 433, 447-48 (1973).

3. "[T]he needs of the Government in conducting an inventory search may be ordinarily accomplished without the serious intrusion into the locked trunk of an automobile. Absent a special justification for more extensive intrusion, the routine search of a locked automobile trunk is unreasonable under the Fourth Amendment." *United States v. Wilson,* 636 F.2d 1161, 1165 (8th Cir. 1980).

4. "[I]n conducting an inventory search pursuant to standard police practice, an officer may search those places within an automobile where, under the facts of the particular case, he can reasonably conclude that personal property may be located." *United States v. Edwards,* 577 F.2d 883, 885 (5th Cir.), *cert. denied,* 439 U.S. 968 (1978).

5.   "[A] legitimate seizure does not automatically justify an unlimited search of an automobile, and...the search must still be reasonable in light of the facts and circumstances of the particular case.... Here...no reason existed to limit the inventory search to the passenger area of the vehicle. After discovering the large amount of money in the cab, and in light of the absence of the owner, the need under *Opperman* for a reasonable police procedure for 'protection of the owner's property' justified police in examining and making an inventory of the entire vehicle, including the locked camper, to assure that any other valuable property would be recorded and kept safe." *United States v. Maier,* 691 F.2d 421, 423-24, 425 (8th Cir. 1982), *cert. denied,* ____U.S.____(1984).

6.   "Of course, a routine automobile inventory search must be limited to the purposes for which it was effectuated.... [The] decision to inventory and secure each and every item contained within the Corvette, including the contents of the unsecured brown paper bag, protected the bag's contents from falling out and being lost.... '[I]f a container which is to be inventoried is not securely closed so that the articles within could possibly fall out, it may be wiser for police to itemize the articles.' In addition, [the] decision to itemize the unknown contents of the unsecured brown paper bag allowed the Indiana State Police Department to verify the bag's contents, and thus prevent false claims of lost or stolen property." *United States v. Griffin,* 729 F.2d 475, 483, 485 (7th Cir. 1984).

7.   "Counsel would escape the rule of *Opperman* by pointing out that the glove compartment in *Opperman* was unlocked, and that the [car's] trunk in the instant case had to be opened with a key. This argument overlooks the fact that though the glove compartment in *Opperman* was unlocked, the car itself was locked.... Therefore, in both

Opperman and the instant case a key had to be used before access could be made to the particular area where the search later complained about was effected. We found no real difference between *Opperman* and the instant case." *United States v. Martin,* 566 F.2d 1143, 1145 (10th Cir. 1977).

D.   Booking Searches: A custodial search of an arrestee's personal effects may be justified as an inventory procedure.

1.   "[I]t is not 'unreasonable' for police, as part of the routine procedure incident to incarcerating an arrested person, to search any container or article in his possession, in accordance with established inventory procedures." *Illinois v. Lafayette,* 462 U.S. 640,____(1983).

2.   "A range of governmental interests support an inventory process. . . . A standardized procedure for making a list or inventory as soon as reasonable after reaching the stationhouse not only deters false claims but also inhibits theft or careless handling of articles taken from the arrested person. Arrested persons have also been known to injure themselves—or others—with belts, knives, drugs or other items on their person while being detained. Dangerous instrumentalities—such as razor blades, bombs, or weapons—can be concealed in innocent-looking articles taken from the arrestee's possession. . . . Examining all the items removed from the arrestee's person or possession and listing or inventorying them is an entirely reasonable administrative procedure. It is immaterial whether the police actually fear any particular package or container; the need to protect against such risks arises independent of a particular officer's subjective concerns. . . . Finally, inspec-

tion of an arrestee's personal property may assist the police in ascertaining or verifying his identity." *Illinois v. Lafayette,* 462 U.S. 640,____(1983).

3. "[O]nce the accused is lawfully arrested and is in custody, the effects in his possession at the place of detention that were subject to search at the time and place of his arrest may lawfully be searched and seized without a warrant even though a substantial period of time has elapsed between the arrest and subsequent administrative processing, on the one hand, and the taking of the property for use as evidence, on the other hand. This is true where the clothing or effects are immediately seized upon arrival at the jail, held under the defendant's name in the 'property room' of the jail, and at a later time searched and taken for use at the subsequent criminal trial." *United States v. Edwards,* 415 U.S. 800, 807 (1974).

4. "[S]earches of an individual and his wallet or other personal property at this stage of the arrest [incarceration] have been upheld both as incident to a lawful arrest when conducted shortly afterward at the jail or place of detention and for the purpose of discovering concealed weapons. Likewise, such search has been upheld as being part of the necessary inventory of an accused's personal property both to preserve the accused's belongings while he is incarcerated and to safeguard the police from a later groundless claim that some item has not been returned to him." *United States v. Gardner,* 480 F.2d 929, 931 (10th Cir.), *cert. denied,* 414 U.S. 977 (1973).

5. "It can not be denied that to prevent escape, self-injury, or harm to others, the police have a legitimate interest in separating the accused from the property found in his possession. An inventory is then necessary both to preserve the property of the accused while he is in jail and

to forestall the possibility that the accused may later claim that some item has not been returned to him." *United States v. Lipscomb,* 435 F.2d 795, 800 (5th Cir. 1970), *cert. denied,* 401 U.S. 980 (1971).

Chapter 14

Plain View

A. Location of Police: The police officer must be at a location where he has a legal right to be.

1. "The plain view doctrine is grounded on the proposition that once police are lawfully in a position to observe an item first-hand, its owner's privacy interest in that item is lost; the owner may retain the incidents of title and possession but not privacy." *Illinois v. Andreas,* 463 U.S. 765,____(1983).

2. "[T]he police officer must lawfully make an 'initial intrusion' or otherwise properly be in a position from which he can view a particular area.... '[P]lain view' provides grounds for seizure of an item when an officer's access to an object has some prior justification under the Fourth Amendment." *Texas v. Brown,* 460 U.S.730, 737(1983).

3. "[O]bjects falling in the plain view of an officer who has a right to be in the position to have that view are subject to seizure and may be introduced in evidence." *Harris v. United States,* 390 U.S. 234, 236 (1968).

4. "[T]he police officer...[must have] had a prior justification for an intrusion in the course of which he came inadvertently across a piece of evidence incriminating the accused...[T]his initial intrusion is justified by a warrant or by an exception such as 'hot pursuit' or search incident to a lawful arrest, or by an extraneous valid reason for the

officer's presence." *Coolidge v. New Hampshire,* 403 U.S. 443, 466-67 (1971).

5. "The primary requisite for the application of the plain view doctrine is that the police officer has a right to be where he is when he sees the evidence." *United States v. Blalock,* 578 F.2d 245, 248 (9th Cir. 1978).

6. "Just as what an officer sees when lawfully present is considered nonintrusive plain view, what he hears while so stationed is similarly not a search and seizure and is thus *per se* lawful. . . . [A]n agent could lawfully stand with his ear pressed against a wall and. . .such a presence may be reasonably anticipated by defendants." *United States v. Mankani,* 738 F.2d 538, 543 (2d Cir. 1984).

7. "Ordinarily, 'only items described in a search warrant may be seized.' However, when in the course of performing a lawful search for an item listed on the warrant, the officers come across other articles of an incriminatory character, that property may be seized under the plain view doctrine." *United States v. Johnson,* 713 F.2d 654, 660 (11th Cir. 1983), *cert. denied,* ____U.S.____(1984).

B. Nature of Discovery: The discovery of the seized item must be inadvertent.

1. "[T]he police must discover incriminating evidence 'inadvertently,' which is to say, they may not 'know in advance the location of [certain] evidence and intend to seize it,' relying on the plain view doctrine only as a pretense." *Texas v. Brown,* 460 U.S. 730, 737(1983).

2. "[T]he police [cannot] know in advance the location of the evidence and intend to seize it...." *Coolidge v. New Hampshire,* 403 U.S. 443, 470 (1971).

3. "[Plain view] allows the seizure of 'incriminating' articles not listed in the warrant but found inadvertently by the officers in executing a valid warrant." *United States v. Ross,* 527 F.2d 984, 985 (4th Cir. 1975), *cert. denied,* 424 U.S. 945 (1976).

4. "[T]he plain view doctrine is properly applied to situations in which a police officer is not searching for evidence against the accused but nevertheless inadvertently comes across an incriminating object." *United States v. Sedillo,* 496 F.2d 151, 152 (9th Cir.), *cert. denied,* 419 U.S. 947 (1974).

C. Nature of Evidence: The seized item must appear to be incriminating.

1. "The plain view doctrine authorizes seizure of illegal or evidentiary items visible to a police officer whose access to the object has some prior Fourth Amendment justification and who has probable cause to suspect that the item is connected with criminal activity." *Illinois v. Andreas,* 463 U.S. 765,____(1983).

2. "[I]t must be 'immediately apparent' to the police that the items they observe may be evidence of a crime, contraband, or otherwise subject to seizure." *Texas v. Brown,* 460 U.S. 730, 737 (1983).

3. "[T]he extension of the original justification is legitimate only where it is immediately apparent to the police

that they have evidence before them." *Coolidge v. New Hampshire,* 403 U.S. 443, 466 (1971).

4. "The 'plain view' exception to the Fourth Amendment warrant requirement permits a law enforcement officer to seize what clearly is incriminating evidence or contraband when it is discovered in a place where the officer has a right to be." *Washington v. Chrisman,* 455 U.S. 1, 5-6 (1982).

5. "[T]he 'immediately apparent' language of *Coolidge* [does not] establish...any requirement that a police officer 'know' that certain items are contraband or evidence of a crime." *Texas v. Brown,* 460 U.S. 730, 741(1983).

6. "Where the initial intrusion by a police officer is justified, the warrantless seizure of inadvertently discovered evidence in plain view does not offend the Constitution if it is immediately apparent to the police officer that he has evidence before him." *United States v. Duckett,* 583 F.2d 1309, 1313 (5th Cir. 1978).

7. "[W]as the evidence incriminating on its face? In answering this question, it is critical to remember that a law enforcement official making evaluations is not bound to the objective knowledge of a reasonable person. Such an agent may rely on his special experience and knowledge in determining whether, for example, reasonable suspicion or probable cause exists." *United States v. Slocum,* 708 F.2d 587, 605 (11th Cir. 1983).

8. "[A]n officer may inspect an item found in plain view to determine whether it is evidence of a crime if he 'has a "reasonable suspicion" to believe that the discovered item is evidence.'" *United States v. Hillyard,* 677 F.2d 1336, 1342 (9th Cir. 1982).

9.   "[T]he plain view doctrine would permit brief perusal of the book's contents and, consequently, its seizure if such perusal gives the examining agent probable cause to believe that the book constitutes evidence. We do not mean to suggest that agents entitled to examine a book or similar item may minutely scrutinize its contents, especially when personal, nonbusiness papers are involved." *United States v. Issacs,* 708 F.2d 1365, 1370 (9th Cir.), *cert. denied,* ____U.S.____(1983).

Chapter 15

Abandonment

A. Act: Abandonment is a voluntary relinquishment of control of property.

1. "[Items] were found in the room's wastepaper basket, where petitioner had put them while packing his belongings and preparing to leave.... He had thrown them away.... There can be nothing unlawful in the Government's appropriation of such abandoned property." *Abel v. United States,* 362 U.S. 217, 241 (1960).

2. "The defendant's own acts, and those of his associates, disclosed the jug, the jar and the bottle—and there was no seizure in the sense of the law when the officers examined the contents of each after it had been abandoned." *Hester v. United States,* 265 U.S. 57, 58 (1924).

3. "The test for abandonment is whether an individual has retained any reasonable expectation of privacy in the object. This determination is to be made by objective standards. An expectation of privacy is a question of intent, which 'may be inferred from words spoken, acts done, and other objective facts.'" *United States v. Jones,* 707 F.2d 1169, 1172 (10th Cir.), *cert. denied,* _____U.S._____(1983).

4. "Abandonment...is not meant in the strict property-right sense, but rests instead on whether the person so relinquished his interest in the property that he no longer retained a reasonable expectation of privacy in it at the

time of the search." *United States v. Jackson,* 544 F.2d
407, 409 (9th Cir. 1976).

5.   "Abandonment is an ultimate fact or conclusion based
generally upon a combination of act and intent. How did the
person who was supposed to have abandoned the property act, that is, what did he do, and, second, what was his
intention? These call for factual determinations." *Friedman
v. United States,* 347 F.2d 697, 704 (8th Cir.), *cert. denied,*
382 U.S. 946 (1965).

6.   "There was no seizure in disregard of any lawful right
when the officers retrieved and examined the packets
which had been dropped in a public place." *Trujillo v.
United States,* 294 F.2d 583, 583-84 (10th Cir. 1961).

7.   "The requisite intent has been held to be present by
such acts as: throwing contraband out of a moving vehicle
when pursued by police...; a denial of ownership when
questioned, [when] the defendant is seen previously in
possession of the item...; and leaving the item behind in a
trash basket at a hotel after checking out...; or in a trash
can next to the sidewalk." *United States v. Cella,* 568 F.2d
1266, 1283-84 (9th Cir. 1978).

8.   "[T]he act of leaving the airport without claiming one's
luggage, without more, does not constitute abandonment."
United States v. Sanders, 719 F.2d 882, 885 (6th Cir.
1983).

**B.   Consequence: An individual who abandons prop-
erty does not retain any expectation of privacy which
is constitutionally protected.**

1.   "The test for abandonment is whether the complaining
party retains a reasonable expectation of privacy in the

premises." *United States v. Akin,* 562 F.2d 459, 464 (7th Cir. 1977), *cert. denied,* 435 U.S. 933 (1978).

2. "The primary question. . .is whether abandonment is to be determined by reference to subjective intent or by reference to the objective manifestation of an individual's intent. . . . Whether a person entertains a reasonable expectation of privacy is to be determined by objective standards." *United States v. Kendall,* 655 F.2d 199, 200-01 (9th Cir. 1981), *cert. denied,* 455 U.S. 941 (1982).

3. "Because no one owns or possesses abandoned property, no one can claim a Fourth Amendment interest in it. . . . The very notion of abandonment. . .implies a renunciation of any reasonable expectation of privacy." *United States v. Alden,* 576 F.2d 772, 777 (8th Cir.), *cert. denied,* 439 U.S. 855 (1978).

4. "To the extent his possession of the explosives might have given him a claim, he lost that claim by abandoning the explosives in a public area. When a person has 'so relinquished his interest in the property that he no longer retains a reasonable expectation of privacy in it at the time of the search' he has no standing to complain of a Fourth Amendment violation." *United States v. McFillin,* 713 F.2d 57, 59 (4th Cir.), *cert. denied,* 454 U.S. 1056 (1981).

5. " '[The Defendant's] denial of ownership should not defeat his legitimate expectation of privacy in the space invaded and thus his right to contest the lawfulness of the search when the government at trial calls upon the jury to reject that denial.' " *United States v. Morales,* 737 F.2d 761, 764 (8th Cir. 1984).

6. "Those circuits that have considered the issue of whether a person has a legitimate expectation of privacy in trash placed for collection in a public area, in close proximity to a public way, or in an outdoors communal trash container serving an apartment building, have consistently denied fourth amendment relief.... 'Having placed the trash in an area particularly suited for public inspection and, in a manner of speaking, public consumption, for the express purpose of having strangers take it, it is inconceivable that the defendant intended to retain a privacy interest in the discarded objects. If he had such an expectation, it was not reasonable.'" *United States v. Michaels,* 726 F.2d 1307, 1312, 1313 (8th Cir. 1984).

Chapter 16

Curtilage

A. The Curtilage Doctrine: The curtilage is afforded the same Fourth Amendment protections as is the home.

1. "[O]nly the curtilage, not the neighboring open fields, warrants the Fourth Amendment protections that attach to the home. At common law, the curtilage is the area to which extends the intimate activity associated with the 'sanctity of a man's home and the privacies of life,'...and therefore has been considered part of home itself for Fourth Amendment purposes. Thus, courts have extended Fourth Amendment protection to the curtilage; and they have defined the curtilage, as did the common law, by reference to the factors that determine whether an individual reasonably may expect that an area immediately adjacent to the home will remain private." *Oliver v. United States,* 466 U.S.____,____(1984).

2. "The sacredness of a person's home and his right of personal privacy and individuality are paramount considerations in our country and are specifically protected by the Fourth Amendment. The Fourth Amendment's protection, however, extends further than just the walls of the physical structure of the home itself. The area immediately surrounding and closely related to the dwelling is also entitled to the Fourth Amendment's protection. In defining the surrounding area entitled to such protection, the courts historically have found helpful the common law concept of curtilage, meaning 'yard, courtyard or other piece of ground

included within the fence surrounding a dwelling house'. . . . When officers have physically invaded this protected area, either to seize evidence or to obtain a view of illegal activities, we have readily condemned such an invasion as violative of the Fourth Amendment." *Fixel v. Wainwright,* 492 F.2d 480, 483 (5th Cir. 1974).

3. "The protection afforded by the Fourth Amendment, insofar as houses are concerned, has never been restricted to the interior of the house, but has extended to open areas immediately adjacent thereto. The differentiation between an immediately protected area and an unprotected open field has usually been analyzed as a problem of determining the extent of the 'curtilage.'" *Wattenberg v. United States,* 388 F.2d 853, 857 (9th Cir. 1968).

4. "The curtilage of the home is formed by the buildings 'constituting an integral part of that group of structures making up the farm home,' or 'the immediate domestic establishment' of the home. The 'outer limits of the curtilage' have been expressly defined to be 'the outer walls of the extreme outbuildings of the curtilage.'" *United States v. Berrong,* 712 F.2d 1370, 1374 (11th Cir. 1983), *cert. denied,* ____U.S.____(1984).

5. "Generally speaking, curtilage has been held to include all buildings in close proximity to a dwelling, which are continually used for carrying on domestic employment; or such place as is necessary and convenient to a dwelling, and is habitually used for family purposes." *United States v. Potts,* 297 F.2d 68, 69 (6th Cir. 1961).

B. The Open Field Doctrine: Fourth Amendment protections do not extend to the "open fields" surrounding the curtilage and the home.

1. "[T]he special protection accorded by the Fourth Amendment to the people in their 'persons, houses, papers, and effects,' is not extended to the open fields. The distinction between the latter and the house is as old as the common law." *Hester v. United States,* 265 U.S. 57, 59 (1924).

2. "It is clear, however, that the term 'open fields' may include any unoccupied or undeveloped area outside of the curtilage. An open field need be neither 'open' nor a 'field' as those terms are used in common speech." *Oliver v. United States,* 466 U.S.____,____n.11 (1984).

3. "The field inspector did not enter the [Defendant's] plant or offices. . . . He had sighted what anyone in the city who was near the plant could see in the sky—plumes of smoke. The Court [has previously] refused to extend the Fourth Amendment to sights seen in 'the open fields'. . . . [T]he inspector may operate within or without the premises but in either case he is well within the 'open fields' exception to the Fourth Amendment." *Air Pollution Variance Board v. Western Alfalfa,* 416 U.S. 861, 864, 865 (1974).

4. "The Fourth Amendment's protections do not extend to the 'open field' area surrounding a dwelling and the immediate adjacent curtilage, and therefore, information gained as a result of civil trespass [by police officers] on an 'open field' area is not constitutionally tainted, nor is the search and seizure which ultimately results from acquiring that information." *United States v. Capps,* 435 F.2d 637, 640 (9th Cir. 1971).

5. "[I]nasmuch as the protection of the Fourth Amendment against unreasonable searches and seizures does not extend to 'open fields,' there is no unreasonable search.... Moreover, even if the officers were trespassing on private property, a trespass does not itself constitute an illegal search." *Atwell v. United States,* 414 F.2d 136, 138 (5th Cir. 1969).

6. "[A]t no time was the dwelling of [Defendant], or the curtilage surrounding the dwelling, invaded for the purposes of the search. It cannot be seriously contended the open fields in question were part of the curtilage. The fields were clearly separated from the farm buildings of [the Defendant] and about one-quarter to one-half mile distant therefrom.... Therefore, a search of open fields, without a search warrant, even if such fields are construed as part of a commercial enterprise, is not constitutionally 'unreasonable.'" *McDowell v. United States,* 383 F.2d 599, 603 (8th Cir. 1967).

C. Legitimate Expectation of Privacy: The determination of whether Fourth Amendment protections will be extended focuses on whether the person challenging the search has a legitimate expectation of privacy in the place that was searched.

1. "[B]y focusing on legitimate expectations of privacy in Fourth Amendment jurisprudence, the Court has not altogether abandoned use of property concepts in determining the presence or absence of the privacy interest protected by that Amendment.... On the other hand, even a property interest in premises may not be sufficient to establish a legitimate expectation of privacy with respect to particular

items located on the premises or activity conducted thereon." *Rakas v. Illinois,* 439 U.S. 128, 144 n.12 (1978).

2.   "[A]n individual may not legitimately demand privacy for activities conducted out of doors in fields, except in the area immediately surrounding the home.... [O]pen fields do not provide the setting for those intimate activities that the Amendment is intended to shelter from government interference or surveillance." *Oliver v. United States,* 466 U.S.____,____(1984).

3.   "[N]o...expectation of privacy extended...to movements of objects such as the drum of chloroform outside the cabin in the 'open fields.' " *United States v. Knotts,* 460 U.S. 276, 282(1983).

4.   "It is sufficient here to observe that whatever expectation of privacy attends a closed but unsecured 'effect' generally is diminished where the 'effect' itself is placed in an area totally without the protection of the fourth amendment such as an open field." *United States v. Ramapuram,* 632 F.2d 1149, 1155 (4th Cir. 1980), *cert. denied,* 450 U.S. 1030 (1981).

5.   "Although the expectations [of privacy] test has done away with outmoded property concepts no longer satisfactory for fourth amendment analysis...the distinction between open fields and curtilage is still helpful in determining the existence or not of reasonable privacy expectations." *United States v. Williams,* 581 F.2d 451, 453 (5th Cir. 1978), *cert. denied,* 440 U.S. 972 (1979).

6.   "Further, even absent the 'open fields' doctrine, aerial surveillance without a warrant of an area such as this large commercial gravel pit tract does not amount to an unconstitutional search, at least where, as here, it is for the purpose

of verifying a particularized, justifiable belief concerning criminal activity associated with the premises." *United States v. Marbury*, 732 F.2d 390, 398 (5th Cir. 1984).

Chapter 17

Consent

A. Voluntariness: The prosecutor has the burden of proving that the defendant's consent to a warrantless search was given freely and voluntarily.

1.   "[W]here the validity of a search rests on consent, the State has the burden of proving that the necessary consent was obtained and that it was freely and voluntarily given, a burden that is not satisfied by showing a mere submission to a claim of lawful authority." *Florida v. Royer,* 460 U.S. 491, 497 (1983).

2.   "The question whether the respondent's consent to accompany the agents was in fact voluntary or was the product of duress or coercion, express or implied, is to be determined by the totality of all the circumstances...and is a matter which the government has the burden of proving." *United States v. Mendenhall,* 446 U.S. 544, 557 (1980).

3.   "The prosecutor...has the burden of proving that the consent was, in fact, freely and voluntarily given." *Bumper v. North Carolina,* 391 U.S. 543, 548 (1968).

4.   "[T]he specifics necessary to sustain the burden required of the government to establish justification for a warrantless [consent] search...may be paraphrased in the following manner: (1) There must be clear and positive testimony that consent was 'unequivocal and specific' and 'freely and intelligently' given; (2) the government must prove consent was given without duress or coercion,

express or implied; and (3) the courts indulge every reasonable presumption against the waiver of fundamental constitutional rights and there must be convincing evidence that such rights were waived." *United States v. Abbott,* 546 F.2d 883, 885 (10th Cir.), *cert. denied,* 430 U.S. 966 (1977).

5. "When attempting to prove voluntary consent to search following an illegal stop, the Government has a much heavier burden to satisfy than when proving consent to search after a legitimate initial stop. In addition to proving valid and voluntary consent to search, the Government must also establish the existence of intervening factors which prove that the consent was sufficiently attenuated from the illegal stop." *United States v. Melendez-Gonzalez,* 727 F.2d 407, 414 (5th Cir. 1984).

6. "In the context of an airport stop 'exceptionally clear evidence' is required to establish voluntary consent to go to an airport office.... Further, the government bears the burden of showing voluntary consent." *United States v. Robinson,* 690 F.2d 869, 875 (11th Cir. 1982).

B. Test: The voluntariness of a person's consent is measured by the totality of the circumstances.

1. "[T]he question whether a consent to a search was in fact 'voluntary' or was a product of duress or coercion, express or implied, is a question of fact to be determined from the totality of all the circumstances." *Schneckloth v. Bustamonte,* 412 U.S. 218, 227 (1973).

2. "Although the Constitution does not require 'proof of knowledge of a right to refuse as the *sine qua non* of an effective consent to a search,'...such knowledge was

highly relevant to the determination that there had been consent." *United States v. Mendenhall,* 446 U.S. 544, 558-59 (1980).

3.   "[I]t would be next to impossible to apply to a consent search the standard of 'an intentional relinquishment or abandonment of a known right or privilege.'" *Schneckloth v. Bustamonte,* 412 U.S. 218, 243 (1973).

4.   "Some of the factors relevant to the consent inquiry are: 'voluntariness of the defendant's custodial status, the presence of coercive police procedure, the extent and level of the defendant's cooperation with police, the defendant's awareness of his right to refuse consent to the search, [and] the defendant's education and intelligence.'" *United States v. Robinson,* 690 F.2d 869, 875 (11th Cir. 1982).

5.   "Ignorance of the right to refuse to consent to a search is a factor to be considered in evaluation of the totality of the circumstances, but it is not dispositive of the issue of voluntariness. '[T]he defendant need not be informed specifically of his Fourth Amendment rights..., nor must the investigating officer state that he will refrain from searching if the defendant refuses to give permission.'" *United States v. Mejia,* 720 F.2d 1378, 1381 (5th Cir. 1983).

6.   "[V]oluntary consent requires an intellectual understanding of exactly what is being requested and a voluntary acquiescence in light of that understanding. More, such an approach requires an analysis of all the facts and circumstances surrounding the defendant's alleged consent and is not predicated upon a single factor or combination of factors less than the whole." *United States v. D'Allerman,* 712 F.2d 100, 104 (5th Cir.), *cert. denied,* ____U.S.____ (1983).

7.   " 'When a law enforcement officer claims authority to search a home under a warrant, he announces in effect that the occupant has no right to resist the search. The situation is instinct with coercion—albeit colorably lawful coercion. Where there is coercion there cannot be consent.'...'*Bumper* may be read to hold that a search can never be justified on the basis of consent when consent has been given after an official has asserted that he or she possesses a warrant.'" *United States v. Alberts,* 721 F.2d 636, 640 (8th Cir. 1983).

8.   " '[A]n undercover police officer's entry by consent, though obtained by deception, is not prohibited by the Fourth Amendment'.... '[M]isrepresentations about the nature of an investigation may be evidence of coercion.' The misrepresentation may even invalidate the consent if the consent was given in reliance on the officer's deceit." *United States v. Briley,* 726 F.2d 1301, 1304 (8th Cir. 1984).

C.   Consent After Arrest: If the consenting party is in custody, the voluntariness of the consent is still measured by the totality of the circumstances, although courts will often analyze the relevant factors more critically.

1.   "[T]he fact of custody alone has never been enough in itself to demonstrate a coerced confession or consent to search. Similarly,...the absence of proof that [Defendant] knew he could withhold his consent, though it may be a factor in the overall judgment, is not to be given controlling significance." *United States v. Watson,* 423 U.S. 411, 424 (1976).

2. "[A]n alleged voluntary consent to search must be viewed with caution and misgivings if given after arrest.... [T]he court must look to all of the facts and circumstances in determining whether consent to search is freely given by one under arrest." *United States v. Shields,* 573 F.2d 18, 23 (10th Cir. 1978).

3. "The fact that the defendant is in custody and lacks knowledge of his right to refuse to consent forms part of the circumstances, but is not determinative in and of itself." *United States v. Townsend,* 510 F.2d 1145, 1146 (9th Cir. 1975).

4. "[Defendant] was not simply asked if he would consent to a search; he was hauled off the street and into a private office and told that if he did not consent to a search he would be held until [the agent] obtained a search warrant. In view of the fact that [Defendant] was threatened with being detained, although [the agent] had no right to hold him, his consent cannot be considered voluntary. It was obtained under duress; the alleged consent does not vitiate the illegality of the arrest." *United States v. Jefferson,* 650 F.2d 854, 858 (6th Cir. 1981).

D. Third Party Consent: Consent for a warrantless search may be given by a third party who shares control of the premises or items to be searched.

1. "[T]he prosecution...is not limited to proof that consent was given by the defendant, but may show that permission to search was obtained from a third party who possessed common authority over or other sufficient relationship to the premises or effects sought to be

inspected." *United States v. Matlock,* 415 U.S. 164, 171 (1974).

2. "Common authority...rests...on mutual use of the property by persons generally having joint access or control for most purposes, so that it is reasonable to recognize that any of the co-inhabitants has the right to permit the inspection in his own right and that the others have assumed the risk that one of their number might permit the common areas to be searched." *United States v. Matlock,* 415 U.S. 164, 171 n.7 (1974).

3. "No less than a tenant of a house, or the occupant of a room in a boarding house,...a guest in a hotel room is entitled to constitutional protection against unreasonable searches and seizures.... That protection would disappear if it were left to depend upon the unfettered discretion of an employee of the hotel. It follows that this search without a warrant was unlawful." *Stoner v. California,* 376 U.S. 483, 490 (1964).

4. "Generally, a lessor cannot consent to a search of leased premises.... However, to the extent that a lessor has the right to enter a room, he can authorize entry by the police.... We do not hold that police must invariably seek consent from the suspect before relying on a third party's consent. However, when the police intentionally bypass a suspect who is present and known by them to possess a superior privacy interest, the validity of third party consent is less certain." *United States v. Impink,* 728 F.2d 1228, 1232, 1234 (9th Cir. 1984).

5. "One who has possession and control of the articles seized or the premises on which they are found may consent to a search which produces incriminating evidence against someone else." *United States v. Brown,* 540 F.2d

1048, 1057 (10th Cir. 1976), *cert. denied,* 429 U.S. 1100 (1977).

6. "We think appellee's exclusive right to use the desk assigned to her made the search of it unreasonable. No doubt a search of it without her consent would have been reasonable if made by some people in some circumstances. Her official superiors might reasonably have searched the desk for official property needed for official use. But...[h]er superiors could not reasonably search the desk for her purse, her personal letters, or anything else that did not belong to the government and had no connection with the work of the office. Their consent did not make such a search by the police reasonable." *United States v. Blok,* 188 F.2d 1019, 1021 (D.C. Cir. 1951).

E. Scope of Consent: A consent search may not exceed the terms of a consent.

1. "When an official search is properly authorized—whether by consent or by the issuance of a valid warrant—the scope of the search is limited by the terms of its authorization. Consent to search a garage would not implicitly authorize a search of an adjoining house." *Walter v. United States,* 447 U.S. 649, 656-57 (1980).

2. "When the basis for a search or seizure is consent, the government must conform to the limitations placed upon the right granted to search, seize or retain the papers or effects." *Mason v. Pulliam,* 557 F.2d 426, 429 (5th Cir. 1977).

3. "The only restraint on a validly authorized search, one conducted pursuant to consent or upon issuance of a

warrant, is that the scope of the search be limited to the terms of its authorization." *United States v. Rackley,* 724 F.2d 1463, 1468 (11th Cir. 1984).

4. "It is clear that a person may limit the consent which he gives to authorities to search his premises.... And 'a consent search is reasonable only if kept within the bounds of the actual consent.'" *United States v. Griffin,* 530 F.2d 739, 744 (7th Cir. 1976).

5. "[T]he defendant's consent set the parameters of the agents' conduct at that which would reasonably be necessary to determine whether he had narcotics in his home. But the agents went beyond what was necessary to determine whether defendant had hidden narcotics among his personal papers; they read through those papers to determine whether they gave any hint that defendant was engaged in criminal activity. This was a greater intrusion into defendant's privacy than he had authorized and the fourth amendment requires that any evidence resulting from this invasion be suppressed." *United States v. Dichiarinte,* 445 F.2d 126, 130 (7th Cir. 1971).

Chapter 18

Border and Immigration Stops and Searches

A. Standard: A reasonable border search may be conducted of all persons and property entering the country.

1. "Travellers may be…stopped in crossing an international boundary because of national self protection reasonably requiring one entering the country to identify himself as entitled to come in, and his belongings as effects which may be lawfully brought in." *Carroll v. United States,* 267 U.S. 132, 154 (1925).

5. "The authority of the United States to search the baggage of arriving international travelers is based on its inherent sovereign authority to protect its territorial integrity. By reason of that authority, it is entitled to require that whoever seeks entry must establish the right to enter and to bring into the country whatever he may carry." *Torres v. Puerto Rico,* 442 U.S. 465, 472-73 (1979).

3. "Border searches,…from before the adoption of the Fourth Amendment, have been considered to be 'reasonable' by the single fact that the person or item in question had entered into our country from outside…. This longstanding recognition that searches at our borders without probable cause and without a warrant are nonetheless 'reasonable' has a history as old as the Fourth Amendment itself." *United States v. Ramsey,* 431 U.S. 606, 619 (1977).

4. "Although courts traditionally have employed the border search exception to uphold warrantless searches of persons or objects entering the United States, the rationale behind this exception applies with equal force to persons or objects leaving the country: the Government has an interest in protecting some interest of United States' citizens, the individual is on notice that his privacy may be invaded when he crosses the border, and the individual will be searched only because of his membership in a morally neutral class." *United States v. Udofot,* 711 F.2d 831, 839 (8th Cir.), *cert. denied,*____U.S.____(1983).

B.   Border Area: The border search exception applies to the immediate vicinity of the border as well as the boundary line itself.

1.   "Practical considerations dictate a certain amount of elasticity in describing the area within which the border search standard is constitutionally appropriate, a determination dependent upon the particular facts of each case. The area has not been limited to the actual confines of an international port or to the border itself. On the contrary, it has been expanded to a 'reasonable extended geographic area in the immediate vicinity of any entry point.'" *United States v. Beck,* 483 F.2d 203, 207-08 (3d Cir. 1973), *cert. denied,* 414 U.S. 1132 (1974).

2.   "The 'border' includes not only the actual border crossing points but also a reasonable extended geographic area in the immediate vicinity of the crossing point.... Moreover, simply because Customs agents inspected a person or his vehicle at the crossing point does not mean that they may not conduct a second border search within the immediate vicinity of the crossing point: a person is not

immune from further examination by Customs agents 'merely because he may momentarily escape detection and pass safely through the first Customs check'...." *United States v. Warner,* 441 F.2d 821, 832-33 (5th Cir.), *cert. denied,* 404 U.S. 829 (1971).

3. " '[B]order area' reasonably includes not only actual land border checkpoints but also the checkpoints at all international ports of entry and a reasonable extended geographic area in the immediate vicinity of any entry point." *United States v. Glaziou,* 402 F.2d 8, 12-13 (2d Cir. 1968), *cert. denied,* 393 U.S. 1121 (1969).

4. " '[T]he right to arrest by Customs agents doesn't cease simply because the suspect may get his foot across on this side of the bridge'.... The right of border search is indeed broad, and the border itself is elastic." *Marsh v. United States,* 344 F.2d 317, 324 (5th Cir. 1965).

C. Functional Equivalents of Borders: The border search exception is also applicable to searches at the functional equivalent of a border.

1. "Whatever the permissible scope of intrusiveness of a routine border search might be, searches of this kind may in certain circumstances take place not only at the border itself, but at its functional equivalents as well. For example, searches at an established station near the border, at a point marking the confluence of two or more roads that extend from the border, might be functional equivalents of border searches. For another example, a search of the passengers and cargo of an airplane arriving at a St. Louis airport after a nonstop flight from Mexico City would clearly

be the functional equivalent of a border search." *Almeida-Sanchez v. United States,* 413 U.S. 266, 272-73 (1973).

2.   " '[A] particular *search* may be the functional equivalent of a search at the border if the object of the search has been kept under constant surveillance from the border to the point of search.' " *United States v. Haley,* 743 F.2d 862, 865 (11th Cir. 1984).

3.   "The 'extended border'...doctrine permits the Government to conduct border searches some time after the border has been crossed. The validity of such a search depends on whether the fact finder, viewing the totality of the circumstances, is reasonably certain that the suspected smuggler did not acquire the contraband after crossing the border...Some of the circumstances that the fact finder should consider include the time and distance between the border crossing and the search, and the continuity of surveillance over the suspected smuggler." *United States v. Caicedo-Guarnizo,* 723 F. 2d 1420, 1422 (9th Cir. 1984).

4.   "Along with other practical difficulties posed to law enforcement agencies by having the boundary at three miles from shore is the fact that some motor watercraft today are able to travel three miles in less than five minutes, increasing the difficulties of enforcement.... Given the practical difficulties in maritime law enforcement and other considerations, we think it is wise to consider the contiguous zone the functional equivalent of the border." *United States v. Hidalgo-Gato,* 703 F.2d 1267, 1272-73 (11th Cir. 1983).

5.   "A border search need not take place at the actual border. It may be conducted at a place considered 'the functional equivalent of the border,' such as the port where a ship docks in this country after entering our territorial

waters from abroad,...or the airport where an international flight lands." *United States v. Richards,* 638 F.2d 765, 771 (5th Cir.), *cert. denied,* 454 U.S. 1097 (1981).

6. "[A] border search is not limited to searches at the actual border itself,...a border search may take place at 'its functional equivalents as well.'" *United States v. King,* 485 F.2d 353, 359 (10th Cir. 1973).

7. "The major factor necessary to an affirmative determination of functional equivalence is the minimal interdiction of domestic traffic.... Because minimal is somewhat qualitative, it has been indicated that should the percentage of domestic travel approach the majority, the checkpoint would not be the functional equivalent of the border.... In addition to minimally interfering with domestic travel, a checkpoint must be permanent.... The third and final consideration is the extent to which the checkpoint is the necessary practical substitute of the border.... Germane to this criteri[on] is the extent to which the access of the border is uncontrolled, the necessity of the checkpoint to monitor the uncontrolled access, and the degree of success the checkpoint has enjoyed." *United States v. Reyna,* 572 F.2d 515, 517 (5th Cir.), *cert. denied,* 439 U.S. 871 (1978).

D. International Mail: Mail arriving from foreign countries may be searched under the rationale justifying border searches.

1. "[N]o different constitutional standard should apply simply because the envelopes were mailed, not carried. The critical fact is that the envelopes cross the border and enter this country, not that they are brought in by one mode

of transportation rather than another." *United States v. Ramsey,* 431 U.S. 606, 620 (1977).

2. "There appears to be no sound reason to distinguish between incoming mail and other property that crosses our border. Affixing a postage stamp to a parcel should not grant it immunity that would not be accorded a package carried by a traveller." *United States v. Richards,* 638 F.2d 765, 772 (5th Cir.), *cert. denied,* 454 U.S. 1097 (1981).

3. "There is no question that the initial opening of the package by customs agents was lawful. Customs officials are authorized to inspect incoming international mail when they have a 'reasonable cause to suspect' that the mail contains contraband. 'Reasonable cause to suspect' is a considerably milder standard than probable cause." *United States v. Dubrofsky,* 581 F.2d 208, 211 (9th Cir. 1978).

4. "Mail sorting rooms at a port of entry like New York are border areas. Thus, the instant search was reasonable simply because the package was searched at a border area after entering this country from Thailand." *United States v. Pringle,* 576 F.2d 1114, 1117 (5th Cir. 1978).

5. "[T]he interception and discovery of the hashish in New York was a legal border search.... Furthermore, controlled or monitored deliveries of intercepted mail packages of foreign origin to the named addressee have been upheld." *United States v. Galvez,* 465 F.2d 681, 687 (10th Cir. 1972).

E. Controlled Deliveries: When law enforcement agents lawfully learn that there is contraband in a

container, they may reseal the container and deliver it to the recipient.

1. "The lawful discovery by common carriers or customs officers of contraband in transit presents law enforcement authorities with an opportunity to identify and prosecute the person or persons responsible for the movement of the contraband. To accomplish this, the police, rather than simply seizing the contraband and destroying it, make a so-called controlled delivery of the container to its consignee, allowing the container to continue its journey to the destination contemplated by the parties. The person dealing in the contraband can then be identified upon taking possession of and asserting dominion over the container." *Illinois v. Andreas,* 463 U.S. 765,____(1983).

2. "The threshold question, then, is whether an individual has a legitimate expectation of privacy in the contents of a previously lawfully searched container. It is obvious that the privacy interest in the contents of a container diminishes with respect to a container that law enforcement authorities have already lawfully opened and found to contain illicit drugs. No protected privacy interest remains in contraband in a container once government officers lawfully have opened that container and identified its contents as illegal. The simple act of resealing the container to enable the police to make a controlled delivery does not operate to revive or restore the lawfully invaded privacy rights." *Illinois v. Andreas,* 463 U.S. 765,____(1983).

3. "The issue then becomes, at what point after an interruption of control or surveillance [should courts] recognize the individual's expectation of privacy in the container as a legitimate right protected by the Fourth Amendment proscription against unreasonable searches. In fashioning a standard, we must be mindful of three

Fourth Amendment principles. First, the standard should be workable for application by rank and file, trained police officers.... Second, it should be reasonable; for example, it would be absurd to recognize as legitimate an expectation of privacy where there is only a minimal probability that the contents of a particular container had been changed. Third, the standard should be objective, not dependent on the belief of individual police officers.... A workable, objective standard that limits the risk of intrusion on legitimate privacy interests is whether there is a substantial likelihood that the contents of the container have been changed during the gap in surveillance. We hold that absent a substantial likelihood that the contents have been changed, there is no legitimate expectation of privacy in the contents of a container previously opened under lawful authority." *Illinois v. Andreas,* 463 U.S. 765,____(1983).

4. "Controlled deliveries of contraband apparently serve a useful function in law enforcement. They most ordinarily occur when a carrier, usually an airline, unexpectedly discovers what seems to be contraband while inspecting luggage to learn the identity of its owner, or when the contraband falls out of a broken or damaged piece of luggage, or when the carrier exercises its inspection privilege because some suspicious circumstance has caused it concern that it may unwittingly be transporting contraband. Frequently, after such a discovery, law enforcement agents restore the contraband to its container, then close or reseal the container, and authorize the carrier to deliver the container to its owner. When the owner appears to take delivery he is arrested and the container with the contraband is seized and then searched a second time for the contraband known to be there." *United States v. Bulgier,* 618 F.2d 472, 476 (7th Cir.), *cert. denied,* 449 U.S. 824 (1980).

5. "[T]he official seizure of the contraband occurred...when the government asserted dominion over it.... Certainly, the seizure meets the Fourth Amendment requirement of probable cause, because the government agents involved knew that the substance was contraband before seizing it. But, the officers' failure to obtain a warrant to seize can be excused only if the circumstances at the time of the seizure were sufficiently exigent to make their course of action imperative.... The...officers had determined with certainty—and without violation of privacy—that the substance submitted for shipment was contraband. At that time, they could have ordered that the substance be detained until a magistrate could issue a warrant to seize it. The time delay required to obtain a warrant, however, might very well have warned the parties to the crime of the government's presence and prevented their apprehension. If the contraband had not been shipped immediately, the...addressee probably would have become suspicious and remained aloof, and the officer's investigation and arrest process would have proven unproductive." *United States v. Ford,* 525 F.2d 1308, 1313 (10th Cir. 1975).

F. Traffic Checkpoint Stops: Border officials may routinely stop vehicles and question passengers at traffic checkpoints without individualized suspicion.

1. "[T]he Border Patrol [may] maintain permanent checkpoints at or near intersections of important roads leading away from the border at which a vehicle may be stopped for brief questioning of its occupants 'even though there is no reason to believe that the particular vehicle contains illegal aliens.'" *United States v. Villamonte-Marquez,* 462 U.S. 579,____(1983).

2. "[A] requirement that stops on major routes inland always be based on reasonable suspicion would be impractical because the flow of traffic tends to be too heavy to allow the particularized study of a given car that would enable it to be identified as a possible carrier of illegal aliens.... While the need to make routine checkpoint stops is great, the consequent intrusion on Fourth Amendment interests is quite limited.... Accordingly, we hold that the stops and questioning at issue may be made in the absence of any individualized suspicion at reasonably located checkpoints." *United States v. Martinez-Fuerte*, 428 U.S. 543, 557, 562 (1976).

3. "Stops at permanent checkpoints may 'be made in the absence of any individualized suspicion....'" *United States v. Fontecha*, 576 F.2d 601, 602 (5th Cir. 1978).

4. "Routine stops for brief questioning concerning the citizenship of the occupants of a vehicle, which are performed at a permanent checkpoint, do not violate the Fourth Amendment." *United States v. Blanford*, 566 F.2d 470, 471 (5th Cir. 1978).

G. Traffic Checkpoint Searches: At traffic checkpoints, border officials may direct a vehicle off to the side and conduct a search only if they have probable cause or consent.

1. "[S]tops for brief questioning routinely conducted at permanent checkpoints are consistent with the Fourth Amendment and need not be authorized by warrant. The principal protection of Fourth Amendment rights at checkpoints lies in appropriate limitations on the scope of the stop.... [C]heckpoint searches are constitutional only if

justified by consent or probable cause to search." *United States v. Martinez-Fuerte*, 428 U.S. 543, 566-67 (1976).

2. "[A]t traffic checkpoints removed from the border and its functional equivalents, officers may not search private vehicles without consent or probable cause." *United States v. Ortiz*, 422 U.S. 891, 896-97 (1975).

3. "It is also clear that the warrantless search of a vehicle at a permanent checkpoint is justified if based upon probable cause...." *United States v. Fontecha*, 576 F.2d 601, 603 (5th Cir. 1978).

4. "A search at a permanent checkpoint is valid if, after stopping the vehicle, the Border Patrol agent finds probable cause to make the search." *United States v. Faulkner*, 547 F.2d 870, 871 (5th Cir 1977).

H. Roving Patrol Stops: Border officials on roving patrol need a reasonable suspicion to stop a vehicle.

1. "Except at the border and its functional equivalents, officers on roving patrol may stop vehicles only if they are aware of specific articulable facts, together with rational inferences from those facts, that reasonably warrant suspicion that the vehicles contain aliens who may be illegally in the country." *United States v. Brignoni-Ponce*, 422 U.S. 873, 884 (1975).

2. "[S]tops by the Border Patrol may be justified under circumstances less than those constituting probable cause for arrest or search.... [T]he test is...whether, based upon the whole picture, they, as experienced Border Patrol agents, could reasonably surmise that the particular vehicle

they stopped was engaged in criminal activity." *United States v. Cortez,* 449 U.S. 411, 421 (1981).

3. "[A] particular vehicle may be stopped when the observations of a roving patrol create a 'reasonable suspicion' that illegal activity is occurring." *United States v. Macias,* 546 F.2d 58, 62 (5th Cir. 1977).

4. "In the immigration field, agents on roving patrol, as here, may properly consider the following factors in determining whether there exist 'specific articulable facts, together with rational inferences from those facts, that reasonably warrant suspicion that the vehicles contain aliens who may be illegally in the country,'...thus justifying the stop of a particular vehicle and the limited questioning of its occupants: (1) the physical characteristics of the area in which the vehicle is stopped; (2) patterns of traffic on the road; (3) proximity to the border; (4) previous experience with alien trafficking in the area; (5) information about recent border crossings; (6) attempts to evade detection; (7) appearance of the vehicle; (8) appearance and behavior of the driver and passengers; and, (9) other relevant information." *United States v. Leyba,* 627 F.2d 1059, 1062-63 (10th Cir.), *cert. denied,* 449 U.S. 987 (1980).

5. "Our decision regarding the reasonableness of this particular stop, however, cannot be controlled by the fact that the agents fully intended to stop every car. 'The legality of the officers' action depends upon the objective facts known to them at the time the appellant's freedom was restricted by the stop, and not upon the officers' subjective reasons for their actions.'" *United States v. Melendez-Gonzalez,* 727 F.2d 407, 412 (5th Cir. 1984).

I. Roving Patrol Searches: Border officials on roving patrol need probable cause or consent to search a stopped vehicle.

1. "[B]ecause of the importance of the governmental interest at stake, the minimal intrusion of a brief stop, and the absence of practical alternatives for policing the border, we hold that when an officer's observations lead him reasonably to suspect that a particular vehicle may contain aliens who are illegally in the country, he may stop the car briefly and investigate the circumstances that provoke suspicion.... [T]he stop and inquiry must be 'reasonably related in scope to the justification for their initiation'.... [B]ut any further detention or search must be based on consent or probable cause." *United States v. Brignoni-Ponce*, 422 U.S. 873, 881-82 (1975).

2. "[T]he search of the [Defendant's] automobile by a roving patrol.... [i]n the absence of probable cause or consent...violated the...Fourth Amendment right to be free of 'unreasonable searches and seizures.'" *Almeida-Sanchez v. United States*, 413 U.S. 266, 273 (1973).

3. "If after a valid investigatory stop probable cause arises, the search may then be made." *United States v. Burgarin-Casas*, 484 F.2d 853, 854 (9th Cir. 1973), *cert. denied*, 414 U.S. 1136 (1974).

J. Border Strip Searches: Border strip searches may be conducted only pursuant to real or reasonable suspicion.

1. "[A]lthough anyone entering or leaving the country may expect to have his luggage and personal effects

examined, he does not expect that his entry or departure, standing alone, will cause him to be subjected to a strip search. Before a border official may insist upon such an extensive invasion of privacy, he should have a suspicion of illegal concealment that is based upon something more than the border crossing, and the suspicion should be substantial enough to make the search a reasonable exercise of authority." *United States v. Asbury*, 586 F.2d 973, 975-76 (2d Cir. 1978).

2. "It is well settled that searches conducted at the international borders of the United States by Customs officials need not be premised upon probable cause.... This court has upheld strip searches at the border meeting the less exacting standard of 'reasonable suspicion,' ...finding that this standard affords the full measure of protection commanded by the Fourth Amendment." *United States v. Barger*, 574 F.2d 1283, 1285 (5th Cir. 1978).

3. " 'Real suspicion' that the person to be searched is smuggling narcotics is required for a border strip search—a search involving visual inspection of body surfaces.... 'Real suspicion' is 'subjective suspicion supported by objective, articulable facts.' " *United States v. Aman*, 624 F.2d 911, 912 (9th Cir. 1980).

4. "The objective, articulable facts must bear some reasonable relationship to suspicion that something is concealed on the body of the person to be searched; otherwise, the scope of the search is not related to the justification for its initiation, as it must be to meet the reasonableness standard of the Fourth Amendment." *United States v. Guadalupe-Garza*, 421 F.2d 876, 879 (9th Cir. 1970).

5.   "A more intrusive search, the strip search, requires a particularized 'reasonable suspicion'.... This standard has been held to have been met if a person behaves in an articulably suspicious manner." *United States v. Vega-Barvo,* 729 F.2d 1341, 1345 (11th Cir. 1984).

K.   Body Cavity Searches: Body cavity searches at the border must be based on a higher standard than strip searches.

1.   " '[T]he greater the intrusion, the greater must be the reason for conducting a search that results in such invasion.' ... Thus, what constitutes 'reasonable suspicion' to justify a particular search may not suffice to justify a more intrusive or demeaning search." *United States v. Afanador,* 567 F.2d 1325, 1328 (5th Cir. 1978).

2.   "It is necessary to show preliminarily that there is a 'clear indication' of the presence of narcotics." *Yanez v. Romero,* 619 F.2d 851, 855 (10th Cir.), *cert. denied,* 449 U.S. 876 (1980).

3.   "More, however, is required for a body cavity search at a border, a search which involves an intrusion 'beyond the body's surface.' ... A 'clear indication' or 'plain suggestion' that the suspect is concealing contraband *in his body cavity* is required for such a search." *United States v. Aman,* 624 F.2d 911, 912, 913 (9th Cir. 1980).

4.   "But we have further held that searches involving a 'serious invasion of personal privacy and dignity,' such as close scrutiny of intimate portions of the body, may proceed only when there is a clear indication or plain suggestion that the individual may be involved in the

importation of contraband." *United States v. Cameron*, 538
F.2d 254, 257 (9th Cir. 1976).

5. "We have...found a violation of the Fourth Amendment since the initiation of the intrusive body cavity search
was unjustified because of the lack of any 'clear indication'
or 'plain suggestion' in the minds of Dr. Salerno and his
rectal invasion squad members, that [Defendant] had any
narcotics cached in his rectal cavity." *Huguez v. United
States*, 406 F.2d 366, 380 (9th Cir. 1968).

6. "At the border, a customs inspector must have a
reasonable suspicion that a person is carrying contraband
internally before a person's stomach may be searched
either by x-ray or by detaining the person until he excretes
his stomach's contents. The reasonable suspicion standard requires a showing of articulable facts which are
particularized as to the person and as to the place that is to
be searched." *United States v. Henao-Castano,* 729 F.2d
1364, 1366 (11th Cir. 1984).

Chapter 19

Immigration and Naturalization Service Searches

A. Seizures of Persons: Fourth Amendment standards govern the stopping, interrogating, and arresting of suspected illegal aliens.

1. "[T]he immigration officer may detain an individual, reasonably believed to be an alien, against his will for the purpose of questioning. We believe the statutory interrogation authority comprehends such detentions, but, because they are far greater intrusions upon personal privacy than the non-forcible approaches, and since aliens in this country are sheltered by the Fourth Amendment in common with citizens, such a reading of the Congressional mandate must be controlled by the constitutional standards governing similar detentions made by other law enforcement officials.... We hold that immigration officers, in accordance with the Congressional grant of authority found in Section 287(a)(1) [of the Immigration and Nationality Act] may make forcible detentions of a temporary nature for the purposes of interrogation under circumstances created by reasonable suspicion, not arising to the level of probable cause to arrest, that the individual so detained is illegally in this country." *Au Yi Lau v. United States Immigration & Naturalization Service*, 445 F.2d 217, 223 (9th Cir.), *cert. denied*, 404 U.S. 864 (1971).

2. "We reject the claim that the entire work forces of the two factories were seized for the duration of the surveys

when the INS placed agents near the exits of the factory sites. . . . [W]orkers were not prevented by the agents from moving about the factories. . . . The obvious purpose of the agents' presence at the factory doors was to insure that all persons in the factories were questioned. . . . If mere questioning does not constitute a seizure when it occurs inside the factory, it is no more a seizure when it occurs at the exits." *Immigration and Naturalization Service v. Delgado,*____U.S.____,____(1984).

3.   "In seizing persons suspected of violations of 8 U.S.C. § 1325, Peoria police have adopted a procedure identical to that described in *Dunaway.* Defendants are walked or driven to the police station and held pending interrogation by the Border Patrol. This seizure constitutes an arrest, and the constitutional standards cannot be avoided by labeling it a mere detention. Prior to invoking this procedure, the police must therefore have probable cause to believe either that illegal entry has occurred or that another offense has been committed. As we have indicated, inability to produce documentation does not in itself provide probable cause." *Gonzales v. City of Peoria,* 722 F.2d 468, 477 (9th Cir. 1983).

4.   "The Spanish surnames and appearance of Mexican ancestry were insufficient to justify INS [street stoppages and interrogations]. . . . Rightly, racial appearance has never been considered sufficient to justify a search or seizure involved in random stops. . . . [A] street stop is justifiable...only when the INS agent has a 'reasonable suspicion based on specific articulable facts that such person is an alien [unlawfully] in the [United States].' " *Illinois Migrant Council v. Pilliod,* 540 F.2d 1062, 1070 (7th Cir. 1976).

5. "Appellant was not arrested until probable cause existed that he was an illegal alien. The informant's tip gave the agent a founded suspicion upon which he could briefly detain and question appellant.... The agent's subsequent observation that appellant matched the informant's description and the detection of the altered I-151 card [make] it clear that when appellant was arrested this founded suspicion had ripened into probable cause." *United States v. Reyes-Oropesa*, 596 F.2d 399, 400 (9th Cir. 1979).

6. "Section 28(a)(2) of Title 8 U.S.C. authorizes an INS officer to arrest without a warrant 'any alien in the United States, if he has reason to believe that the alien so arrested is in the United States in violation of any such law or regulation and is likely to escape before a warrant can be obtained for his arrest....' The phrase 'has reason to believe' has been equated with the constitutional requirement of probable cause." *Tejeda-Mata v. INS*, 626 F.2d 721, 724-25 (9th Cir. 1980), *cert. denied,* 456 U.S. 944 (1982).

7. "A principal purpose of the *Miranda* warnings is to permit the suspect to make an intelligent decision as to whether to answer the government agent's questions.... In deportation proceedings, however—in light of the alien's burden of proof, the requirement that the alien answer non-incriminating questions, the potential adverse consequences to the alien of remaining silent, and the fact that an alien's statement is admissible in the deportation hearing despite his lack of counsel at the preliminary interrogation—*Miranda* warnings would be not only inappropriate but could also serve to mislead the alien." *United States v. Alderete-Deras,* 743 F.2d 645, 648 (9th Cir. 1984).

B. Searches of Private Premises: A warrant is required to search private premises for illegal aliens. Strict probable cause standards are applied for criminal searches, but not for civil administrative searches.

1. "[A]fter [the]...arrest, Jacobs and the other [INS] agents were required to do as best they could to maintain custody of the aliens lawfully arrested and surveillance of the house while a search warrant was being obtained.... [T]he conviction must be reversed because of the...search of the house [without a warrant]." *United States v. Rodriguez*, 532 F.2d 834, 839 (2d Cir. 1976),

2. "The appellees moved to exclude from their trial any evidence of the presence of the aliens obtained during the search, and the testimony of the aliens themselves, on the ground that the affidavit for the search warrant failed to state probable cause to search.... We...hold that the affidavit fails to state facts sufficient to indicate probable cause to search, and that the search warrant was therefore improperly issued." *United States v. Karathanos*, 531 F.2d 26, 29, 32 (2d Cir.), *cert. denied*, 428 U.S. 910 (1976).

3. "First...we think that Congress, in passing the Immigration and Nationality Act, contemplated a vigorous enforcement program that might include INS entries into private premises for the purpose of questioning 'any alien or person believed to be an alien,' and of detaining those aliens believed to be in this country illegally. Second, since an INS search is conducted pursuant to a civil administrative mandate, the warrant issued to permit such a search may therefore be evaluated under a standard of probable cause different from that applied to criminal warrants.... We agree that the District Court's stringent formulation of probable cause was inappropriate in the present situation.... [The definition of probable cause called for

should]...comport with the multiplicity of 'hybrid' administrative law enforcement activities in a non-criminal context." *Blackie's House of Beef, Inc. v. Castillo*, 659 F.2d 1211, 1218-19, 1222 (D.C. Cir. 1981), *cert. denied*, 455 U.S. 940 (1982).

4.   "We conclude that the INS's right to enter commercial premises, with a proper warrant, for the purpose of searching out a suspected violation of the immigration laws derives from its general statutory power to seek out and question suspected illegal aliens.... [T]he court should have examined the warrant and supporting affidavits with an eye to whether the warrant [contained] sufficient specificity and reliability to prevent the exercise of unbridled discretion by law enforcement officials." *Blackie's House of Beef, Inc. v. Castillo*, 659 F.2d 1211, 1222, 1225 (D.C. Cir. 1981), *cert. denied*, 455 U.S. 940 (1982).

C.   Suppression: The exclusionary rule does not bar the admission of illegally seized evidence in deportation hearings.

1.   "At issue here is the exclusion of credible evidence gathered in connection with peaceful arrests by INS officers. We hold that evidence derived from such arrests need not be suppressed in an INS civil deportation hearing." *Immigration and Naturalization Service v. Lopez-Mendoza*, 468 U.S. _____, _____ (1984).

2.   "INS has already taken sensible and reasonable steps to deter Fourth Amendment violations by its officers, and this makes the likely additional deterrent value of the exclusionary rule small. The costs of applying the exclusionary rule in the context of civil deportation hearings are

high. In particular, application of the exclusionary rule in cases such as Sandoval's would compel the courts to release from custody persons who would then immediately resume their commission of a crime through their continuing, unlawful presence in this country. 'There comes a point at which courts, consistent with their duty to administer the law, cannot continue to create barriers to law enforcement in the pursuit of a supervisory role that is properly the duty of the Executive and Legislative Branches.'" *Immigration and Naturalization Service v. Lopez-Mendoza,* 468 U.S. ____, ____ (1984).

Chapter 20

Boat Stops and Searches

A. Standard: The Fourth Amendment applies to stops and searches by the United States government within the jurisdiction of the United States, on the high seas, and in foreign waters.

1. "The Fourth Amendment not only protects all within our bounds; it also shelters our citizens wherever they may be in the world from unreasonable searches by our own government. *Reid v. Covert*, 354 U.S. 1, 5-6 (1957).

2. "[T]he mere existence of a statutory authority to make a search does not obviate the need for Fourth Amendment compliance." *United States v. Conroy*, 589 F.2d 1258, 1268 (5th Cir.), *cert. denied*, 444 U.S. 831 (1979).

B. Documentation Stops in Inland Waters: Customs officials may stop a boat in inland waters and board it to inspect its documentation without reasonable suspicion.

1. "Customs officials acting pursuant to [19 U.S.C § 1581(a) (1976)] and without any suspicion of wrongdoing, [may] board for inspection of documents a vessel that is located in waters providing ready access to the sea." *United States v. Villamonte-Marquez*, 462 U.S. 579,_____ (1983).

2. "In a lineal ancestor to the statute at issue here the First Congress clearly authorized the suspicionless boarding of vessels, reflecting its view that such boardings are not contrary to the Fourth Amendment; this gives the statute before us an impressive historical pedigree. Random stops without any articulable suspicion of vehicles away from the border are not permissible under the Fourth Amendment...but stops at fixed checkpoints or at roadblocks are.... The nature of waterborne commerce in waters providing ready access to the open sea is sufficiently different from the nature of vehicular traffic on highways as to make possible alternatives to the sort of 'stop' made in this case less likely to accomplish the obviously essential governmental purposes involved. The system of prescribed outward markings used by States for vehicle registration is also significantly different [from] the system of external markings on vessels, and the extent and type of documentation requried by federal law is a good deal more variable and more complex than are the state vehicle registration laws. The nature of the governmental interest in assuring compliance with documentation requirements, particularly in waters where the need to deter or apprehend smugglers is great, are substantial.... All of these factors lead us to conclude that the action of the Customs officers in stopping and boarding the *Henry Morgan II* was 'reasonable,' and was therefore consistent with the Fourth Amendment." *United States v. Villamonte-Marquez,* 462 U.S. 579,____(1983).

3. "Customs officers may board a vessel in Customs waters to check its documents even if the boarding serves merely as a pretext for the officers' desire to look for signs of contraband." *United States v. Albano,* 722 F.2d 690, 695 (11th Cir. 1984).

C. Investigatory Stops in Inland Waters: Customs officials with a reasonable suspicion that illegal activity is occurring on a vessel in inland waters may make an investigatory stop.

1. "Customs officers may make investigatory stops of vessels on inland waters 'on facts which justify a reasonable suspicion of illegal activity.'" *United States v. Kent*, 691 F.2d 1376, 1378 (11th Cir. 1982), *cert. denied*, ____ U.S.____(1983).

2. "Limited Customs searches are reasonable under the fourth amendment without a showing of probable cause, although a border crossing has not been proved, because of the diminished expectation of privacy inherent in the maritime setting. Thus such searches do not require proof of a border crossing to establish their fourth amendment reasonableness." *United States v. Herrera,* 711 F.2d 1546, 1552 (11th Cir. 1983).

3. "[A] visual inspection [by] Customs officers from aboard their own boat and their asking a few questions. . .is [a] minimal [intrusion] compared to the governmental interest involved. . . . [T]he initial stop and inquiry by the Customs officers of inland waters was within their statutory authority and was reasonable within the meaning of the Fourth Amendment [because they had] reasonable suspicion of illegal activity." *United States v. Gollwitzer*, 697 F.2d 1357, 1362 (11th Cir. 1983).

4. "Customs officers may make an investigatory stop of a vessel on inland waters adjacent to the open Gulf of Mexico under 19 U.S.C.A. § 1581(a) on facts that justify a reasonable suspicion of illegal activity. The evidence need not support suspicion on a border crossing, but only of the presence of contraband." *United States v. D'Antignac*, 628

F.2d 428, 434 (5th Cir. 1980), *cert. denied*, 450 U.S. 967 (1981).

5. "With regard to the officers coming alongside the Red Baron and immediately stepping onto the deck, '[w]e are persuaded that a boarding is a necessary element of many vessel investigatory stops, given the sound and motion of water, the often significant size differential between the government's boat and the investigated vessel, and the extreme mobility of water craft.'" *United States v. Maybusher,* 735 F.2d 366, 372 (9th Cir. 1984).

6. "A stop and boarding after dark must be for cause, requiring at least a reasonable and articulable suspicion of noncompliance, or must be conducted after administrative standards so drafted that the decision to search is not left to the sole discretion of the Coast Guard officer." *United States v. Eagon,* 707 F.2d 362, 365 (9th Cir. 1982), *cert. denied,* ____U.S.____(1983).

D. Warrantless Searches in Inland Waters: Warrantless searches in inland waters are permissible when probable cause and exigent circumstances exist.

1. "[T]he circumstances and exigencies of the maritime setting afford people on a vessel a lesser expectation of privacy than in their homes, obviating the usual Fourth Amendment requirements of a warrant." *United States v. Green*, 671 F.2d 46, 53 (1st Cir.), *cert. denied*, 457 U.S. 1135 (1982).

2. "The inherent mobility of a vessel and the attendant possibility of flight or disposal of evidence certainly amount to exigent circumstances." *United States v. D'Antignac,*

628 F.2d 428, 434 (5th Cir. 1980), *cert. denied*, 450 U.S. 967 (1981).

E. Border Searches: A search of a vessel that has crossed into the territory of the United States is subject to border search standards if it takes place in an area contiguous to, or a functional equivalent of, the border.

1.   "Given the practical difficulties in Maritime law enforcement and other considerations, we think it wise to consider the contiguous zone [3 to 12 miles from the shoreline] the functional equivalent of the border.... The standard applied to searches in the contiguous zone will be prescribed by border search standards."*United States v. Hidalgo-Gato*, 703 F.2d 1267, 1273 (11th Cir. 1983).

2.   "[A] search in customs waters is a functional border search when the vessel has crossed from territorial waters of the United States and there is sufficient evidence to convince a fact finder, to a reasonable certainty, that any contraband which might be found at the time of the search was also aboard at the border crossing." *United States v. Stanley*, 545 F.2d 661, 667 (9th Cir. 1976), *cert. denied*, 436 U.S. 917 (1978).

3.   "[A] search without probable cause pursuant to 19 U.S.C. § 1581(a) of a vessel in a harbor may be valid under the Fourth Amendment as a border search at the functional equivalent of the border...where there are articulable facts to support a reasonably certain conclusion by the customs officers that a vessel had crossed the border and entered our territorial waters." *United States v. Tilton*, 534 F.2d 1363, 1366 (9th Cir. 1976).

F. Administrative Inspections of United States Vessels on the High Seas: United States registered vessels on the high seas are subject to routine safety or documentation inspections.

1. "The Coast Guard has plenary authority to board American vessels beyond the twelve mile limit with neither probable cause nor even particularized suspicion [under 14 U.S.C. § 89(a)]. . . . After legally boarding the vessel, [the officer] noticed the flooding and entered the cabin under his authority to conduct a safety inspection. The bales [of marijuana], in plain view, and the odor emanating from them clearly established probable cause sufficient to justify a full and complete search."*United States v. Hicks*, 624 F.2d 32, 33 (5th Cir. 1980).

2. "14 U.S.C. § 89(a) confers on the Coast Guard 'plenary power to stop and board any American flag vessel anywhere on the high sea in the complete absence of suspicion of criminal activity,' at least for the purpose of conducting an administrative inspection. . . . If the administrative inspection gives rise to a suspicion of criminal activity, a full search may be conducted. . . . A search warrant is not necessary." *United States v. Robbins*, 623 F.2d 418, 420 (5th Cir. 1980).

G. Stop and Search of Foreign Vessels on the High Seas: The Coast Guard may stop and search a foreign vessel on the high seas if it has a reasonable suspicion that those aboard the vessel are involved in criminal activity.

1. "[14 U.S.C.] section 89(a) authorizes the Coast Guard to seize a foreign vessel in international waters if the Coast

Guard first has a reasonable suspicion that those aboard the vessel are engaged in a conspiracy to smuggle contraband into the United States." *United States v. Williams*, 617 F.2d 1063, 1074 (5th Cir. 1980).

2. "[A]n officer having a reasonable suspicion, based on articulable, objective facts, that criminal activity is afoot may make an investigatory stop that is reasonable both in its duration and its intrusiveness on the individual's legitimate privacy expectations.... [D]iffering expectations of privacy in various kinds of...vessels may result in differences in the balancing of the interests relevant in assessing the reasonableness of an investigatory stop, but they do not make inapplicable the principles which require that balancing be done." *United States v. Streifel*, 665 F.2d 414, 422-23 (2d Cir. 1981).

3. "[A] Coast Guard helicopter had surprised the *Persistence*...in a rendezvous with a fishing vessel. The ships had taken off in different directions. A different Coast Guard cutter had caught up with the *Persistence* later that day, boarded, and found a man who was the subject of a Drug Enforcement Administration warrant. Three days later, the Coast Guard had located the fishing vessel...with marijuana residue in the hold.... [When sighted] the *Persistence*...was riding sluggishly, low in the water, and heavy in the bow.... [S]he did not respond until after two hours to the Coast Guard's efforts to hail her by radio. The response then...[was] contradictory. These facts, when taken together, gave the officers a reasonable and articulable suspicion that the *Persistence* was carrying marijuana below deck." *United States v. Green*, 671 F.2d 46, 54 (1st Cir. 1982), *cert. denied,* 457 U.S. 1135 (1982).

4. "[T]he Coast Guard's failure to obtain Honduras' consent to search a Honduran ship on the high seas did

not require suppression of the evidence found. The purpose of international law's 'consent' requirement is to protect nations, not individuals; and, if the nation does not care, the individual cannot raise 'lack of consent' as a ground for suppression." *United States v. Kincaid,* 712 F.2d 1, 3 (1st Cir. 1983).

H. Stop and Search of United States Vessels in Foreign Waters: The Coast Guard has the authority to stop and search American vessels in foreign waters, unless the sovereign power involved objects, on a showing of probable cause coupled with exigent circumstances.

1. "The pattern of legislation...and the subsequent congressional action [of 14 U.S.C § 89(a)]...make it clear that, in the absence of objection by the sovereign power involved, Congress intended the Coast Guard to have authority to stop and search American vessels on foreign waters as well as on the high sea and in territorial waters." *United States v. Conroy,* 589 F.2d 1258, 1266-67 (5th Cir.), *cert. denied,* 444 U.S. 831 (1979).

2. "[The statute, 14 U.S.C § 89(a), is] a grant of plenary authority to stop and board United States vessels on the high seas for either a safety-and-document inspection or to check for obvious customs and narcotics violations. Once aboard, if probable cause arises to suspect the presence of narcotics, a search can then be made of the vessel." *United States v. Conroy,* 589 F.2d 1258, 1268 (5th Cir.), *cert. denied,* 444 U.S. 831 (1979).

I. Scope of Searches: The Coast Guard may not search a private area of a ship unless it has a reasonable suspicion that the area contains seizable items.

1. "[T]he fourth amendment requires at least a reasonable suspicion that contraband or evidence of criminal activity will be found before the Coast Guard may, pursuant to section 89(a), search a 'private' area of the *hold* of a vessel in international waters for the purpose of finding such items. It follows, of course, that, in the context of such searches, the fourth amendment does *not* require a search warrant." *United States v. Williams*, 617 F.2d 1063, 1087 (5th Cir. 1980).

2. "The only limit upon the Coast Guard's authority to search vessels lawfully boarded is that it may not search 'private' areas for the purpose of finding evidence of criminal activity without reason to suspect the existence there of such evidence." *United States v. Robbins*, 623 F.2d 418, 420 (5th Cir. 1980).

Chapter 21

Administrative Searches

A. Rule: A search warrant is generally required to make a search or inspection to check compliance with regulatory statutes.

1. "Searches for administrative purposes, like searches for evidence of crime, are encompassed by the Fourth Amendment.... The officials may be health, fire, or building inspectors. Their purpose may be to locate and abate a suspected public nuisance, or simply to perform a routine periodic inspection. The privacy that is invaded may be sheltered by the walls of a warehouse or other commercial establishment not open to the public.... These deviations from the typical police search are...clearly within the protection of the Fourth Amendment." *Michigan v. Tyler*, 436 U.S. 499, 506, 504-05 (1978).

2. "The Warrant Clause of the Fourth Amendment protects commercial buildings as well as private homes. To hold otherwise would belie the origin of that Amendment, and the American colonial experience...." *Marshall v. Barlow's, Inc.*, 436 U.S. 307, 311 (1978).

3. "The basic purpose of [the Fourth] Amendment...is to safeguard the privacy and security of individuals against arbitrary invasions by governmental officials.... [O]ne governing principle, justified by history and by current experience, has consistently been followed: except in certain carefully defined classes of cases, a search of private property without a proper consent is 'unreasonable'

unless it has been authorized by a valid search warrant."
Camara v. Municipal Court, 387 U.S. 523, 528-29 (1967).

4. "[W]e see no justification for. . .relaxing Fourth Amendment safeguards where the official inspection is intended
to aid enforcement of laws prescribing minimum physical
standards for commercial premises. . . . The businessman,
like the occupant of a residence, has a constitutional right
to go about his business free from unreasonable official
entries upon his private commercial property. The businessman, too, has that right placed in jeopardy if the
decision to enter and inspect for a violation of regulatory
laws can be made and enforced by the inspector in the
field without official authority evidenced by a warrant." *See
v. City of Seattle*, 387 U.S. 541, 543 (1967).

5. "[A]dministrative searches generally require warrants.
. . . If reasonable privacy interests remain in the fire-dam-
aged property, the warrant requirement applies, and any
official entry must be made pursuant to a warrant in the
absence of consent or exigent circumstances." *Michigan v.
Clifford*, 464 U.S. _____, _____(1984).

6. "[T]he fourth amendment prohibition against unreasonable searches protects against warrantless intrusions
during civil as well as criminal investigations. The reason is
found in the 'basic purpose of this Amendment. . .[which] is
to safeguard the privacy and security of individuals against
arbitrary invasions by government officials.' . . . If the government intrudes on a person's property, the privacy
interest suffers whether the government's motivation is to
investigate violations of criminal laws or breaches of other
statutory or regulatory standards." *Franks v. Smith*, 717
F.2d 183, 186 (5th Cir. 1983).

7. "[W]here fire fighters are pursuing a purpose less clearly defined as one of the core duties with which they are charged, searches of a burned dwelling for that purpose, after the fire has been extinguished, do not fall within the exigent circumstances created by the fire and thus are unlawful in the absence of a warrant.... We therefore hold that searches for and seizures of valuables in a burned dwelling neither fall within the inventory search exception nor the same exigent circumstances exception to the warrant requirement that justifies entry to extinguish and ascertain the cause of a fire. Prior to undertaking such searches, absent consent or the presence of other exceptions to the warrant requirement, warrants should be obtained pursuant to the procedures governing administrative searches." *United States v. Parr,* 716 F.2d 796, 812, 816 (11th Cir. 1983).

B. Standard: To obtain an administrative search warrant, the government must show that reasonable administrative standards for conducting inspections are being followed with respect to the premises to be searched.

1. "Whether the Secretary proceeds to secure a warrant or other process, with or without prior notice, ... [p]robable cause in the criminal law sense is not required. For purposes of an administrative search such as this, probable cause justifying the issuance of a warrant may be based not only on specific evidence of an existing violation but also on a showing that 'reasonable legislative or administrative standards for conducting an...inspection are satisfied with respect to a particular [establishment]." *Marshall v. Barlow's, Inc.*, 436 U.S. 307, 320 (1978).

2. "The agency's particular demand for access will of course be measured, in terms of probable cause to issue a warrant, against a flexible standard of reasonableness that takes into account the public need for effective enforcement of the particular regulation involved." *See v. City of Seattle*, 387 U.S. 541, 545 (1967).

3. "[W]e think that a number of persuasive factors combine to support the reasonableness of [administrative] inspection. First, such programs have a long history of judicial and public acceptance.... Second, the public interest demands that all dangerous conditions be prevented or abated, yet it is doubtful that any other canvassing technique would achieve acceptable results.... Finally, because the inspections are neither personal in nature nor aimed at the discovery of evidence of crime, they involve a relatively limited invasion of the...citizen's privacy." *Camara v. Municipal Court*, 387 U.S. 523, 537 (1967).

4. "First...we think that Congress, in passing the Immigration and Nationality Act, contemplated a vigorous enforcement program that might include INS entries into private premises for the purpose of questioning 'any alien or person believed to be an alien,' and of detaining those aliens believed to be in this country illegally. Second, since an INS search is conducted pursuant to a civil administrative mandate, the warrant issued to permit such a search may therefore be evaluated under a standard of probable cause different from that applied to criminal warrants.... We agree that the District Court's stringent formulation of probable cause was inappropriate in the present situation.... [The definition of probable cause called for should] comport with the multiplicity of 'hybrid' administrative law enforcement activities in a non-criminal context." *Blackie's House of Beef, Inc. v. Castillo*, 659 F.2d 1211, 1218-22 (D.C. Cir. 1981), *cert. denied*, 455 U.S. 940 (1982).

5. "We conclude that the INS's right to enter commercial premises, with a proper warrant, for the purpose of searching out a suspected violation of the immigration laws derives from its general statutory power to seek out and question suspected illegal aliens. . . . [T]he court should have examined the warrant and supporting affidavits with an eye to whether the warrant [contained] sufficient specificity and reliability to prevent the exercise of un-bridled discretion by law enforcement officials." *Blackie's House of Beef, Inc. v. Castillo*, 659 F.2d 1211, 1222-25 (D.C. Cir. 1981), *cert. denied*, 455 U.S. 940 (1982).

6. "If the primary object is to determine the cause and origin of a recent fire, an administrative warrant will suffice. To obtain such a warrant, fire officials need show only that a fire of undetermined origin has occurred on the premises, that the scope of the proposed search is reasonable and will not intrude unnecessarily on the fire victim's privacy, and that the search will be executed at a reasonable and convenient time. If the primary object of the search is to gather evidence of criminal activity, a criminal search warrant may be obtained only on a showing of probable cause to believe that relevant evidence will be found in the place to be searched. If evidence of criminal activity is discovered during the course of a valid administrative search, it may be seized under the 'plain view' doctrine." *Michigan v. Clifford,* 464 U.S. ____, ____ (1984).

C. Closely Regulated Industries: Industries with a long history of pervasive governmental regulation can be inspected without a warrant.

1. "[A] warrant may not be constitutionally required when Congress has reasonably determined that warrantless

searches are necessary to further a regulatory scheme and
the federal regulatory presence is sufficiently comprehen-
sive and defined that the owner of commercial property
cannot help but be aware that his property will be subject to
periodic inspections undertaken for specific purposes."
Donovan v. Dewey, 452 U.S. 594, 600 (1981).

2. "Certain industries have such a history of government oversight [*sic*] that no reasonable expectation of
privacy. . .could exist for a proprietor over the stock of such
an enterprise. Liquor. . .and firearms. . .are industries of this
type; when an entrepreneur embarks upon such a business, he has voluntarily chosen to subject himself to a full
arsenal of governmental regulation." *Marshall v. Barlow's,
Inc.*, 436 U.S. 307, 313 (1978).

3. "In determining whether warrantless searches in a
closely regulated industry are reasonable we must decide
whether the regulatory scheme, 'in terms of the certainty
and regularity of its application, provides a constitutionally
adequate substitute for a warrant.' " *Balilo v. Baldridge*, 724
F.2d 753, 765-66 (9th Cir. 1984).

4. "The determinative factors to be considered are
whether the industry affected is so closely regulated as to
provide notice of the prospect of governmental intrusion
and whether the statutory scheme enacted 'provides an
adequate substitute for a warrant in terms of the certainty
and regularity of its application'. . . . To satisfy the 'certainty
and regularity' requirement, the inspection program must
define clearly what is to be searched, who can be
searched, and the frequency of such searches. . . . [T]he
degree and extent of past regulation comprise but a part,
albeit a substantial part, of a determination of a 'reasonable
expectation of privacy' under the Fourth Amendment.
Otherwise, no protections at all would be appropriate in

closely regulated industries. The Fourth Amendment requires that a determination of the 'reasonableness' of the intrusion be made. Even in closely regulated industries, the inspection provisions still must be tailored to the state's proper objectives, and they must minimize the dangers inherent in the unbridled exercise of administrative discretion." *Bionic Auto Parts & Sales, Inc. v. Fahner,* 721 F.2d 1072, 1078, 1079 (7th Cir. 1983).

5. "Federal regulation of the interstate traffic in firearms is not as deeply rooted in history as governmental control of the liquor industry, but close scrutiny of this traffic is undeniably of central importance to federal efforts to prevent violent crime. . . . It is also apparent that if [the Gun Control Act] is to be properly enforced and inspection made effective, inspections without warrant must be deemed reasonable official conduct under the Fourth Amendment. . . . We have little difficulty in concluding that. . .the inspection may proceed without a warrant where specifically authorized by statute." *United States v. Biswell,* 406 U.S. 311, 315, 316, 317 (1972).

6. "We agree that Congress has broad power to design such powers of inspection under the liquor laws as it deems necessary to meet the evils at hand. The general rule. . .'that administrative entry, without consent, upon the portions of commercial premises which are not open to the public may only be compelled through prosecution or physical force within the framework of a warrant procedure'—is therefore not applicable here." *Colonnade Corp. v. United States,* 397 U.S. 72, 76 (1970).

7. "[T]he warrantless inspections required by the Mine Safety and Health Act do not offend the Fourth Amendment. . . . [I]t is undisputed that there is a substantial federal interest in improving the health and safety conditions in the

Nation's underground and surface mines." *Donovan v. Dewey*, 452 U.S. 594, 602 (1981).

8. *"Barlow's*...affirmed the validity of warrantless searches of premises occupied by businesses that historically have been subject to pervasive governmental regulation. Persons engaging in such businesses have no reasonable expectation of privacy." *Marshall v. Sink*, 614 F.2d 37, 38 (4th Cir. 1980).

D.   Emergencies: In emergency situations a warrant is not required.

1. "[I]n the regulatory field, our cases have recognized the importance of 'prompt inspections, even without a warrant, ... in emergency situations.'" *Michigan v. Tyler*, 436 U.S. 499, 509 (1978).

2. "[P]rovision for a hearing before seizure and condemnation and destruction of food which is unwholesome and unfit for use is not necessary. The right to so seize is based upon the right and duty of the State to protect and guard, as far as possible, the lives and health of its inhabitants, and...it is proper to provide that food which is unfit for human consumption should be summarily seized and destroyed to prevent the danger which would arise from eating it." *North American Storage Co. v. Chicago*, 211 U.S. 306, 315 (1908).

3. "[A]n entry to fight a fire requires no warrant, and...once in the building, officials may remain there for a reasonable time to investigate the cause of the blaze. Thereafter, additional entries to investigate the cause of fire must be made pursuant to the warrant procedures

governing administrative searches." *Michigan v. Tyler*, 436 U.S. 499, 511 (1978).

4. "The object of the search is important even if exigent circumstances exist. Circumstances that justify a warrantless search for the cause of a fire may not justify a search to gather evidence of criminal activity once that cause has been determined." *Michigan v. Clifford*, 464 U.S. ____, ____(1984).

5. "If an acute emergency occurs precluding reference to a court or magistrate, public officials must take such steps as are necessary to protect the public. But absent such emergency, health laws are enforced by the police power and are subject to the same constitutional limitations as are other police powers." *District of Columbia v. Little*, 178 F.2d 13, 20 (D.C. Cir. 1949), *aff'd on other grounds*, 339 U.S. 1 (1950).

6. "During the course of their investigation, fire officials discovered a large quantity of chemicals used in the manufacture of fireworks. Since the firemen were not trained in the handling of explosive materials, they summoned police officers with the necessary expertise to aid in the investigation. While the mere occurrence of a fire at a residence does not give police officers *carte blanche* to enter the premises,...we hold that the firemen's delegation of these 'render safe' operations to the bomb squad officers and the ATF agent was eminently reasonable, and thus the warrantless entry by these officers was justified as a continued response to the exigency created by the fire itself.... Once inside, the officers had the right to seize objects of apparent evidentiary value which were in plain view." *United States v. Urban*, 710 F.2d 276, 279 (6th Cir. 1983).

E. Vital Government Interest: Warrantless administrative searches which further vital government interests are reasonable if the public interest is great and the intrusion small.

1. "Those cases that sustain limited searches of persons seeking to enter sensitive facilities recognize an exception to the general requirement of the Fourth Amendment that searches are proper only if conducted pursuant to a lawful warrant.... The search must be clearly necessary to secure a vital governmental interest, such as protecting sensitive facilities from a real danger of violence.... The search must be limited and no more intrusive than necessary to protect against the danger to be avoided.... The inspection must be conducted for a purpose other than the gathering of evidence for criminal prosecutions. To indicate this, we have designated limited searches at sensitive facilities as 'administrative searches.' " *McMorris v. Alioto*, 567 F.2d 897, 899 (9th Cir. 1978).

2. "[T]he public interest in preventing the introduction of dangerous material into the particular area involved was sufficiently strong to make it reasonable for the government (without a warrant or traditional probable cause) to condition access by any person seeking to enter the area upon submission by that person to an administrative inspection no more intrusive than necessary to meet the need to exclude the dangerous material from the restricted area." *United States v. Miles*, 480 F.2d 1217, 1219 (9th Cir.), *cert. denied*, 414 U.S. 1008 (1973).

3. "[T]he dangers to federal property and personnel were imminent.... To require that an officer obtain a warrant to examine the packages of each of hundreds of persons entering the building or determine as to each person the existence of probable cause would as a practical matter

seriously impair the power of government to protect itself against ruthless forces bent upon its destruction. We find here no violation of the Fourth Amendment...." *Downing v. Kunzig*, 454 F.2d 1230, 1232, 1233 (6th Cir. 1972).

Chapter 22

Airport Searches

A. Seizure of the Person: An airport stop must constitute a seizure for the Fourth Amendment to apply.

1. "If there is no detention—no seizure within the meaning of the Fourth Amendment—then no constitutional rights have been infringed." *Florida v. Royer,* 460 U.S. 491, 498 (1983).

2. "[A] person has been 'seized' within the meaning of the Fourth Amendment only if, in view of all of the circumstances surrounding the incident, a reasonable person would have believed that he was not free to leave. Examples of circumstances that might indicate a seizure, even where the person did not attempt to leave, would be the threatening presence of several officers, the display of a weapon by an officer, some physical touching of the person of the citizen, or the use of language or tone of voice indicating that compliance with the officer's request might be compelled.... In the absence of some such evidence, otherwise inoffensive contact between a member of the public and the police cannot, as a matter of law, amount to a seizure of that person." *United States v. Mendenhall,* 446 U.S. 544, 554-55 (1980).

3. "[I]t is submitted that the entire encounter was consensual and hence [Defendant] was not being held against his will at all. We find this submission untenable. Asking for and examining [Defendant's] ticket and his driver's license were no doubt permissible in themselves, but when the

officers identified themselves as narcotics agents, told [him] that he was suspected of transporting narcotics, and asked him to accompany them to the police room, while retaining his ticket and driver's license and without indicating in any way that he was free to depart, [Defendant] was effectively seized for the purposes of the Fourth Amendment. These circumstances surely amount to a show of official authority such that 'a reasonable person would have believed he was not free to leave.'" *Florida v. Royer,* 460 U.S. 491, 501-02 (1983).

4. "When, on the other hand, an individual is 'free to choose whether to enter or continue an encounter with police and elects to do so,' we have held that there is no seizure.... The determination of whether such a freedom of choice exists often requires a 'refined judgment,' especially when no force, physical restraint, or blatant show of authority is involved." *United States v. Elmore,* 595 F.2d 1036, 1041-42 (5th Cir. 1979), *cert. denied,* 447 U.S. 910 (1980).

5. "Agent Demnik began his inquiry by simply asking the appellant if he would answer a few questions. This nonthreatening approach has been deemed something less than a seizure and, thus, placed within the bounds of the type of initial encounter in *Mendenhall.*" *United States v. Saperstein,* 723 F.2d 1221, 1226 (6th Cir. 1983).

6. "[T]here has been no seizure, within the meaning of the Fourth Amendment, when DEA agents employing a drug courier profile request airline passengers to produce their ticket and some form of identification, so long as the passenger's cooperation is voluntary and not the product of coercion, force, or other use of authority." *United States v. Pulvano,* 629 F.2d 1151, 1155 (5th Cir. 1980).

7. "[A] request by police that a suspect accompany them to a separate office raises the presumption of a seizure: 'Only exceptionally clear evidence of consent should overcome a presumption that a person requested to accompany an agent to an office no longer would feel free to leave.'" *United States v. Waksal,* 709 F.2d 653, 659 (11th Cir. 1983).

B.   Grounds for Stop: An airport stop must be based on reasonable suspicion; a "drug courier profile" alone may not supply reasonable suspicion.

1.   "[N]ot all seizures of the person must be justified by probable cause to arrest for a crime.... [C]ertain seizures are justifiable under the Fourth Amendment if there is articulable suspicion that a person has committed or is about to commit a crime." *Florida v. Royer,* 460 U.S. 491, 498 (1983).

2.   "Because of the inherently transient nature of drug courier activity at airports, allowing police to make brief investigative stops of persons at airports on reasonable suspicion of drug-trafficking substantially enhances the likelihood that police will be able to prevent the flow of narcotics into distribution channels." *United States v. Place,* 462 U.S. 696, _____ (1983).

3.   "We agree with the State that when the officers discovered that [Defendant] was travelling under an assumed name, this fact, and the facts already known to the officers—paying cash for a one-way ticket, the mode of checking the two bags, and [Defendant's] appearance and conduct in general—were adequate grounds for suspecting [Defendant] of carrying drugs and for temporarily detaining

him and his luggage while they attempted to verify or dispel their suspicions in a manner that did not exceed the limits of an investigative detention." *Florida v. Royer,* 460 U.S. 491, 502 (1983).

4.   "[I]f the respondent was 'seized' when the DEA agents approached her on the concourse and asked questions of her, the agents' conduct in doing so was constitutional only if they reasonably suspected the respondent of wrongdoing." *United States v. Mendenhall,* 446 U.S. 544, 551-52 (1980).

5.   "[T]he [lower] court thought it relevant that (1) the petitioner had arrived from Fort Lauderdale, which the agent testified is a principal place of origin of cocaine sold elsewhere in the country, (2) the petitioner arrived in the early morning, when law enforcement activity is diminished, (3) he and his companion appeared to the agent to be trying to conceal the fact that they were traveling together, and (4) they apparently had no luggage other than their shoulder bags. [T]he agent could not, as a matter of law, have reasonably suspected the petitioner of criminal activity on the basis of these observed circumstances. Of the evidence relied on, only the fact that the petitioner preceded another person and occasionally looked backward at him as they proceeded through the concourse relates to their particular conduct. The other circumstances described a very large category of presumably innocent travelers, who would be subject to virtually random seizures were the Court to conclude that as little foundation as there was in this case could justify a seizure.... The agent's belief that the petitioner and his companion were attempting to conceal the fact that they were traveling together, a belief that was more an 'inchoate and unparticularized suspicion or "hunch" '... than a fair inference in the light of his experience, is simply too slender a reed to

support the seizure in this case." *Reid v. Georgia,* 448 U.S. 438, 440-41 (1980).

6. "[T]he 'drug courier profile,' by itself, provides no probable cause to arrest an individual. In addition, while a set of facts may arise in which the existence of certain profile characteristics constitutes reasonable suspicion, the circumstances of this case do not provide 'specific and articulable facts which, taken together with rational inferences from those facts, reasonably warrant[ed]' the intrusion of an investigatory stop." *United States v. McCaleb,* 552 F.2d 717, 720 (6th Cir. 1977).

7. "The standard by which this circuit judges a warrantless seizure... is by now clear: [the] stop will be deemed justified if (1) it can be demonstrated solely upon specific and articulable facts, and the rational inferences to be drawn therefrom, that the intrusion was based on a reasonable suspicion and was necessary, and (2) the intrusion fits within the narrow category of minimally intrusive seizures recognized in *Terry v. Ohio....* We must also be guided by three criteria in determining whether the facts and inferences support a reasonable suspicion. First, [the agent's] observations must be viewed as a whole, not as discrete and separate facts.... Second, [the agent's] observations must be viewed through the eyes of an agent who... is trained and experienced in discerning in ostensibly innocuous behavior the indicia of narcotics trafficking.... Third, the fact that conduct is as consistent with innocence as with guilt does not preclude that conduct from supporting a reasonable suspicion of criminal activity." *United States v. Forero-Rincon,* 626 F.2d 218, 221-22 (2d Cir. 1980).

**C. Arrest: An airport arrest must be based on proba-
ble cause.**

1. "[P]robable cause to arrest [Defendant] did not exist at
the time he consented to the search of his luggage. The
facts are that a nervous young man with two American
Tourister bags paid cash for an airline ticket to a 'target
city.' These facts led to inquiry, which in turn revealed that
the ticket had been bought under an assumed name. The
proffered explanation did not satisfy the officers. We
cannot agree with the State, if this is its position, that every
nervous young man paying cash for a ticket to New York
City under an assumed name and carrying two heavy
American Tourister bags may be arrested and held to
answer for a serious felony charge." *Florida v. Royer,* 460
U.S. 491, 507 (1983).

2. "[T]he rule has emerged that the characteristics of the
drug courier profile are not alone enough to provide
probable cause to arrest nor necessarily enough to create
a reasonable suspicion to stop under *Terry.* The compo-
nents of the profile may be considered, however, along
with the other relevant information known to the officer in
evaluating whether he had probable cause to arrest or
reasonable suspicion to stop." *United States v. Smith,* 574
F.2d 882, 884 (6th Cir. 1978).

3. "Nor can it be said that the elements of the courier
profile, considered alone or in conjunction with the tip, were
sufficient to provide probable cause [for arrest]." *United
States v. Ballard,* 573 F.2d 913, 915 (5th Cir. 1978).

4. "The investigative stop rapidly developed evidence
sufficient to justify appellant's arrest. He denied having an
airline ticket and repeated the untruthful statement that he

was at the airport to meet his sister." *United States v. Rico*, 594 F.2d 320, 326 (2d Cir. 1979).

5. "[W]hen [the agent] requested [Defendant] to come with him to the Delta office, the interrogation could no longer be characterized as 'brief' or 'on-the-spot.' Rather, the request signaled the beginning of a more extended interrogation which was to occur in a place other than where it began. Second,.... [Defendant] was never informed that he was 'free to go,' and the circumstances surrounding the request indicate that [he] would have been physically restrained if he had refused to accompany [the agent] or had tried to escape his custody. Third, ...the circumstances indicate that the detention involved here was for the purpose of interrogation. In sum, the scope of the intrusion involved in [the agent's] request for [Defendant] to accompany him to the Delta office was significantly greater than that involved in a brief *Terry* stop, and therefore amounted to an arrest." *United States v. Hill*, 626 F.2d 429, 435-36 (5th Cir. 1980).

6. "Appellant contends that the act of directing him to proceed to an interview room constituted an arrest and that probable cause should have existed at that time. We disagree. Founded suspicion based on the facts then known to the agent justified the interrogation, and it was not improper, in absence of protest or coercive circumstances, to arrange that it take place free from public view with its attendant embarrassment." *United States v. Chatman*, 573 F.2d 565, 567 (9th Cir. 1977).

D. Consent: Contraband found during a consent search may be suppressed if it is the "fruit" of an unlawful stop or arrest.

1. "[I]t is submitted that the entire encounter was consensual and hence [Defendant] was not being held against his will at all. We find this submission untenable. Asking for and examining [Defendant's] ticket and his driver's license were no doubt permissible in themselves, but when the officers identified themselves as narcotics agents, told [him] that he was suspected of transporting narcotics and asked him to accompany them to the police room, while retaining his ticket and driver's license and without indicating in any way that he was free to depart, [Defendant] was effectively seized for the purposes of the Fourth Amendment. These circumstances surely amount to a show of official authority such that 'a reasonable person would have believed he was not free to leave.'... [Defendant] was being illegally detained when he consented to the search of his luggage, we agree that the consent was tainted by the illegality and was ineffective to justify the search." *Florida v. Royer,* 460 U.S. 491, 501, 502 (1983).

2. "[T]he totality of the evidence in this case was plainly adequate to support the District Court's finding that the respondent voluntarily consented to accompany the officers to the DEA office. The respondent had twice unequivocally indicated her consent to the search, and when assured by the police officer that there would be no problem if nothing were turned up by the search, she began to undress without further comment." *United States v. Mendenhall,* 446 U.S. 544, 558, 559 (1980).

3. "[T]he very nature of [airport] stops may render them intimidating. The nervousness that air flight often engenders, the need quickly to make connections for continuing one's journey, the mere surprise from being accosted in a crowded airport concourse by a law enforcement officer for no apparent reason, and the pressure to cooperate with police to avoid an untoward scene before the crowds of

people, all make it easy for implicit threats or subtle coercion to exert tremendous pressure on an individual to acquiesce to the officer's wishes. In such a situation it would be easy to misinterpret acquiescence to an officer's demands as consent; acquiescence cannot, of course, substitute for free consent." *United States v. Berry,* 670 F.2d 583, 596 (5th Cir. 1982).

4. "Despite the obvious irony, it is apparent that suspects can, and often do, voluntarily consent to a search even when it must be clear to them that incriminating evidence will be disclosed." *United States v. Price,* 599 F.2d 494, 503 (2d Cir. 1979).

5. "[A] voluntary consent to search does not remove the taint of an illegal seizure. Rather, voluntariness is merely a threshold requirement. The 'causal connection' between the illegal seizure and the consent to search must be independently examined...." *United States v. Robinson,* 625 F.2d 1211, 1220 (5th Cir. 1980).

6. "We... find that trial court erred when it held [Defendant's] consent to have been voluntarily given. Although in this circuit, consent can, in proper circumstances, validate a search following an illegal arrest, those circumstances are not present here.... When trying to establish that there was a voluntary consent after an illegal stop, the government has a much heavier burden to carry than when the consent is given after a permissible stop.... In this case, the government has failed to establish the existence of any intervening circumstances which would serve to show that the consent was sufficiently attenuated from the illegal stop." *United States v. Ballard,* 573 F.2d 913, 916 (5th Cir. 1978).

E. Boarding Passengers and Luggage: Warrantless searches of boarding passengers and their luggage are justified by the strong public interest in preventing air piracy.

1. "The appropriate standards for evaluating the airport search program under the Fourth Amendment are found in a series of Supreme Court cases relating to 'administrative' searches.... The need to prevent airline hijacking is unquestionably grave and urgent.... A pre-boarding screening of all passengers and carry-on articles sufficient in scope to detect the presence of weapons or explosives is reasonably necessary to meet...the administrative need that justifies it." *United States v. Davis,* 482 F.2d 893, 908, 910 (9th Cir. 1973).

2. "The reasonableness of a warrantless search depends...on balancing the need for a search against the offensiveness of the intrusion. We need not labor the point with respect to need; the success of the FAA's [Federal Aviation Agency] anti-hijacking program should not obscure the enormous dangers to life and property from terrorists, ordinary criminals, or the demented. The search of carry-on baggage...involves not the slightest stigma.... To brand such a search as unreasonable would go beyond any fair interpretation of the Fourth Amendment." *United States v. Edwards,* 498 F.2d 496, 500 (2d Cir. 1974).

3. "[A]irport security checkpoints and loading gates are sui generis under the fourth amendment. Due to the intense danger of air piracy, we have long held that these areas, like international borders, are 'critical zones' in which special fourth amendment considerations apply." *United States v. Herzbrun,* 723 F.2d 773, 775 (11th Cir. 1984).

4. "Due to the gravity of the air piracy problem, we think that the airport, like the border crossing, is a critical zone in which special fourth amendment considerations apply. It is the one channel through which all hijackers must pass before being in a position to commit their crime. It is also the one point where airport security officials can marshal their resources to thwart such acts before the lives of an airplane's passengers and crew are endangered." *United States v. Moreno,* 475 F.2d 44, 51 (5th Cir.), *cert. denied,* 414 U.S. 840 (1973).

5. "In view of the magnitude of the crime sought to be prevented, the exigencies of time which clearly precluded the obtaining of a warrant, the use of the magnetometer is in our view a reasonable caution." *United States v. Bell,* 464 F.2d 667, 673 (2d Cir.), *cert. denied,* 409 U.S. 991 (1972).

6. "[Defendant] had a choice of traveling by air or by some other means. The signs in the terminal gave him fair notice that if in the course of the total screening process a physical inspection of his hand luggage should be considered necessary to assure the safety of the traveling public, he could be required to submit it for that purpose. When he then voluntarily entered upon the screening process [Defendant] acquiesced in its full potential scope as represented to him, including physical inspection if, as developed, that should be requested. Allowing him to withdraw his luggage when the x-ray raised the suspicions of the security officers would frustrate the regulation's purpose of deterring hijacking." *United States v. DeAngelo,* 584 F.2d 46, 47-48 (4th Cir. 1978), *cert. denied,* 440 U.S. 935 (1979).

7. "[A] party may revoke his consent to be searched any time prior to boarding the plane, even when he has passed beyond the initial screening point, if he agrees to leave the

boarding area. Other decisions of this court have also recognized that a passenger always maintains the option of leaving." *United States v. Homburg,* 546 F.2d 1350, 1352 (9th Cir. 1976), *cert. denied,* 431 U.S. 940 (1977).

8.   "[T]he authorities can conduct a security search outside the perimeter of the security area of one who has attempted to enter the security area.... '[T]he limits of a constitutional search are not necessarily defined by the perimeter of a particular security system. The marshals' specified authority should not bar further investigation if, in the exercise of their professional judgment, their reasonable suspicions [have] not been allayed by the routine security check.'" *United States v. Herzbrun,* 723 F.2d 773, 777 (11th Cir. 1984).

F.   Dogs: Using a dog to sniff a container at an airport to detect contraband does not normally constitute a search; thus, Fourth Amendment protections do not apply.

1.   "[W]e conclude that the particular course of investigation that the agents intended to pursue here—exposure of respondent's luggage, which was located in a public place, to a trained canine—did not constitute a 'search' within the meaning of the Fourth Amendment." *United States v. Place,* 462 U.S. 696,____(1983).

2.   "We have affirmed that a person possesses a privacy interest in the contents of personal luggage that is protected by the Fourth Amendment.... A 'canine sniff' by a well-trained narcotics detection dog, however, does not require opening the luggage. It does not expose noncontraband items that otherwise would remain hidden from public

view, as does, for example, an officer's rummaging through the contents of the luggage. Thus, the manner in which information is obtained through this investigative technique is much less intrusive than a typical search. Moreover, the sniff discloses only the presence or absence of narcotics, a contraband item. Thus, despite the fact that the sniff tells the authorities something about the contents of the luggage, the information obtained is limited. This limited disclosure also ensures that the owner of the property is not subjected to the embarrassment and inconvenience entailed in less discriminate and more intrusive investigative methods." *United States v. Place,* 462 U.S. 696, _____ (1983).

3. "[I]t [can]not be considered a search within the protection of the Fourth Amendment for a dog to sniff bags handled by an airline. There can be no reasonable expectation of privacy when any passenger's bags may be subjected to close scrutiny for the protection of public safety.... [H]aving defendants' luggage sniffed by [the dog] was not a search." *United States v. Sullivan,* 625 F.2d 9, 13 (4th Cir. 1980), *cert. denied,* 450 U.S. 923 (1981).

4. "It is well settled that the olfactory activities of a trained police dog legitimately on the premises do not constitute a search.... As of the time of their arrest, appellants' legitimate expectations with regard to the locked briefcase were that it would remain unopened absent warrant authorization. The dog's mere sniffing of such did not offend constitutional guarantees." *United States v. Burns,* 624 F.2d 95, 101 (10th Cir.), *cert. denied,* 449 U.S. 954 (1980).

5. "It is because [the dog's] sniff did not constitute a search within the meaning of the Fourth Amendment that we hold that reasonable and articulable suspicion is not

required before a DEA agent may use a canine trained in drug detection to sniff luggage in the custody of a common carrier." *United States v. Goldstein,* 635 F.2d 356, 361-62 (5th Cir.), *cert. denied,* 452 U.S. 962 (1981).

G. Seizure of Luggage: If reasonable suspicion exists that a traveler's luggage contains seizable items, a limited seizure of the luggage may be permissible.

1. "In the ordinary case, the Court has viewed a seizure of personal property as *per se* unreasonable within the meaning of the Fourth Amendment unless it is accomplished pursuant to a judicial warrant issued upon probable cause and particularly describing the items to be seized. . . . Where law enforcement authorities have probable cause to believe that a container holds contraband or evidence of a crime, but have not secured a warrant, the Court has interpreted the Amendment to permit seizure of the property, pending issuance of a warrant to examine its contents, if the exigencies of the circumstances demand it or some other recognized exception to the warrant requirement is present." *United States v. Place,* 462 U.S. 696,____(1983).

2. "[T]he Government asks us to recognize the reasonableness under the Fourth Amendment of warrantless seizures of personal luggage from the custody of the owner on the basis of less than probable cause, for the purpose of pursuing a limited course of investigation, short of opening the luggage, that would quickly confirm or dispel the authorities' suspicion. Specifically, we are asked to apply the principles of *Terry v. Ohio,* [392 U.S. (1968)], to permit such seizures on the basis of reasonable, articulable suspicion, premised on objective facts, that the luggage

contains contraband or evidence of a crime. In our view, such application is appropriate." *United States v. Place,* 462 U.S. 696,____(1983).

3. "Given the fact that seizures of property can vary in intrusiveness, some brief detentions of personal effects may be so minimally intrusive of Fourth Amendment interests that strong countervailing governmental interests will justify a seizure based only on specific articulable facts that the property contains contraband or evidence of a crime." *United States v. Place,* 462 U.S. 696,____(1983).

4. "[S]uch a seizure can effectively restrain the person since he is subjected to the possible disruption of his travel plans in order to remain with his luggage or to arrange for its return. Therefore, when the police seize luggage from the suspect's custody, we think the limitations applicable to investigative detentions of the person should define the permissible scope of an investigative detention of the person's luggage on less than probable cause. Under this standard, it is clear that the police conduct here exceeded the permissible limits of a *Terry*-type investigative stop. The length of the detention of respondent's luggage alone precludes the conclusion that the seizure was reasonable in the absence of probable cause.... [T]he New York agents knew the time of [Defendant's] scheduled arrival at LaGuardia, had ample time to arrange for their additional investigation at that location, and thereby could have minimized the intrusion on respondent's Fourth Amendment interests." *United States v. Place,* 462 U.S. 696,____(1983).

5. "In the airport setting, privacy and possessory interests in luggage are often high.... Air travelers for many reasons may simply be unable to function if they arrive without their luggage. If a DEA agent seizes an air traveler's luggage,

the seizure may be, for all practical purposes, tantamount to a seizure of the traveler himself, even an arrest.... Because police seizure of an air traveler's luggage may effectively stop or even arrest the traveler, the fourth amendment applies to protect the traveler's reasonable possessory interest in his luggage." *United States v. Puglisi,* 723 F.2d 779, 786 (11th Cir. 1984).

6. "[I]f the police possess reasonable suspicion to stop someone under *Terry,* they may also seize any luggage he may be carrying, for a brief, investigatory purpose. Even though such detention restricts the possessor's freedom of movement, the seizure is permissible if the police possess reasonable, articulable suspicion, in view of the totality of the circumstances, that the luggage contains contraband or evidence of a crime." *United States v. Puglisi,* 723 F.2d 779, 785 (11th Cir. 1984).

Chapter 23

Mail Searches

A. First Class Mail: First class mail is accorded full Fourth Amendment protection and may only be opened pursuant to a search warrant.

1. "[First class] letters and sealed packages of this kind in the mail are as fully guarded from examination and inspection, except as to their outward form and weight, as if they were retained by the parties forwarding them in their own domiciles. The constitutional guaranty of the right of the people to be secure in their papers against unreasonable searches and seizures extends to their papers, thus closed against inspection, wherever they may be. Whilst in the mail, they can only be opened and examined under like warrant, issued upon similar oath or affirmation, particularly describing the thing to be seized, as is required when papers are subjected to search in one's own household." *Ex parte Jackson,* 96 U.S. 727, 733 (1878).

2. "The significant Fourth Amendment interest was in the privacy of this first-class mail; and that privacy [could] not [be] disturbed or invaded until the approval of the magistrate was obtained." *United States v. Van Leeuwen,* 397 U.S. 249, 253 (1970).

3. "But, indisputably, the privacy of a sealed item bearing the proper amount of postage for a first class item is protected from warrantless opening, not because it is given the appellation 'first class' but because the Constitution

commands that result." *United States v. Phillips,* 478 F.2d 743, 748 (5th Cir. 1973).

4.   "Any user of the mails, entrusting papers or effects to the Post Office Department, is entitled to rely upon their being received on this basis. The matter mailed is, of course, subject to being searched and seized on proper warrant, but this is true no matter where it may be, including the owner's personal possession." *Oliver v. United States,* 239 F.2d 818, 823 (8th Cir. 1957).

5.   "[T]he package in question was mailed as first-class mail and...under applicable law it was not subject to opening and inspection by the Post Office Department without a search warrant." *Collins v. Wolff,* 467 F.2d 359, 360 (8th Cir. 1972).

6.   "In our view, the mail cover at issue in the instant case is indistinguishable in any important respect from the pen register at issue in *Smith.* This mail cover did not include an examination of the contents of any mail. The postal officer merely recorded information appearing on the outside of mail addressed to the boxes which were the subject of the mail cover. The persons who sent or received mail knew or ought to have known that postal employees must examine the outside of the mail in order to deliver it. Furthermore, even if the plaintiffs did harbor a subjective expectation of privacy, that expectation was unreasonable. Persons who sent mail to the plaintiffs voluntarily exposed the information on the outside of the envelopes to postal employees." *Vreeken v. Davis,* 718 F.2d 343, 347–48 (10th Cir. 1983).

7.   "[P]robable cause is not needed to support a brief segregation and delay of a mailed package. While 'theoretically' an unduly long detention of mail could become unreasonable enough to intrude upon privacy interests

protected by the Fourth Amendment,...the main Fourth Amendment interest in a mailed package attaches to the privacy of its contents, not the speed with which it is delivered.... For this reason, the Court ruled that no interest protected by the Fourth Amendment is invaded by forwarding a package on the following day rather than the day it is deposited." *United States v. Hillison,* 733 F.2d 692, 695–96 (9th Cir. 1984).

8. "[A] seizure occurred when Drug Enforcement Administration agents took custody of a package and its contents from employees of a private carrier. '[T]he decision by governmental authorities to exert dominion and control over the package for their own purposes clearly constituted a "seizure." '...a package in the mail may be detained on the basis of reasonable suspicion to believe it contains contraband pending further investigation directed toward establishing probable cause which will support issuance of a search warrant." *Garmon v. Foust,* 741 F.2d 1069, 1072 (8th Cir. 1984).

B. Other Mail: Mail which is not first class is not accorded the protection of the Fourth Amendment.

1. "[F]irst-class mail such as letters and sealed packages subject to letter postage—as distinguished from newspapers, magazines, pamphlets, and other printed matter—is free from inspection by postal authorities, except in the manner provided by the Fourth Amendment." *United States v. Van Leeuwen,* 397 U.S. 249, 251 (1970).

2. "[U]nlike first class mail, there is no expectation of privacy in the forwarding of fourth class mail. Such classification is not altered by the availability of 'preferential

handling to the extent practicable in dispatch and delivery'
by payment of a special handling fee." *United States v.
Riley,* 554 F.2d 1282, 1283 (4th Cir. 1977).

3. "[I]nspection by the Post Office Department of an
unsealed package not having upon it stamps sufficient to
qualify it as first class mail was not an invasion of
appellant's immunity from unreasonable search and seizure...." *Webster v. United States,* 92 F.2d 462, 462 (6th
Cir. 1937).

4. "[T]he package was not first-class but must have been
accepted as either third- or fourth-class mail.... The
appellant might have protected the privacy of his package
by marking it first class.... [W]e see no constitutional
question under the unreasonable search and seizure
provision of the Fourth Amendment." *Santana v. United
States,* 329 F.2d 854, 856 (1st Cir.), *cert. denied,* 377 U.S.
990 (1964).

5. "[T]he possibility that Federal Express would for some
purpose open the package, be it for reasons of security, an
accident or damage, is a risk that must, or at least should
have been, considered by [Defendant] when he decided to
use their services. [Defendant] chose to accept this risk.
That decision could only serve to reduce his subjective
expectation of privacy in the parcel he consigned." *United
States v. Barry,* 673 F.2d 912, 919 (6th Cir.), *cert. denied,*
459 U.S. 927 (1982).

**C.   International Mail: Mail arriving from foreign coun-
tries may be searched without a warrant under the
rationale which justifies border searches.**

1. "[C]ustoms officials could search, without probable
cause and without a warrant, envelopes carried by an

entering traveler, whether in his luggage or on his person.... Surely no different constitutional standard should apply simply because the envelopes were mailed, not carried. The critical fact is that envelopes cross the border and enter this country, not that they are brought in by one mode of transportation rather than another." *United States v. Ramsey,* 431 U.S. 606, 620 (1977).

2. "There appears to be no sound reason to distinguish between incoming mail and other property that crosses our border. Affixing a postage stamp to a parcel should not grant it immunity that would not be accorded a package carried by a traveller." *United States v. Richard,* 638 F.2d 765, 772 (5th Cir.), *cert. denied,* 454 U.S. 1097 (1981).

3. "There is no question that the initial opening of the package by customs agents was lawful. Customs officials are authorized to inspect incoming international mail when they have a 'reasonable cause to suspect' that the mail contains contraband.... 'Reasonable cause to suspect' is a considerably milder standard than probable cause." *United States v. Dubrofsky,* 581 F.2d 208, 211 (9th Cir. 1978).

4. "Mail sorting rooms at a port of entry like New York are border areas. Thus, the instant search was reasonable simply because the package was searched at a border area after entering this country from Thailand." *United States v. Pringle,* 576 F.2d 1114, 1117 (5th Cir. 1978).

5. "[T]he interception and discovery of the hashish in New York was a legal border search.... Furthermore, controlled or monitored deliveries of intercepted mail packages of foreign origin to the named addressee have

been upheld." *United States v. Galvez,* 465 F.2d 681, 687 (10th Cir. 1972).

D. Controlled Deliveries: When law enforcement agents lawfully learn that there is contraband in a container, they may reseal the container and deliver it to the recipient.

1.   "The lawful discovery by common carriers or customs officers of contraband in transit presents law enforcement authorities with an opportunity to identify and prosecute the person or persons responsible for the movement of the contraband. To accomplish this, the police, rather than simply seizing the contraband and destroying it, make a so-called controlled delivery of the container to its consignee, allowing the container to continue its journey to the destination contemplated by the parties. The person dealing in the contraband can then be identified upon taking possession of and asserting dominion over the container." *Illinois v. Andreas,* 463 U.S. 765,____(1983).

2.   "The threshold question, then, is whether an individual has a legitimate expectation of privacy in the contents of a previously lawfully searched container. It is obvious that the privacy interest in the contents of a container diminishes with respect to a container that law enforcement authorities have already lawfully opened and found to contain illicit drugs. No protected privacy interest remains in contraband in a container once government officers lawfully have opened that container and identified its contents as illegal. The simple act of resealing the container to enable the police to make a controlled delivery does not operate to revive or restore the lawfully invaded privacy rights." *Illinois v. Andreas,* 463 U.S. 765,____(1983).

3. "The issue then becomes, at what point after an interruption of control or surveillance [should courts] recognize the individual's expectation of privacy in the container as a legitimate right protected by the Fourth Amendment proscription against unreasonable searches. In fashioning a standard, we must be mindful of three Fourth Amendment principles. First, the standard should be workable for application by rank and file, trained police officers.... Second, it should be reasonable; for example, it would be absurd to recognize as legitimate an expectation of privacy where there is only a minimal probability that the contents of a particular container had been changed. Third, the standard should be objective, not dependent on the belief of individual police officers.... A workable, objective standard that limits the risk of intrusion on legitimate privacy interests is whether there is a substantial likelihood that the contents of the container have been changed during the gap in surveillance. We hold that absent a substantial likelihood that the contents have been changed, there is no legitimate expectation of privacy in the contents of a container previously opened under lawful authority." *Illinois v. Andreas,* 463 U.S. 765,____(1983).

4. "Controlled deliveries of contraband apparently serve a useful function in law enforcement. They most ordinarily occur when a carrier, usually an airline, unexpectedly discovers what seems to be contraband while inspecting luggage to learn the identity of its owner, or when the contraband falls out of a broken or damaged piece of luggage, or when the carrier exercises its inspection privilege because some suspicious circumstance has caused it concern that it may unwittingly be transporting contraband. Frequently, after such a discovery, law enforcement agents restore the contraband to its container, then close or reseal the container, and authorize the carrier to deliver the container to its owner. When the owner

appears to take delivery he is arrested and the container with the contraband is seized and then searched a second time for the contraband known to be there." *United States v. Bulgier,* 618 F.2d 472, 476 (7th Cir.), *cert. denied,* 449 U.S. 824 (1980).

5. "[T]he official seizure of the contraband occurred...when the government asserted dominion over it.... Certainly, the seizure meets the Fourth Amendment requirement of probable cause, because the government agents involved knew that the substance was contraband before seizing it. But, the officers' failure to obtain a warrant to seize can be excused only if the circumstances at the time of the seizure were sufficiently exigent to make their course of action imperative.... The...officers had determined with certainty—and without violation of privacy—that the substance submitted for shipment was contraband. At that time, they could have ordered that the substance be detained until a magistrate could issue a warrant to seize it. The time delay required to obtain a warrant, however, might very well have warned the parties to the crime of the government's presence and prevented their apprehension. If the contraband had not been shipped immediately, the...addressee probably would have become suspicious and remained aloof, and the officers' investigation and arrest process would have proven unproductive." *United States v. Ford,* 525 F.2d 1308, 1313 (10th Cir. 1975).

Chapter 24

Canine Searches

A. Private Property: Dogs' sniffing of private property located in public and semi-public places does not constitute a search.

1. "The purpose for which respondent's luggage was seized, of course, was to arrange its exposure to a narcotics detection dog. Obviously, if this investigative procedure is itself a search requiring probable cause, the initial seizure of respondent's luggage for the purpose of subjecting it to the sniff test—no matter how brief—could not be justified on less than probable cause.... The Fourth Amendment 'protects people from unreasonable government intrusions into their legitimate expectations of privacy.'... We have affirmed that a person possesses a privacy interest in the contents of personal luggage that is protected by the Fourth Amendment.... A 'canine sniff' by a well-trained narcotics detection dog, however, does not require opening the luggage. It does not expose noncontraband items that otherwise would remain hidden from public view, as does, for example, an officer's rummaging through the contents of the luggage. Thus, the manner in which information is obtained through this investigative technique is much less intrusive than a typical search. Moreover, the sniff discloses only the presence or absence of narcotics, a contraband item. Thus, despite the fact that the sniff tells the authorities something about the contents of the luggage, the information obtained is limited. This limited disclosure also ensures that the owner of the property is not subjected to the embarrassment and inconvenience

entailed in less discriminate and more intrusive investigative methods. In these respects, the canine sniff is *sui
generis.* We are aware of no other investigative procedure
that is so limited both in the manner in which the
information is obtained and in the content of the information revealed by the procedure. Therefore, we conclude
that the particular course of investigation that the agents
intended to pursue here—exposure of respondent's luggage, which was located in a public place, to a trained
canine—did not constitute a 'search' within the meaning of
the Fourth Amendment." *United States v. Place,* 462 U.S.
696,____(1983).

2.   "It is well settled that the olfactory activities of a trained
police dog legitimately on the premises do not constitute a
search.... 'If the police officers here had detected the
aroma of the drug through their olfactory senses, there
could be no serious contention that their sniffing in the area
of the bags would be tantamount to an unlawful search....'
The dog's mere sniffing of [the locked briefcase] did not
offend constitutional guarantees." *United States v. Burns,*
624 F.2d 95, 101 (10th Cir.), *cert. denied,* 449 U.S. 954
(1980).

3.   "The reasonableness of a detention of luggage for the
purpose of conducting a 'sniff test' is dependent on the
facts of each case...in light of the three main factors
discussed in *Place:*
"1) the diligence of officers in pursuing their investigation
so as to minimize the intrusion;
"2) the brevity of the detention; and
"3) the information afforded the suspect regarding the
detention and return of the luggage."
United States v. West, 731 F.2d 90, 92 (1st Cir. 1984).

4. "[T]he dogs' sniffing of student lockers in public hallways and automobiles parked in public parking lots...did not constitute a search." *Horton v. Goose Creek Ind. School Dist.,* 690 F.2d 470, 477 (5th Cir. 1982), *cert. denied,* ____U.S.____(1983).

5. "The odor of a drug emanated from a source located in an area where privacy cannot be expected. Thus, [the dog's] sniffing was in no fashion an intrusion upon the privacy of 'persons, houses, papers and effects....'" *U.S. v. Sullivan,* 625 F.2d 9, 12 (4th Cir. 1980), *cert. denied,* 450 U.S. 923 (1981).

B. Persons: Dogs' sniffing of persons constitutes a search protected by the Fourth Amendment.

1. "The use of the dogs to sniff the students...presents an entirely different problem [from dogs' sniffing of lockers and automobiles]. After all, the fourth amendment 'protects people, not places.'" *Horton v. Goose Creek Ind. School Dist.,* 690 F.2d 470, 477 (5th Cir. 1982), *cert. denied,* ____ U.S.____(1983).

2. "[S]ociety recognizes the interest in the integrity of one's person, and the fourth amendment applies with its fullest vigor against any intrusion on the human body.... [W]e hold that sniffing by dogs of the students' persons...i.e., sniffing around each child, putting his nose *on* the child and scratching and manifesting other signs of excitement in the case of an alert...is a search within the purview of the fourth amendment." *Horton v. Goose Creek Ind. School Dist.,* 690 F.2d 470, 478, 479 (5th Cir. 1982), *cert. denied,* ____U.S.____(1983).

C. Dog Reactions as Probable Cause: In order for a dog's reaction to a person or container to provide probable cause to search or arrest, the reliability of the dog must be established.

1. "[T]he statement in the affidavit that [the dog] was a 'trained, certified marijuana sniffing dog' [is sufficient]...to show probable cause that there was marijuana or heroin in defendant's locker." *United States v. Venema,* 563 F.2d 1003, 1007 (10th Cir. 1977).

2. "The response by [the trained police dog] during his inspection, moreover, provided sufficient probable cause, particularly when coupled with the other facts laid out in the affidavit, to support the issuance of the search warrant." *United States v. Sullivan,* 625 F.2d 9, 13 (4th Cir. 1980), *cert. denied,* 450 U.S. 923 (1981).

3. "When the dog alerted the authorities to defendants' luggage, probable cause was then established.... [T]he dog's reliability as a drug detector...[is established by] the affiant's representation to the magistrate that the dog 'graduated from a training class in drug detection in October 1978' and 'has proven reliable in detecting drugs and narcotics on prior occasions.'" *United States v. Klein,* 626 F.2d 22, 27 (7th Cir. 1980).

4. "Trained dogs were brought in which appeared to respond to the presence of narcotics in the six suitcases.... The affidavit stat[ing] that one of the dogs had successfully discovered drugs on 409 occasions, another in over 100 instances...surely created probable cause to believe that the suitcases contained cocaine, heroin, or a like substance." *United States v. Viera,* 644 F.2d 509, 510, 511-12 (5th Cir.), *cert. denied,* 454 U.S. 867 (1981).

5.   "[The state] need not show that the dogs are infallible or even that they are reliable enough to give...probable cause; instead, the dogs must be reasonably reliable. It will not, however, be enough to show that the dogs are reasonably reliable in indicating the presence or recent presence of contraband. If the reaction is to justify a search, it must give rise to reasonable suspicion that the search will produce something—i.e., reasonable suspicion that contraband is *currently* present." *Horton v. Goose Creek Ind. School Dist.,* 690 F.2d 470, 482 (5th Cir. 1982), *cert. denied,* ____U.S.____(1983).

Chapter 25

Electronic Surveillance

A. Standard: The Fourth Amendment governs electronic surveillance that infringes on an individual's expectation of privacy.

1. "[T]he Fourth Amendment protects people, not places. What a person knowingly exposes to the public, even in his own home or office, is not a subject of Fourth Amendment protection.... But what he seeks to preserve as private, even in an area accessible to the public, may be constitutionally protected.... The Government's activities in electronically listening to and recording the petitioner's words violated the privacy upon which he justifiably relied while using the telephone booth and thus constituted a 'search and seizure' within the meaning of the Fourth Amendment. The fact that the electronic device employed to achieve that end did not happen to penetrate the wall of the booth can have no constitutional significance." *Katz v. United States,* 389 U.S. 347, 351, 353 (1967).

2. "[C]onversation [is] within the Fourth Amendment's protections, and...the use of electronic devices to capture it [is] a 'search' within the meaning of the Amendment...." *Berger v. New York,* 388 U.S. 41, 51 (1967).

3. "This case thus presents the question whether the monitoring of a beeper in a private residence, a location not open to visual surveillance, violates the Fourth Amendment rights of those who have a justifiable interest in the privacy of the residence. Contrary to the submission of the United

States, we think that it does." *United States v. Karo,* 468
U.S.____,____(1984).

4.   "[T]he principles enunciated in *Katz* are applicable to
situations involving visual, as well as auditory, surveillance." *United States v. Taborda,* 635 F.2d 131, 138 n.7
(2d Cir. 1980).

5.   "[T]he proper focal point for inquiry is whether the
government, in searching out information not otherwise
available, invades an individual's 'right of personal security,
personal liberty, and private property'...and violates 'the
privacy upon which he justifiably relied'.... By this approach, courts are able to distinguish visual surveillance
from electronic surveillance, eavesdropping from wiretapping, a plain view from a breaking and entering." *United
States v. Michael,* 622 F.2d 744, 752 (5th Cir. 1980), *cert.
denied,* 454 U.S. 950 (1981).

**B.   Warrant Requirements: A warrant authorizing elec-
tronic surveillance must be based on probable cause
and meet particularity requirements.**

1.   "The Fourth Amendment commands that a warrant
issue not only upon probable cause supported by oath or
affirmation, but also 'particularly describing the place to be
searched, and the persons or things to be seized'.... The
need for particularity and evidence of reliability in the
showing required when judicial authorization of a search is
sought is especially great in the case of eavesdropping. By
its very nature eavesdropping involves an intrusion on
privacy that is broad in scope." *Berger v. New York,* 338
U.S. 41, 55, 56 (1967).

2. "The government agents here ignored 'the procedure of antecedent justification...that is central to the Fourth Amendment,' a procedure that we hold to be a constitutional precondition of the kind of electronic surveillance involved in this case. Because the surveillance here failed to meet that condition, and because it led to the petitioner's conviction, the judgment must be reversed." *Katz v. United States,* 389 U.S. 347, 359 (1967).

3. "Yet the inescapable fact is that this restraint was imposed by the agents themselves, not by a judicial officer. They were not required, before commencing the search, to present their estimate of probable cause for detached scrutiny by a neutral magistrate. They were not compelled, during the conduct of the search itself, to observe precise limits established in advance by a specific court order. Nor were they directed, after the search had been completed, to notify the authorizing magistrate in detail of all that had been seized. In the absence of such safeguards, this Court has never sustained a search upon the sole ground that officers reasonably expected to find evidence of a particular crime and voluntarily confined their activities to the least intrusive means consistent with that end." *Katz v. United States,* 389 U.S. 347, 356-57 (1967).

4. "[Statutes which give] broadside authorization rather than being 'carefully circumscribed' so as to prevent unauthorized invasions of privacy actually permit general searches by electronic devices.... [T]he statute here is equally offensive. First,...eavesdropping is authorized without requiring belief that any particular offense has been or is being committed; nor that the 'property' sought, the conversations, be particularly described.... Secondly, authorization of eavesdropping for a two-month period is the equivalent of a series of intrusions, searches, and seizures pursuant to a single showing of probable cause. Prompt

execution is also avoided. . . . Third, the statute places no termination date on the eavesdrop once the conversation sought is seized. . . . Finally, the statute's procedure, necessarily because its success depends on secrecy, has no requirement for notice as do conventional warrants, nor does it overcome this defect by requiring some showing of special facts. . . . Nor does the statute provide for a return on the warrant thereby leaving full discretion in the officer as to the use of seized conversations of innocent as well as guilty parties. In short, the statute's blanket grant of permission to eavesdrop is without adequate judicial supervision or protective procedures." *Berger v. New York*, 388 U.S. 41, 58-60 (1967).

5. "[W]e find nothing to persuade us that the Court of Appeals was wrong in its rejection of [the minimization] claim. Forty percent of the calls were clearly narcotics related. . . . Many of the remaining calls were very short, such as wrong-number calls, [and] calls to persons who were not available to come to the phone. . . . In a case such as this, involving a wide-ranging conspiracy with a large number of participants, even a seasoned listener would have been hard pressed to determine with any precision the relevancy of many of the calls before they were completed. A large number were ambiguous in nature, making characterization virtually impossible until the completion of these calls. And some of the nonpertinent conversations were one-time conversations. Since these calls did not give the agents an opportunity to develop a category of innocent calls which should not have been intercepted, their interception cannot be viewed as a violation of the minimization requirement." *Scott v. United States,* 436 U.S. 128, 141-42 (1978).

6. "[T]he statute's failure to describe with particularity the conversation sought gives the officer a roving commission

to 'seize' any and all conversations. It is true that the statute requires the naming of 'the person or persons whose communications, conversations or discussions are to be overheard or recorded. . . .' But this does no more than identify the person whose constitutionally protected area is to be invaded rather than 'particularly describing' the communications, conversations, or discussions to be seized. As with general warrants this leaves too much to the discretion of the officer executing the order." *Berger v. New York*, 388 U.S. 41, 59 (1967).

7.   "[T]he overriding principle in both *Berger* and *Katz* was the necessity for judicial control over electronic surveillance and a neutral predetermination of the scope of the search." *Kilgore v. Mitchell*, 623 F.2d 631, 635 (9th Cir. 1980).

8.   "We do not believe that evidence relating to crimes other than those specified in a wiretap warrant must be discovered 'inadvertently' or take officers by 'surprise' in order for a court properly to authorize the use of such evidence pursuant to [18 U.S.C.] section 2517(5). Congress intended that evidence relating to unauthorized offenses should be given retroactive judicial approval under section 2517(5) if the 'original [wiretap warrant] was lawfully obtained, . . .was sought in *good faith and not as a subterfuge search,* and that the communication was in fact *incidentally* intercepted during the course of a lawfully executed order.'. . . Evidence of crimes other than those authorized in a wiretap warrant are intercepted 'incidentally' when they are the byproduct of a bona fide investigation of crimes specified in a valid warrant." *United States v. McKinnon,* 721 F.2d 19, 22, 23 (1st Cir. 1983).

C. Exceptions: There are some electronic surveillance devices and techniques which do not invade a reasonable expectation of privacy.

1. "The governmental surveillance conducted by means of the beeper in this case amounted principally to the following of an automobile on public streets and highways. ... Nothing in the Fourth Amendment prohibited the police from augmenting the sensory faculties bestowed upon them at birth with such enhancement as science and technology afforded them in this case.... [T]here is no indication that the beeper was used in any way to reveal information as to the movement of the drum within the cabin, or in any way that would not have been visible to the naked eye from outside the cabin.... [D]id monitoring the beeper signals complained of by respondent invade any legitimate expectation of privacy on his part?... [W]e hold they did not. Since they did not, there was neither a 'search' not a 'seizure' within the contemplation of the Fourth Amendment." *United States v. Knotts,* 460 U.S. 276, 281, 282, 285 (1983).

2. "[P]etitioner in all probability entertained no actual expectation of privacy in the phone numbers he dialed, and...even if he did, his expectation was not 'legitimate.' The installation and use of a pen register, consequently, was not a 'search,' and no warrant was required." *Smith v. Maryland,* 442 U.S. 735, 745-46 (1979).

3. "It is clear that the actual placement of the beeper into the can violated no one's Fourth Amendment rights. The can into which the beeper was placed belonged at the time to the DEA, and by no stretch of the imagination could it be said that respondents then had any legitimate expectation of privacy in it." *United States v. Karo,* 468 U.S.____, ____ (1984).

4. "Neither the Constitution nor any Act of Congress requires that official approval be secured before conversations are overheard or recorded by Government agents with the consent of one of the conversants." *United States v. Caceres*, 440 U.S. 741, 744 (1979).

5. "The Fourth Amendment does not prohibit *per se* a covert entry performed for the purpose of installing otherwise legal electronic bugging equipment." *Dalia v. United States*, 441 U.S. 238, 248 (1979).

6. "[L]istening in to a telephone conversation on an extension, with the consent of one party, does not violate the rights of the other party under the fourth amendment." *United States v. Miller,* 720 F.2d 227, 228 (1st Cir. 1983), *cert. denied,* ____U.S.____(1984).

7. "An individual has no legitimate expectation that the person to whom he is speaking will not relate the conversation to the legal authorities, either by repetition or by the recording of the conversation." *United States v. Haimowitz,* 725 F.2d 1561, 1582 (11th Cir. 1984).

8. "[N]ot all activities conducted in [Defendant's] home were automatically entitled to Fourth Amendment protection, [but not] every object or activity viewable through a telescope because [Defendant] failed to close the curtains was beyond Fourth Amendment protection.... [O]bservation of objects and activities inside a person's home by unenhanced vision from a location where the observer may properly be does not impair a legitimate expectation of privacy. However, any enhanced viewing of the interior of a home does impair a legitimate expectation of privacy and encounters the Fourth Amendment's warrant requirement, unless circumstances create a traditional exception to that

requirement." *United States v. Taborda*, 635 F.2d 131, 139 (2d Cir. 1980).

9. "The residents of the...[r]anch would, no doubt, have been aware of these routine [helicopter] flights and any reasonable person, cognizant of the ranch's proximity to the coastline and the Coast Guard's well-known function of sea-coast patrol and surveillance, could expect that government officers conducting such flights would be aided by sophisticated electronic equipment. As such, the residents could not reasonably bear a subjective expectation of privacy from the Coast Guard's airborne telephotographic scrutiny...." *United States v. Allen*, 633 F.2d 1282, 1290 (9th Cir. 1980), *cert. denied*, 454 U.S. 833 (1981).

10. "Permissible techniques of surveillance include more than just the five senses of officers and their unaided physical abilities. Binoculars, dogs that track and sniff out contraband, searchlights, fluorescent powders, automobiles and airplanes, burglar alarms, radar devices, and bait money contribute to surveillance without violation of the Fourth Amendment in the usual case. On the other hand, wiretaps, breaking and entering, and many other searches and seizures fall on the other side of the line." *United States v. Dubrofsky*, 581 F.2d 208, 211 (9th Cir. 1978).

11. "[A]ll courts that have squarely confronted the issue have concluded that warrantless electronic surveillance of foreign agents does not violate the Fourth Amendment provided its primary purpose is not to gather evidence for a criminal prosecution." *Ellsberg v. Mitchell,* 709 F.2d 51, 65 (D.C. Cir. 1983), *cert. denied*, ____ U.S. ____ (1984).

Chapter 26

Beeper Searches

A. Definition: A beeper is a device that transmits radio signals. It can reveal locations but cannot record or transmit conversations.

1. "A beeper is a radio transmitter, usually battery operated, which emits periodic signals that can be picked up by a radio receiver." *United States v. Knotts,* 460 U.S. 276, 277 (1983).

2. "Visual surveillance...would have sufficed to reveal all of these facts to the police. The fact that the officers in this case relied not only on visual surveillance, but also on the use of the beeper to signal the presence of Petschen's automobile to the police receiver, does not alter the situation. Nothing in the Fourth Amendment prohibited the police from augmenting the sensory faculties bestowed upon them at birth with such enhancement as science and technology afforded them in this case." *United States v. Knotts,* 460 U.S. 276, 282 (1983).

3. "An electronic tracking device—also called a 'beeper,' 'beacon,' or 'transponder'—is a miniature, battery-powered radio transmitter that emits a recurrent signal at a set frequency. When monitored by directional finders, the beeper provides information as to the location and movement of the object to which it is attached. A beeper is incapable of transmitting conversation or recording sounds.... For this reason, beepers do not fall within the

definition of wiretapping devices." *United States v. Butts,* 710 F.2d 1139, 1142-43 (5th Cir. 1983).

B. Installation: Warrantless installations of beepers by methods that do not violate reasonable expectations of privacy are permissible.

1.   "It is clear that the actual placement of the beeper into the can violated no one's Fourth Amendment rights. The can into which the beeper was placed belonged at the time to the DEA, and by no stretch of the imagination could it be said that respondents then had any legitimate expectation of privacy in it." *United States v. Karo,* 468 U.S. ____, ____ (1984).

2.   "We conclude that no Fourth Amendment interest of Karo or of any other respondent was infringed by the installation of the beeper." *United States v. Karo,* 468 U.S. ____, ____ (1984).

3.   "Although the can may have contained an unknown and unwanted foreign object, it cannot be said that anyone's possessory interest was interfered with in a meaningful way. At most, there was a technical trespass on the space occupied by the beeper. The existence of a physical trespass is only marginally relevant to the question of whether the Fourth Amendment has been violated." *United States v. Karo,* 468 U.S. ____, ____ (1984).

4.   "The mere transfer to Karo of a can containing an unmonitored beeper infringed no privacy interest. It conveyed no information that Karo wished to keep private, for it conveyed no information at all. To be sure, it created a *potential* for an invasion of privacy, but we have never held

that potential, as opposed to actual, invasions of privacy constitute searches for purposes of the Fourth Amendment." *United States v. Karo,* 468 U.S. ____, ____ (1984).

5 "We find that the DEA agents' reasonable suspicion that Michael was engaged in criminal activity justified the placement and monitoring of the beeper. The actual installation of the beeper was much less intrusive than the typical stop and frisk. Michael was in the pizza restaurant when the installation took place. He was not detained or questioned; he suffered no indignity; nothing from the interior of the van was seized or searched; indeed, nothing even from the van's exterior was removed." *United States v. Michael,* 645 F.2d 252, 258 (5th Cir. 1981).

6. "Applying this dual privacy and intrusiveness analysis to the facts of the instant case, we hold that the minimal intrusion involved in the attachment of a beeper to Michael's van, parked in a public place, was sufficiently justified so as to satisfy any of Michael's fourth amendment expectation of privacy concerns." *United States v. Michael,* 645 F.2d 252, 256 (5th Cir. 1981).

C. Monitoring in a Public Place: Warrantless monitoring in a public place of a beeper's transmissions does not violate the Fourth Amendment.

1. "[D]id monitoring the beeper signals complained of by respondent invade any legitimate expectation of privacy on his part? . . . [W]e hold it did not. Since it did not, there was neither a 'search' nor a 'seizure' within the contemplation of the Fourth Amendment." *United States v. Knotts,* 460 U.S. 276, 285 (1983).

2.   "*Knotts* teachs us here that monitoring signals from an electronic tracking device that tells officers no more than that a specific aircraft is flying in the public airspace does not violate any reasonable expectation of privacy. Because this is so, no Fourth Amendment violation results from such public detection. The movement of an airplane in the sky, like that of an automobile on a highway, is not something in which a person can claim a reasonable expectation of privacy." *United States v. Butts,* 729 F.2d 1514, 1517 (5th Cir. 1984).

3.   "The subsequent monitoring also did not violate Michael's reasonable expectation of privacy. The beeper only aided the agents in the performance of their lawful surveillance. The van traveled public roads and was exposed to public view. Monitoring the beeper while the agents had reasonable suspicion to believe Michael was conspiring to manufacture MDA did not violate his fourth amendment rights." *United States v. Michael,* 645 F.2d 252, 258 (5th Cir. 1981).

D.   Monitoring in a Home: Warrantless monitoring of a beeper surreptitiously introduced into a home violates the Fourth Amendment.

1.   "This case thus presents the question whether the monitoring of a beeper in a private residence, a location not open to visual surveillance, violates the Fourth Amendment rights of those who have a justifiable interest in the privacy of the residence. . . . [W]e think that it does." *United States v. Karo,* 468 U.S. ____, ____ (1984).

2.   "In this case, had a DEA agent thought it useful to enter the Taos residence to verify that the ether was

actually in the house and had he done so surreptitiously and without a warrant, there is little doubt that he would have engaged in an unreasonable search within the meaning of the Fourth Amendment. For purposes of the Amendment, the result is the same where, without a warrant, the Government surreptitiously employs an electronic device to obtain information that it could not have obtained by observation from outside the curtilage of the house. The beeper tells the agent that a particular article is actually located at a particular time in the private residence and is in the possession of the person or persons whose residence is being surveilled." *United States v. Karo,* 468 U.S. ____, ____ (1984).

3.   "Indiscriminate monitoring of property that has been withdrawn from public view would present far too serious a threat to privacy interests in the home to escape entirely some sort of Fourth Amendment oversight." *United States v. Karo,* 468 U.S. ____, ____ (1984).

Chapter 27

Body Searches

A. Exterior Intrusions: Intrusions on the body's surface (swabbing, hair samples, retrieval of evidence from the mouth, etc.) do not normally require a search warrant.

1. "The respondent appealed his conviction, claiming that the fingernail scrapings were the product of an unconstitutional search under the Fourth and Fourteenth Amendments.... On the facts of this case, considering the existence of probable cause, the very limited intrusion undertaken incident to the station house detention, and the ready destructibility of the evidence, we cannot say that this search violated the Fourth and Fourteenth Amendments." *Cupp v. Murphy*, 412 U.S. 291, 292, 296 (1973).

2. "In *Schmerber [v. California*, 483 U.S. 757 (1966)] the Court held that certain official intrusions into an individual's person require a search warrant in order for the intrusions to be deemed reasonable and not violative of the Fourth Amendment unless the exigencies of the circumstances of a case justify the failure to obtain a search warrant in that case. This holding does not comprehend that all official intrusions into an individual's person require, in the absence of extenuating circumstances, a search warrant in order to be reasonable. Some official in-custody investigative techniques designed to uncover incriminating evidence from a person's body are such minor intrusions into or upon the 'integrity of an individual's person'...that they are not, in the absence of a search warrant, unreasonable intru-

"

sions. '[T]he relevant test is not whether it is reasonable to procure a search warrant, but whether the search was reasonable.'" *United States v. D'Amico*, 408 F.2d 331, 333 (2d Cir. 1969).

3. "It is apparent that had the agents not swabbed Bridges' hands at the time, the opportunity may not have knocked again, especially if Bridges washed his hands. Accordingly, we find that the swabbing was no more offensive to Bridges' person than fingerprinting or photographing him.... We hold that the swabbing was not an unreasonable search...." *United States v. Bridges*, 499 F.2d 179, 184 (7th Cir.),*cert. denied*, 419 U.S. 1010 (1974).

4. "There can be little doubt that an inspection of one's hands, under an ultraviolet lamp, is the kind of governmental intrusion into one's private domain that is protected by the Fourth Amendment.... If the reach of the Fourth Amendment extends to fingerprinting,...and a search of one's clothing or personal effects,...it should certainly encompass a detailed inspection, by special instrument, of one's skin.... The protection afforded an individual by the Fourth Amendment would be eviscerated if, under authority of a warrant to search premises, government agents could scan an individual's body with sensitive instruments capable of picking up the most minute or intimate object lodged thereon." *United States v. Kenann*, 496 F.2d 181, 182-83 (1st Cir. 1974).

5. "[T]he [warrantless] search was reasonable since it was obviously necessary to conduct the test as promptly as possible because of the ease with which the evidence could be destroyed by a thorough washing. The simplicity of the [benzadine] test [conducted by swabbing the penis] makes it unnecessary to have it conducted by a physician. It is a chemical test not a medical test and was properly

administered by a trained police technician. His qualifications were not questioned." *United States v. Smith*, 470 F.2d 377, 379 (D.C. Cir. 1972).

6. "Appellant also contends that a [warrantless] penis scraping which revealed menstrual blood of the victim's type violated his Fourth Amendment rights. This, too, is devoid of merit, as the scraping constituted a permissible search of the person incident to a lawful arrest and involved no intrusion of the body surface. Additionally, there was threat of imminent destruction of the evidence of menstrual blood." *Brent v. White*, 398 F.2d 503, 505 (5th Cir. 1968), *cert. denied*, 393 U.S. 1123 (1969).

7. "Unquestionably the clipping of the few strands of appellant's hair by a federal agent constituted a 'seizure' that might conceivably be subject to the 'constraints of the Fourth Amendment,' ...but the fact that the officer failed to obtain a search warrant before cutting off the hairs does not necessarily require that we hold that this 'seizure' was an unconstitutional one.... Here there was only the slightest intrusion (if indeed there was any intrusion at all): the clipping by the officer of the few strands of hair from appellant's head was so minor an imposition that appellant suffered no true humiliation or affront to his dignity. We hold that a search warrant was not required to justify the officer's act." *United States v. D'Amico*, 408 F.2d 331, 332-33 (2d Cir. 1969).

B. Interior Intrusions: Intrusions into the body (blood tests, stomach pumping, surgery, etc.) are permitted by the Fourth Amendment only if they are conducted pursuant to a warrant, or if exigent circumstances

exist and there is a clear indication that desired evidence will be found.

1. "Search warrants are ordinarily required for searches of dwellings, and, absent an emergency, no less could be required where intrusions into the human body are concerned.... The importance of informed, detached and deliberate determinations of the issue whether or not to invade another's body in search of evidence of guilt is indisputable and great." *Schmerber v. California*, 384 U.S. 757, 770 (1966).

2. "The interests in human dignity and privacy which the Fourth Amendment protects forbid any such intrusions [into the body] on the mere chance that desired evidence might be obtained. In the absence of a clear indication that in fact such evidence will be found, these fundamental human interests require law officers to suffer the risk that such evidence may disappear unless there is an immediate search." *Schmerber v. California*, 384 U.S. 757, 769-70 (1966).

3. "It would be a stultification of the responsibility which the course of constitutional history has cast upon this Court to hold that in order to convict a man the police cannot extract by force what is in his mind but can extract what is in his stomach.... [T]he proceedings by which this conviction was obtained do more than offend some fastidious squeamishness or private sentimentalism about combatting crime too energetically. This is conduct that shocks the conscience. Illegally breaking into the privacy of the petitioner, the struggle to open his mouth and remove what was there, the forcible extraction of his stomach's contents—this course of proceeding by agents of government to obtain evidence is bound to offend even hardened sensibilities. They are methods too close to the rack and

the screw to permit of constitutional differentiation." *Rochin v. California*, 342 U.S. 165, 172-73 (1952).

4. "The officer in the present case, however, might reasonably have believed that he was confronted with an emergency, in which the delay necessary to obtain a warrant, under the circumstances, threatened 'the destruction of evidence.' ... We are told that the percentage of alcohol in the blood begins to diminish shortly after drinking stops, as the body functions to eliminate it from the system.... Given these special facts, we conclude that the [test] to secure evidence of blood-alcohol content in this case was an appropriate incident to petitioner's arrest." *Schmerber v. California*, 384 U.S. 757, 770-71 (1966).

5. "[T]here is nothing 'brutal' or 'offensive' in the taking of a sample of blood when done, as in this case, under the protective eye of a physician.... The blood test procedure has become routine in our everyday life.... We therefore conclude that a blood test taken by a skilled technician is not such 'conduct that shocks the conscience,'...nor such a method of obtaining evidence that it offends a 'sense of justice....'" *Breithaupt v. Abram*, 352 U.S. 432, 435-37 (1957).

6. "The integrity of an individual's person is a cherished value of our society. That we today hold that the Constitution does not forbid the States minor intrusions into an individual's body under stringently limited conditions in no way indicates that it permits more substantial intrusions, or intrusions under other conditions." *Schmerber v. California*, 384 U.S. 757, 772 (1966).

7. "It is possible that the conduct here is a violation of the Fourth-Fourteenth Amendments, but it is also a possible violation of the due process clause of the Fifth Amend-

ment. That was the basis for the Supreme Court's ruling in *Rochin*.... Our view is that the stronger argument for exclusion is the Fifth Amendment prohibition which is somewhat broader than the limitation provided by the Fourth Amendment.... It is to be gleaned from the evidence that the practice of either threatening to use a catheter or the actual use of it is not an infrequent occurrence in New Mexico. While this may not be shocking to the extent that it was in the *Rochin* case, it is nevertheless an undesirable practice which is ultimately likely to produce a fact situation which will be ruled shocking and unlawful. We are not, however, justified in reaching this conclusion in the present case because of the fact that the *Rochin* decision pretty much stands by itself and is limited to its particular facts. This is not to say that you would have to have a stomach pump in order to satisfy the requirements, but there would have to be something akin to it plus gross circumstances...." *Yanez v. Romero*, 619 F.2d 851, 853, 854 (10th Cir.), *cert. denied*, 449 U.S. 876 (1980).

8. "We hold therefore that personal indignity suffered by the individual searched controls the level of suspicion required to make the search reasonable.... [W]e have isolated three factors which contribute to the personal indignity endured by the person searched: (1) physical contact between the searcher and the person searched; (2) exposure of intimate body parts; and (3) use of force. These factors tend to control the level of insult to personal privacy visited upon the victim of a search.... [A]s medical danger increases because of a search procedure, so must the reasons for conducting the procedure." *United States v. Vega-Barvo*, 729 F.2d 1341, 1346, 1348 (11th Cir. 1984).

9. "[Defendant] cannot complain that his rights were violated by his being taken to a hospital where a stomach

pump was used to extract heroin. At the time he appeared to be unconscious or semi-conscious and the officers acted in good faith to prevent further harm to him." *United States v. Owens*, 475 F.2d 759, 760 (5th Cir. 1973).

10.   "Once the Customs officers developed reasonable suspicion that Marin was an internal carrier, they could permit nature to run its course or ask Marin to speed up the process by taking the laxative. The fourth amendment erects no bar to either procedure so long as neither is physically forced on the suspected carrier." *United States v. Saldarriaga-Marin,* 734 F.2d 1425, 1428 (11th Cir. 1984).

11.   "[I]n all cases, the investigating officer should request the suspect's consent to take the blood sample. . . . If. . .the suspect refuses consent, he or she should be placed under arrest prior to taking the blood sample. The arrest, as well as the removal of blood, must be supported by probable cause. If the officer does not receive a refusal to the request, and considering the physical and mental condition of the suspect, it may be assumed that the suspect is not lucid. In that case, a formal arrest is not required, but, again, the seizure of the person and the blood must be supported by probable cause." *United States v. Harvey*, 701 F.2d 800, 806 (9th Cir. 1983).

12.   "The basic principle is that, once the state has demonstrated the relevancy of evidence and the inability to obtain it otherwise, the reasonableness of removing it forcibly from a person's body is judged by the extent of the surgical intrusion and the extent of the risks to the subject. . . . The judicial inquiry is not to make the medical estimate in medical terms, but is whether, under the totality of the circumstances presented, the procedure proposed by the state is constitutionally unreasonable. Viewed starkly, the state proposes to drug this citizen—not yet convicted of a

criminal offense—with narcotics and barbiturates into a state of unconsciousness, then surgically to open his chest and there to explore for a bullet that may or may not be probative in the trial of the crimes with which he is charged. We hold that this goes beyond the police practices which the state can legitimately undertake within the bounds of the fourth amendment." *Lee v. Winston,* 717 F.2d 888, 899, 901 (4th Cir. 1983), *cert. granted,* April 16, 1984.

13. "[W]e are not here called upon to give general approval of surgical operations in search of evidence. We are concerned only with the procedures followed in this case. We think those procedures were reasonable and justified in the circumstances. We repeat and summarize the factors that lead us to this conclusion: (1) the evidence sought was relevant, could have been obtained in no other way, and there was probable cause to believe that the operation would produce it; (2) the operation was minor, was performed by a skilled surgeon, and every possible precaution was taken to guard against any surgical complications, so that the risk of permanent injury was minimal; (3) before the operation was performed the District Court held an adversary hearing at which the defendant appeared with counsel; (4) thereafter and before the operation was perfomed the defendant was afforded an opportunity for appellate review by this court." *United States v. Crowder,* 543 F.2d 312, 316 (D.C. Cir. 1976) (en banc), *cert. denied,* 429 U.S. 1062 (1977).

C. Strip and Body Cavity Searches: Strip searches and body cavity searches occur primarily in prisons or jails. They must be conducted in a reasonable manner and must be justified under the circumstances.

1. "We do not underestimate the degree to which these searches may invade the personal privacy of inmates. . . .

The searches must be conducted in a reasonable manner.
... But we deal here with the question whether visual body-cavity inspections as contemplated by the [prison] rules can *ever* be conducted on less than probable cause. Balancing the significant and legitimate security interests of the institution against the privacy interests of the inmates, we conclude that they can." *Bell v. Wolfish*, 441 U.S. 520, 560 (1979).

2.   "When a person is lawfully arrested for this reason [possession of controlled substances], of course, post-arrest searches of the body to discover the controlled substances are generally permissible." *Salinas v. Breier*, 695 F.2d 1073, 1083 (7th Cir. 1982), *cert. denied*, _____U.S. _____ (1984).

3.   "Strip searches of detainees are constitutionally con-strained by due process requirements of reasonableness under the circumstances.... [Defendant's] strip search bore no...discernible relationship to security needs at the Detention Center that, when balanced against the ultimate invasion of personal rights involved, ...could reasonably be thought justified. At no time would [Defendant] or similar [DWI] detainees be intermingled with the general jail population; her offense, though not a minor traffic offense, was nevertheless one not commonly associated by its very nature with the possession of weapons or contraband...." *Logan v. Shealy*, 660 F.2d 1007, 1013 (4th Cir. 1981), *cert. denied*, 455 U.S. 942 (1982).

4.   "The [strip] searches were conducted upon all such offenders who were detained overnight in the... County jail due to an unwillingness or inability to post bond before their initial appearance in court. The searches were conducted

despite the absence of any probable cause to believe that the detainees were concealing contraband or weapons on their bodies. The district court ruled that the appellants' practices violated the Fourth...and Fourteenth Amendments.... We affirm the judgment of the district court,...and adopt the district court's Memorandum and Order as the decision of this court." *Tinetti v. Wittke*, 620 F.2d 160, 160-61 (7th Cir. 1980).

5.   "[I]t is our view that a reasonable suspicion standard should govern strip searches of correction officers working in correctional facilities.... [W]e believe that, as applied to correction officers, society is prepared to recognize that the expectation of being free from the indignity of warrantless visual body-cavity searches continues to exist even within the confines of correctional facilities. In contrast to the legitimate governmental interests asserted for strip searches, we believe that the governmental interests vis-á-vis visual body-cavity searches are diminished severely.... [W]e hold that before the Department may conduct a visual body-cavity search, it must obtain a search warrant based on probable cause from a judicial officer." *Security and Law Enforcement Employees, District Council 82 v. Carey*, 737 F.2d 187, 204, 208 (2d Cir. 1984).

6.   "[Searches were conducted]...with probable cause to believe that a controlled substance [was] hidden in a person's rectum or vagina, without first obtaining a warrant and without obtaining the services of a doctor under sanitary conditions, [as well as requiring] the person, without the use of force, to bend forward deeply at the waist so as to expose her rectum and vagina to visual inspection.... The ultimate question is whether a body search limited to these steps is constitutionally permissible when the person searched is in custody following a lawful arrest and when there is probable cause to believe that a

controlled substance is hidden on or within the person's body. We think the answer is clear. Such limited measures in these circumstances are valid under the fourth amendment as it is incorporated within the due process clause of the fourteenth amendment. Such a search [was] reasonable, in the constitutional sense, and performed in a reasonable manner." *Salinas v. Breier*, 695 F.2d 1073, 1085 (7th Cir. 1982), *cert. denied,* _____ U.S. _____ (1984).

7. "[T]he fourth amendment imposes a stricter standard on the 'means and procedures' of a body search than does the due process clause.... Any body search, if it is to comport with the reasonableness standard of the fourth amendment, must be conducted with regard for the subject's privacy and be designed to minimize emotional and physical trauma." *United States v. Cameron*, 538 F.2d 254, 258 (9th Cir. 1976).

8. "A court order compelling a person to submit to an x-ray examination is the equivalent of a search warrant for a body cavity search.... 'Clear indication' means more than real suspicion but less than probable cause.... A clear indication or plain suggestion that the suspect is concealing contraband within his body is required before a search beyond the body's surface may be authorized." *United States v. Mendez-Jimenez,* 709 F.2d 1300, 1302 (9th Cir. 1983).

D. Strip Searches at the Border: Strip searches at the border may be conducted only pursuant to real or reasonable suspicion.

1. "[A]lthough anyone entering or leaving the country may expect to have his luggage and personal effects

examined, he does not expect that his entry or departure, standing alone, will cause him to be subjected to a strip search. Before a border official may insist upon such an extensive invasion of privacy, he should have a suspicion of illegal concealment that is based upon something more than the border crossing, and the suspicion should be substantial enough to make the search a reasonable exercise of authority." *United States v. Asbury*, 586 F.2d 973, 975-76 (2d Cir. 1978).

2. "Reasonable suspicion to justify a strip search can only be met by a showing of articulable facts which are particularized as to the person and as to the place to be searched." *United States v. Vega-Barvo,* 729 F.2d 1341, 1349 (11th Cir. 1984).

3. "It is well settled that searches conducted at the international borders of the United States by Customs officials need not be premised upon probable cause.... This Court has upheld strip searches at the border meeting the less exacting standard of 'reasonable suspicion,'...finding that this standard affords the full measure of protection commanded by the fourth amendment." *United States v. Barger*, 574 F.2d 1283, 1285 (5th Cir. 1978).

4. " 'Real suspicion' that the person to be searched is smuggling narcotics is required for a border strip search—a search involving visual inspection of body surfaces.... 'Real suspicion' is 'subjective suspicion supported by objective, articulable facts.'" *United States v. Aman*, 624 F.2d 911, 912 (9th Cir. 1980).

5. "The objective, articulable facts must bear some reasonable relationship to suspicion that something is concealed on the body of the person to be searched;

otherwise, the scope of the search is not related to the justification for its initiation, as it must be to meet the reasonableness standard of the Fourth Amendment." *United States v. Guadalupe-Garza*, 421 F.2d 876, 879 (9th Cir. 1970).

6. "At the border, a customs inspector must have a reasonable suspicion that a person is carrying contraband internally before a person's stomach may be searched either by x-ray or by detaining the person until he excretes his stomach's contents. The reasonable suspicion standard requires a showing of articulable facts which are particularized as to the person and as to the place that is to be searched." *United States v. Henao-Castano,* 729 F.2d 1364, 1366 (11th Cir. 1984).

E. Body Cavity Searches at the Border: Body cavity searches at the border must be based on a higher standard than strip searches.

1. " '[T]he greater the intrusion, the greater must be the reason for conducting a search that results in such invasion'. . . . Thus, what constitutes 'reasonable suspicion' to justify a particular search may not suffice to justify a more intrusive or demeaning search." *United States v. Afanador,* 567 F.2d 1325, 1328 (5th Cir. 1978).

2. "It is necessary to show preliminarily that there is a 'clear indication' of the presence of narcotics [in the body cavity]." *Yanez v. Romero,* 619 F.2d 851, 855 (10th Cir.), *cert. denied,* 449 U.S. 876 (1980).

3. "More, however, is required for a body cavity search at a border, a search which involves an intrusion 'beyond the

body's surface'.... A 'clear indication' or 'plain suggestion' that the suspect is concealing contraband *in his body cavity* is required for such a search." *United States v. Aman*, 624 F.2d 911, 912 (9th Cir. 1980).

4.   "We have...found a violation of the Fourth Amendment since the initiation of the intrusive body cavity search was unjustified because of the lack of any 'clear indication' or 'plain suggestion' in the minds of Dr. Salerno and his rectal invasion squad members that Huguez had any narcotics cached in his rectal cavity." *Huguez v. United States*, 406 F.2d 366, 380 (9th Cir. 1968).

5.   "We disagree...that the removal of an artificial leg for inspection is as intrusive as a body-cavity search....[T]he exposure of the stump to which the prosthetic device is attached, accompanied by a temporary lack of mobility, constitutes an embarrassment. But done in a medical setting, unaccompanied by exposure of intimate bodily parts, and without physical force...is clearly less intrusive than a body-cavity search." *United States v. Sanders*, 663 F.2d 1, 3 (2d Cir. 1981).

6.   "We recognize that the force of the seven cases decided today may well present the person entering the United States with somewhat of a *Hobson's* choice. Once a particularized suspicion arises that you are an internal carrier, the agents can conduct a search sufficient to determine the accuracy of that suspicion, the type of search depending in part on what you consent to. In the absence of consent, the agents can detain you until nature reveals the truth or falsity of their suspicions. This is the reason, in our judgment, that the cases should not rest solely on whether there was consent or waiver in a particular case. Consent may heavily influence the determination as to the reasonableness of the manner of the

search, but it does not completely foreclose the question of whether it was constitutional to search in some manner. A *Hobson's* choice may render a consent to an otherwise unconstitutional search ineffective. But it may render valid a search that could not otherwise be physically forced." *United States v. Pino,* 729 F.2d 1357, 1360 (11th Cir. 1984).

Chapter 28

Non-Governmental Violations of Individual Rights

A. No Constitutional Protection: Actions by private individuals are not within the purview of the Fourth Amendment.

1. "The Fourth Amendment gives protection against unlawful searches and seizures, and as shown in...previous cases, its protection applies to governmental action. Its origin and history clearly show that it was intended as a restraint upon the activities of sovereign authority, and was not intended to be a limitation upon other than governmental agencies...." *Burdeau v. McDowell*, 256 U.S. 465, 475 (1921).

2. "It is well established...that the exclusionary rule, as a deterrent sanction, is not applicable where a private party or a foreign government commits the offending act." *United States v. Janis*, 428 U.S. 433, 456 n.31 (1976).

3. "The exclusionary rules were fashioned 'to prevent, not to repair,' and their target is official misconduct." *Coolidge v. New Hampshire*, 403 U.S. 443, 488 (1971).

4. "[A] wrongful search or seizure by a private party does not violate the Fourth Amendment or deprive the government of the right to use evidence it has lawfully obtained from a private party." *United States v. Bonfiglio,* 713 F.2d 932, 939 (2d Cir. 1983).

5.   "[T]he Fourth Amendment proscribes only governmental action, and does not apply to a search or seizure, even an unreasonable one, effected by a private individual not acting as an agent of the government or with the participation or knowledge of any governmental official.... Since the police did not instigate, encourage, or participate in the search of the truck, the search by [the private party] was outside the scope of the fourth amendment." *United States v. Coleman*, 628 F.2d 961, 964, 965 (6th Cir. 1980).

B.   No Remedy: The exclusionary rule does not apply to evidence seized illegally by a private individual.

1.   "The papers having come into the possession of the Government without a violation of petitioner's rights by governmental authority, we see no reason why the fact that individuals, unconnected with the Government, may have wrongfully taken them, should prevent them from being held for use in prosecuting an offense where the documents are of an incriminatory character." *Burdeau v. McDowell*, 256 U.S. 465, 476 (1921).

2.   "[A] wrongful search or seizure conducted by a private party does not violate the Fourth Amendment and...such private wrongdoing does not deprive the government of the right to use evidence that it has acquired lawfully...." *Walter v. United States*, 447 U.S. 649, 656, 657 (1980).

3.   "It is well settled that independent searches by private citizens are unaffected by Fourth Amendment prohibitions against unreasonable searches and seizures, and that results thereof constitute admissible evidence." *United States v. Thomas*, 613 F.2d 787, 792 (10th Cir.), *cert. denied*, 449 U.S. 888 (1980).

C. Government Involvement: If a government official aids in a search or seizure by a private citizen, the Fourth Amendment applies.

1. "The decisive factor...is the actuality of a share by a federal official in the total enterprise of securing and selecting evidence by other than sanctioned means. It is immaterial whether a federal agent originated the idea or joined in it while the search was in progress. So long as he was in it before the object of the search was completely accomplished, he must be deemed to have participated in it....Evidence secured through such federal participation is inadmissable...." *Lustig v. United States*, 388 U.S. 74, 79 (1949).

2. "This Court has consistently held that searches by private individuals undertaken without 'collusion with federal officers'...or 'at the behest of Government officials'...do not implicate the Fourth Amendment inasmuch as no Governmental action is involved." *United States v. Andrews*, 618 F.2d 646, 652 (10th Cir.), *cert. denied*, 449 U.S. 824 (1980).

3. "Although the surreptitious search of premises by a private party does not violate the Fourth Amendment, if, in conducting the search, the searcher is acting as an instrument or agent of the Government, there is a Fourth Amendment transgression.... However, '[a] private person cannot act unilaterally as an agent or instrument of the state; there must be some degree of governmental knowledge and acquiescence.'" *United States v. Bennett,* 709 F.2d 803, 805 (2d Cir. 1983).

4. "To determine whether a private person acted as a government agent in an illegal search and seizure, this court considers '(1) whether the government knew of and

acquiesced in the intrusive conduct, and (2) whether the party performing the search intended to assist law enforcement efforts or to further his own ends.' ... The burden of establishing government involvement in a private search rests on the party objecting to the evidence." *United States v. Snowadzki,* 723 F.2d 1427, 1429 (9th Cir. 1984).

5.   "Mrs. Ford does not question the right and duty of an air carrier to inspect any package or article submitted for shipment if it has reason to believe the package does not conform to tariff regulations. But, if government officers participated in this inspection, it became a warrantless government search, per se unreasonable unless falling within one of the carefully defined exceptions." *United States v. Ford*, 525 F.2d 1308, 1311 (10th Cir. 1975).

6.   "But the evidence would be excludable in the present case even if the TWA employee had not acted solely to satisfy the government's interest in viewing the contents of the package, but instead had initiated and participated in the search for reasons contemplated by the inspection clause in TWA's tariff. The customs agents joined actively in the search. They held open the flaps of the large package; removed, opened, and inspected the contents of the small boxes which it contained; and marked the small boxes for future identification. Thus, at the very least, the search of appellant's package was a joint operation of the customs agents and the TWA employee. When a federal agent participates in such a joint endeavor, 'the effect is the same as though he had engaged in the undertaking as one exclusively his own.'" *Corngold v. United States*, 367 F.2d 1, 5-6 (9th Cir. 1966).

Chapter 29

Institutional Searches

A. Military: The Fourth Amendment governs military searches, but does not limit the military's right to conduct inspections.

1. "GIs are entitled to the protection of the Fourth Amendment as are all other American citizens.... 'To strike the proper balance between legitimate military needs and individual liberties we must inquire whether "conditions peculiar to military life" dictate affording different treatment to activity arising in a military context.' [Here] warrantless...inspections...are reasonable and constitutionally permissible under the Fourth Amendment." *Committee for G.I. Rights v. Callaway*, 518 F.2d 466, 476, 477 (D.C. Cir. 1975).

2. "While the traditional military inspection which looks at the overall fitness of a unit to perform its military mission is a permissible deviation from what may be tolerated in civilian society generally—recognizing that such procedure is a reasonable intrusion which a serviceperson must expect in a military society—the 'shakedown inspection' as earlier defined in search specifically of criminal goods or evidence is not such a permissible intrusion into a person's reasonable expectation of privacy, even in the military setting." *United States v. Roberts*, 2 M.J. 31, 36 (CMA 1976).

3. "[A]n 'inspection' cannot be used as a pretext to cover up unlawful invasions of the personal rights of members of

the armed services." *United States v. Lange*, 35 C.M.R. 458, 462 (1965).

B. Parolees and Probationers: Parolees and probationers receive only limited Fourth Amendment protection.

1.   " 'A probation condition [warrantless searches of probationer's person and property] is not necessarily invalid simply because it affects a probationer's ability to exercise constitutionally protected rights.' ... 'The conditions must be "reasonably related" to the purposes of the [Federal Probation Act, 18 U.S.C. § 3651]. Consideration of three factors is required to determine whether a reasonable relationship exists: 1) the purposes sought to be served by probation; 2) the extent to which constitutional rights enjoyed by law-abiding citizens should be accorded to probationers; and 3) the legitimate needs of law enforcement.' " *Owens v. Kelley*, 681 F.2d 1362, 1366 (11th Cir. 1982).

2.   "We think that one of [the] restrictions, necessary to the effective operation of the parole system, is that the parolee and his home are subject to search by the parole officer when the officer reasonably believes that such search is necessary in the performance of his duties.... His decision may be based upon specific facts, though they be less than sufficient to sustain a finding of probable cause. It may even be based on a 'hunch,' arising from what he has learned or observed about the behavior and attitude of the parolee. To grant such powers to the parole officer is not, in our view, unreasonable under the Fourth Amendment." *Latta v. Fitzharris*, 521 F.2d 246, 250 (9th Cir.), *cert. denied*, 423 U.S. 897 (1975).

3. "The status of parolees in our legal system is unique;
they are 'neither physically imprisoned nor free to move at
will.'... Because of this unique position, a parolee 'possess[es] fewer constitutional rights' than ordinary citizens.... A parolee's diminished Fourth Amendment protection regarding searches by a parole officer arises from
the necessity for effective parole supervision and the
unique relationship of the parole officer and the parolee....
A parolee's diminished expectation of privacy would necessarily be further diminished while he is in his parole officer's
office. Even an ordinary citizen's expectation of privacy is
less in a public office than in a residence. The expectation
of privacy of a parolee in a parole officer's office would be
at its lowest ebb." *United States v. Thomas,* 729 F.2d 120,
123-24 (2d Cir. 1984).

4. "While it must be recognized that probationers, like
parolees and prisoners, properly are subject to limitations
from which ordinary persons are free, it is also true that
these limitations in the aggregate must serve the ends of
probation. Conditions that unquestionably restrict otherwise inviolable constitutional rights may properly be subject
to special scrutiny to determine whether the limitation does
in fact serve the dual objectives of rehabilitation and public
safety." *United States v. Consuelo-Gonzalez,* 521 F.2d
259, 265 (9th Cir. 1975).

5. "[A] parolee is released on the assumption that not
only will he meet the conditions of his parole, but that he
will 'live and remain at liberty without violating the law'.... A
parole officer is charged with the duty of enforcing these
conditions. To hold that evidence obtained by a parole
officer in the course of carrying out this duty cannot be
utilized in a subsequent prosecution because evidence
obtained directly by the police in such a manner would be
excluded, would unduly immunize parolees from convic-

tion." *United States ex rel. Santos v. New York State Board of Parole*, 441 F.2d 1216, 1218 (2d Cir. 1971), *cert. denied,* 404 U.S. 1025 (1972).

C. Prisoners: Prisoners receive very limited Fourth Amendment protection.

1. "It may well be argued that a person confined in a detention facility has no reasonable expectation of privacy with respect to his room or cell and that therefore the Fourth Amendment provides no protection for such a person.... In any case, given the realities of institutional confinement, any reasonable expectation of privacy that a detainee retained necessarily would be of a diminished scope.... Assuming, *arguendo*, that a pretrial detainee retains such a diminished expectation of privacy after commitment to a custodial facility, we nonetheless find that the room-search rule does not violate the Fourth Amendment." *Bell v. Wolfish*, 441 U.S. 520, 556-57 (1979).

2. "A detention facility is a unique place fraught with serious security dangers. Smuggling of money, drugs, weapons, and other contraband is all too common an occurrence. And inmate attempts to secrete these items into the facility by concealing them in body cavities are documented in this record.... We do not underestimate the degree to which these searches may invade the personal privacy of inmates. Nor do we doubt, as the District Court noted, that on occasion a security guard may conduct the search in an abusive fashion.... Such abuse cannot be condoned. The searches must be conducted in a reasonable manner.... But we deal here with the question whether visual body-cavity inspections as contemplated by the [prison] rules can *ever* be conducted on less than

probable cause. Balancing the significant and legitimate security interests of the institution against the privacy interests of the inmates, we conclude that they can." *Bell v. Wolfish,* 441 U.S. 520, 559-60 (1979).

3.   "[W]e hold that society is not prepared to recognize as legitimate any subjective expectation of privacy that a prisoner might have in his prison cell and that, accordingly, the Fourth Amendment proscription against unreasonable searches does not apply within the confines of the prison cell. The recognition of privacy rights for prisoners in their individual cells simply cannot be reconciled with the concept of incarceration and the needs and objectives of penal institutions." *Hudson v. Palmer,* 468 U.S. _____, _____ (1984).

4.   "[W]e have previously considered not only a Fourth Amendment challenge but a due process challenge to a room search procedure almost identical to that used at Central Jail, and we sustained the practice on both scores. We have no reason to reconsider that issue; the identical arguments made by respondents here were advanced by the respondents in [*Bell v.*] *Wolfish.* The security concerns that we held justified the same restriction in *Wolfish...*are no less compelling here." *Block v. Rutherford,* 468 U.S. _____, _____ (1984).

5.   "Prisoners enjoy at least minimal fourth amendment protection in cell-search situations.... However, prisoners do not retain the same measure of protection afforded nonincarcerated individuals.... The prisoners' reduced measure of fourth amendment protection stems from legitimate institutional needs as well as prisoners' diminished expectations of privacy." *Olson v. Klecker,* 642 F.2d 1115, 1116-17 (8th Cir. 1981).

6. "While it is true that inmates do not enjoy the full range of constitutional rights possessed by unincarcerated individuals,...the Fourth Amendment still requires that searches—even those in the prison context—be reasonable. As *Bell* [*v. Wolfish*] itself makes clear, '[c]ourts must consider the scope of the particular intrusion, the manner in which it is conducted, the justification for initiating it, and the place in which it is conducted.'" *Hodges v. Stanley,* 712 F.2d 34, 35 (2d Cir. 1983).

7. "Although prisoners do not forfeit all their Fourth Amendment rights upon incarceration, they do not retain the same measure of protection afforded non-incarcerated individuals.... The reduced measure of Fourth Amendment protection afforded prisoners stems from legitimate institutional needs,...as well as prisoners' diminished expectations of privacy." *United States v. Stumes,* 549 F.2d 831, 832 (8th Cir. 1977).

8. "[F]emale guards do not conduct full searches [on male prisoners], but merely pat down the clothing over the inmates' neck, back, stomach, arms and legs.... [T]he state has a strong interest in avoiding sex discrimination in its hiring practices at the prison. In light of this interest and given the limited scope of the search,...allowing female officers to perform the search [does] not violate plaintiff's constitutional rights." *Smith v. Fairman,* 678 F.2d 52, 53 (7th Cir. 1982).

9. "Roy's presence in Rocky Hill on December 3 was also wrongful, since he was an escapee from the MCC in Chicago.... At the time of the search and seizure, Roy was no more than a trespasser on society.... We consider an escapee to be in constructive custody for the purpose of determining his legitimate expectations of privacy; he should have the same privacy expectations in property in

his possession inside and outside the prison." *United States v. Roy,* 734 F.2d 108, 111 (2d Cir. 1984).

D. Schools: Students receive limited Fourth Amendment protection.

1. "In carrying out searches and other disciplinary functions pursuant to such policies, school officials act as representatives of the State, not merely as surrogates for the parents, and they cannot claim the parents' immunity from the strictures of the Fourth Amendment.... [T]he Fourth Amendment applies to searches conducted by school authorities." *New Jersey v. T.L.O.,* ____U.S.____, ____ (1985).

2. "A search of a child's person or of a closed purse or other bag carried on her person, no less than a similar search carried out on an adult, is undoubtedly a severe violation of subjective expectations of privacy.... [S]choolchildren may find it necessary to carry with them a variety of legitimate, noncontraband items, and there is no reason to conclude that they have necessarily waived all rights to privacy in such items merely by bringing them onto school grounds. Against the child's interest in privacy must be set the substantial interest of teachers and administrators in maintaining discipline in the classroom and on school grounds.... [T]he accommodation of the privacy interests of schoolchildren with the substantial need of teachers and administrators for freedom to maintain order in the schools does not require strict adherence to the requirement that searches be based on probable cause to believe that the subject of the search has violated or is violating the law. Rather, the legality of a search of a student should depend simply on the reasonableness,

under all the circumstances, of the search." *New Jersey v. T.L.O.,* ____U.S.____, ____(1985).

3. "Under ordinary circumstances, a search of a student by a teacher or other school official will be 'justified at its inception' when there are reasonable grounds for suspecting that the search will turn up evidence that the student has violated or is violating either the law or the rules of the school. Such a search will be permissible in its scope when the measures adopted are reasonably related to the objectives of the search and not excessively intrusive in light of the age and sex of the student and the nature of the infraction." *New Jersey v. T.L.O.,* ____U.S.____, ____ (1985).

4. "The courts have encountered substantial difficulty in accommodating the fourth amendment to the special situation presented by the public schools, where school officials have both a right and a duty to provide a safe environment conducive to education. At one time, it was not uncommon for a court to view the school official who searched a student as acting under authority derived from the parent and therefore as a private party not subject to the constraints of the fourth amendment. . . . [However,] [a]s courts in most recent cases have decided, we think it beyond question that the school official, employed and paid by the state and supervising children who are, for the most part, compelled to attend, is an agent of the government and is constrained by the fourth amendment." *Horton v. Goose Creek Ind. School Dist.,* 690 F.2d 470, 480 (5th Cir. 1982), *cert. denied,*____U.S.____(1983).

5. "The public school presents special circumstances that demand...accommodations of the usual fourth amendment requirements. When society requires large groups of students, too young to be considered capable of

mature restraint in their use of illegal substances or dangerous instrumentalities, it assumes a duty to protect them from dangers posed by anti-social activities—their own and those of other students—and to provide them with an environment in which education is possible. To fulfill that duty, teachers and school administrators must have broad supervisory and disciplinary powers." *Horton v. Goose Creek Ind. School Dist.,* 690 F.2d 470, 480 (5th Cir. 1982), *cert. denied,*____U.S.____(1983).

6.   "When the school official acts in furtherance of his duty to maintain a safe environment conducive to education, the usual accommodation is to require that the school official have "reasonable cause" for his action. Although the standard is less stringent than that applicable to law enforcement officers, it requires more of the school official than good faith or minimal restraint. The Constitution does not permit good intentions to justify objectively outrageous intrusions on student privacy." *Horton v. Goose Creek Ind. School Dist.,* 690 F.2d 470, 481 (5th Cir. 1982), *cert. denied,*____U.S.____(1983).

7.   "It is beyond peradventure that school children do not shed their constitutional rights at the school house gate. It is well recognized that school officials are subject to constitutional restraints as state officials. School officials, employed and paid by the state and supervising children, are agents of the government and are constrained by the Fourth Amendment. . . . We hold that a school official or teacher's reasonable search of a student's person does not violate the student's fourth amendment rights, if the school official has reasonable cause to believe the search is necessary in the furtherance of maintaining school discipline and order, or his duty to maintain a safe environment conducive to education. We note that not only must there be a reasonable ground to institute the search,

the search itself must be reasonable." *Tarter v. Raybuck,* 742 F.2d 977, 981, 982 (6th Cir. 1984).

8.   "The basic theory is that although a student has rights under the Fourth Amendment, these rights must yield to the extent that they interfere with the school admininstration's fundamental duty to operate the school as an educational institution and that a reasonable right to inspect is necessary in the performance of its duties, even though it may infringe, to some degree, on a student's Fourth Amendment rights. The courts which have considered this question have noted that the doctrine *in loco parentis* expands the authority to school officials, even to the extent that it may conflict with the rules set forth in the Fourth Amendment." *Zamora v. Pomeroy,* 639 F.2d 662, 670 (10th Cir. 1981).

9.   "The logical explanation for all of this is that the school authorities have, on behalf of the public, an interest in these lockers and a duty to police the school, particularly where possible serious violations of the criminal laws exist. There is no merit in the contention that a school locker is the property of the student who occupies it *pro tem."* *Zamora v. Pomeroy,* 639 F.2d 662, 670-71 (10th Cir. 1981).

Chapter 30

Forfeiture

A.   Fourth Amendment: The prohibition against unreasonable searches and seizures and the exclusionary rule apply to forfeiture proceedings.

1.   "[T]he [quasi-criminal] nature of a forfeiture proceeding...and the reasons which led the Court to hold that the exclusionary rule...is obligatory upon the States...support the conclusion that the exclusionary rule is applicable to forfeiture proceedings such as the one involved here." *One 1958 Plymouth Sedan v. Pennsylvania,* 380 U.S. 693, 702 (1965).

2.   "Because forfeiture proceedings are quasi-criminal in character and meant to penalize the commission of an offense against the law, the exclusionary rule applies to such proceedings, barring evidence obtained in violation of the fourth amendment." *United States v. One 1977 Mercedes Benz,* 708 F.2d 444, 448 (9th Cir. 1983), *cert. denied,* ____ U.S. ____ (1984).

3.   "[A]n illegal seizure does not immunize the goods from forfeiture. Although 'any evidence which is the product of an illegal search or seizure must be excluded at trial,...forfeiture may proceed if the Government can satisfy the requirements for forfeiture with untainted evidence.'" *United States v. An Article of Device Theramatic,* 715 F.2d 1339, 1341 (9th Cir. 1983), *cert. denied,* ____ U.S. ____(1984).

4. "[A]n object illegally seized cannot in any way be used either as evidence or as the basis for jurisdiction. Therefore, evidence derived from a search in violation of the fourth amendment must be excluded at a forfeiture proceeding. In the case at bar, all evidence of probable cause was developed independent of the seizure of the vehicle. Thus, even if a warrant were required, the failure to secure it would not bar the forfeiture of the vehicle." *United States v. One 1978 Mercedes Benz Four-Door Sedan,* 711 F.2d 1297, 1303 (5th Cir. 1983).

B. Showing Required: The government must show probable cause to believe the item subject to forfeiture was involved in criminal wrongdoing.

1. "Under 19 U.S.C. § 1615, which is made applicable to these proceedings by 21 U.S.C. § 881(d), the government has the initial burden of showing probable cause for the institution of the forfeiture suit. Once probable cause for believing that the property was involved in criminal wrongdoing is established, the burden shifts to the claimant to show that the property was not used in violation of the law." *United States v. $13,000 in United States Currency,* 733 F.2d 581, 584 (8th Cir. 1984).

2. "The probable cause which the government must show is: 'a reasonable ground for belief of guilt, supported by less than prima facie proof but more than mere suspicion.' In making its probable cause showing, however, the government must also establish a nexus 'between the property to be forfeited and the criminal activity defined by the statute;' i.e., the exchange of a controlled substance." *United States v. $22,287.00 United States Currency,* 709 F.2d 442, 446-47 (6th Cir. 1983).

3. "[A] vehicle is subject to forfeiture no matter how small the quantity of contraband found.... For purposes of forfeiture, positive results in a field test furnish sufficient proof as to the existence of contraband." *United States v. One 1982 28' International Vessel,* 741 F.2d 1319, 1322 (11th Cir. 1984).

4. "[T]he cases establish that under § 881 it is not necessary for the subject vehicle either to have transported the illegal substance (or the purchase money) or to have served as the location for the transaction. The subject vehicle in this case was used to transport the 'pivotal figure in the transaction.'" *United States v. One 1979 Porsche Coupe,* 709 F.2d 1424, 1427 (11th Cir. 1983).

C. Standing: A claimant of property which the government seeks to forfeit must demonstrate a possessory interest in the property.

1. "[A] party seeking to challenge the government's forfeiture of money or property used in violation of federal law must first demonstrate an interest in the seized item sufficient to satisfy the court of its standing to contest the forfeiture." *United States v. $364,960.00 in United States Currency,* 661 F.2d 319, 326 (5th Cir. 1981).

2. " '[A] "claimant" is one who claims to own the article or merchandise or to have an interest therein'.... [U]nder the fourth amendment a seizure of property occurs 'when there is some meaningful interference with an individual's possessory interest in that property.'... It is not necessary therefore that a claimant under the forfeiture statute allege ownership. A lesser property interest such as possession

creates standing."*United States v. 1982 Sanger 24' Spectra Boat,* 738 F.2d 1043, 1046 (9th Cir. 1984).

D.   Remission of Forfeitures: To obtain the return of forfeited property, the claimant must show that he was not involved in criminal activity and that he exercised due care in controlling the forfeited property.

1.   "When the forfeiture statutes are viewed in their entirety, it is manifest that they are intended to impose a penalty only upon those who are significantly involved in a criminal enterprise." *United States v. United States Coin and Currency,* 401 U.S. 715, 721–22 (1971).

2.   "[I]t would be difficult to reject the constitutional claim of an owner...who proved not only that he was uninvolved in and unaware of the wrongful activity, but also that he had done all that reasonably could be expected to prevent the proscribed use of his property." *Calero-Toledo v. Pearson Yacht Leasing Co.,* 416 U.S. 663, 689 (1974).

3.   "[T]o obtain remission or mitigation of forfeiture, the claimant has the burden of proving that he exercised due care in entrusting another with possession of his property." *United States v. One 1972 Chevrolet Blazer,* 563 F.2d 1386, 1389 (9th Cir. 1977).

4.   "[T]he Supreme Court acknowledged the existence of an innocent owner defense in forfeiture proceedings, but in so doing placed a heavy burden of proof upon such an owner." *United States v. One 1982 28' International Vessel,* 741 F.2d 1319, 1322 (11th Cir. 1984).

Chapter 31

Standing

A. Requirement: To object to the introduction of evidence obtained by unlawful search and seizure, the defendant must have been personally aggrieved by the search.

1. "Fourth Amendment rights are personal rights which, like some other constitutional rights, may not be vicariously asserted." *Alderman v. United States,* 394 U.S. 165, 174 (1969).

2. "Our Fourth Amendment decisions have established beyond any doubt that the interest in deterring illegal searches does not justify the exclusion of tainted evidence at the instance of a party who was not the victim of the challenged practices.... [A] court may not exclude evidence under the Fourth Amendment unless it finds that an unlawful search or seizure violated the defendant's own constitutional rights." *United States v. Payner,* 447 U.S. 727, 731, 735 (1980).

3. "A person who is aggrieved by an illegal search and seizure only through the introduction of damaging evidence secured by a search of a third person's premises or property has not had any of his Fourth Amendment rights infringed.... And...it is proper to permit only defendants whose Fourth Amendment rights have been violated to benefit from the [exclusionary] rule's protections." *Rakas v. Illinois,* 439 U.S. 128, 134 (1978).

4. "[T]he supervisory power does not authorize a federal court to suppress otherwise admissible evidence on the ground that it was seized unlawfully from a third party not before the court." *United States v. Payner,* 447 U.S. 727, 735 (1980).

5. "The Fourth Amendment 'affords protection against the uninvited ear[;] oral statements, if illegally overheard,...are...subject to suppression'.... This suppression remedy, however, can only be invoked in a criminal trial, by the victim of the illegality, to prevent the use of the tainted evidence against him.... The reason for these limitations is that the purpose of the Fourth Amendment suppression remedy 'is not to redress the injury to the privacy of the search victim[,]...[but] to deter future unlawful police conduct'.... In the present case the challenged evidence is not to be used against the nonparty movants.... [E]ven though the nonparties are allegedly the victims of illegality, they cannot move to suppress the evidence in the defendants' trial on the basis of the Fourth Amendment." *United States v. Dorfman,* 690 F.2d 1217, 1225-26 (7th Cir. 1982).

B. Standard: The person challenging the constitutionality of a search must show a legitimate expectation of privacy in the premises searched or the item seized.

1. "[T]he question is whether the challenged search and seizure violated the Fourth Amendment rights of a criminal defendant who seeks to exclude the evidence obtained during it. That inquiry in turn requires a determination of whether the disputed search and seizure has infringed an interest of the defendant which the Fourth Amendment

was designed to protect." *Rakas v. Illinois,* 439 U.S. 128, 140 (1978).

2.   "[T]he defendant's Fourth Amendment rights are violated only when the challenged conduct invaded *his* legitimate expectation of privacy rather than that of a third party." *United States v. Payner,* 447 U.S. 727, 731 (1980).

3.   "Petitioner, of course, bears the burden of proving not only that the search...was illegal, but also that he had a legitimate expectation of privacy." *Rawlings v. Kentucky,* 448 U.S. 98, 104 (1980).

4.   "[T]his Court uniformly has held that the application of the Fourth Amendment depends on whether the person invoking its protection can claim a 'justifiable,' a 'reasonable,' or a 'legitimate expectation of privacy' that has been invaded by government action.... This inquiry...normally embraces two discrete questions. The first is whether the individual, by his conduct, has 'exhibited an actual (subjective) expectation of privacy'.... The second question is whether the individual's subjective expectation of privacy is one that society is prepared to recognize as 'reasonable',...whether...the individual's expectation, viewed objectively, is 'justifiable' under the circumstances." *Smith v. Maryland,* 442 U.S. 735, 740 (1979).

5.   "[T]he mere legitimate presence on the searched premises, by invitation or otherwise, is insufficient in itself to create a protectible expectation. A defendant must also establish a legitimate expectation of privacy in the particular area searched in order for a fourth amendment challenge to be allowed." *United States v. Meyer,* 656 F.2d 979, 981 (5th Cir. 1981).

6. "[O]ne who resides at a private residence with permission of the owner as a guest or invitee may demonstrate an expectation of privacy in the premises legally sufficient to support a challenge to a police search.... In effect, he steps into the shoes of the homeowner, whose ongoing interest in the privacy of his home permits him to challenge any intrusion,...whether he was present or not." *United States v. Cassity,* 720 F.2d 451, 458 (6th Cir. 1983).

7. "[A] guest at a party has no expectation of privacy and therefore no standing to raise a fourth amendment claim regarding the search of the premises or the seizure of items found there." *United States v. Adamo,* 742 F.2d 927, 947–48 (6th Cir. 1984).

8. "*Rakas* holds that a mere passenger in an automobile ordinarily does not have the legitimate expectation of privacy necessary to challenge the search of that automobile." *United States v. Durant,* 730 F.2d 1180, 1182 (8th Cir. 1984).

9. "Appellant had no reasonable expectation of privacy with respect to a room from which he had been justifiably ejected.... Once ejected for good cause, the room reverted to the control of the management, and the former occupant had no continuing right to privacy in the room." *United States v. Haddad,* 558 F.2d 968, 975 (9th Cir. 1977).

10. "No one circumstance is talismanic to the *Rakas* inquiry. 'While property ownership is clearly a factor to be considered in determining whether an individual's Fourth Amendment rights have been violated, property rights are neither the beginning nor the end of...[the] inquiry'.... Other factors to be weighed include whether the defendant has a possessory interest in the thing seized or the place searched, whether he has the right to exclude others from

that place, whether he has exhibited a subjective expectation that it would remain free from governmental invasion,
whether he took normal precautions to maintain his privacy
and whether he was legitimately on the premises." *United
States v. Pitt,* 717 F.2d 1334, 1337 (11th Cir. 1983), *cert.
denied,* ____ U.S. ____ (1984).

**C. Possession or Ownership: Possession or owner-
ship of a seized item will not automatically confer
standing, absent a showing of a legitimate expectation
of privacy.**

1. "The person in legal possession of a good seized
during an illegal search has not necessarily been subject to
a Fourth Amendment deprivation. . . . [L]egal possession of
a seized good is not a proxy for determining whether the
owner had a Fourth Amendment interest for it does not
invariably represent the protected Fourth Amendment
interest. This Court has repeatedly repudiated the notion
that 'arcane distinctions developed in property and tort law'
ought to control our Fourth Amendment inquiry." *United
States v. Salvucci,* 448 U.S. 83, 91 (1980).

2. "[C]apacity to claim the protection of the Fourth
Amendment depends not upon a property right in the
invaded place but upon whether the person who claims the
protection of the Amendment has a legitimate expectation
of privacy in the invaded place." *Rakas v. Illinois,* 439 U.S.
128, 143 (1978).

3. "While property ownership is clearly a factor to be
considered in determining whether an individual's Fourth
Amendment rights have been violated,. . .property rights

are neither the beginning nor the end of this Court's inquiry." *United States v. Salvucci,* 448 U.S. 83, 91 (1980).

4. "Capacity to claim the protection of the [Fourth] Amendment depends not upon a property right in the invaded place but upon whether the area was one in which there was a reasonable expectation of freedom from governmental intrusion." *Mancusi v. DeForte,* 392 U.S. 364, 368 (1963).

5. "[In *Jones v. United States,* 362 U.S. 257 (1960)] the Court held that the defendant was not obliged to establish that his own Fourth Amendment rights had been violated, but only that the search and seizure of the evidence was unconstitutional. Upon such a showing, the exclusionary rule would be available to prevent the admission of the evidence against the defendant. We are convinced that the automatic standing rule of *Jones* has outlived its usefulness in this Court's Fourth Amendment jurisprudence. The doctrine now serves only to afford a windfall to defendants whose Fourth Amendment rights have *not* been violated. We are unwilling to tolerate the exclusion of probative evidence under such circumstances since we adhere to the view...that the values of the Fourth Amendment are preserved by a rule which limits the availability of the exclusionary rule to defendants who have been subjected to a violation of their Fourth Amendment rights." *United States v. Salvucci,* 448 U.S. 83, 87, 95 (1980).

6. "While petitioner's ownership of the drugs is undoubtedly one fact to be considered in this case, *Rakas* emphatically rejected the notion that 'arcane' concepts of property law ought to control the ability to claim the protections of the Fourth Amendment." *Rawlings v. Kentucky,* 448 U.S. 98, 105 (1980).

7. "[A] bare assertion of property interest, without a supporting expectation of privacy, will not give rise to a cognizable Fourth Amendment claim." *United States v. Kelly,* 529 F.2d 1365, 1369 (8th Cir. 1976).

Chapter 32

Derivative Evidence: The "Fruit of the Poisonous Tree" Doctrine

A. Rule: Indirect as well as direct evidence obtained by illegal police conduct is inadmissible.

1. "In order to make effective the fundamental constitutional guarantees of sanctity of the home and inviolability of the person...this Court held nearly half a century ago that evidence seized during an unlawful search could not constitute proof against the victim of the search.... The exclusionary prohibition extends as well to the indirect as the direct products of such invasions." *Wong Sun v. United States,* 371 U.S. 471, 484 (1963).

2. "Under the exclusionary rule, evidence obtained in violation of the fourth amendment cannot be used in a criminal trial against the victim of the illegal search and seizure. The Constitution does not require this remedy; it is a doctrine of judicial design. Excluded evidence oftentimes is quite reliable and the 'most probative information bearing on the guilt or innocence of the defendant'.... Nonetheless, the rule's prohibition applies to such direct evidence as well as to 'fruit of the poisonous tree'—secondary evidence derived from the illegally seized evidence itself." *United States v. Houltin,* 566 F.2d 1027, 1030 (5th Cir.), *cert. denied,* 439 U.S. 826 (1978).

3. "There is a principle of constitutional law that evidence *seized* in a facially constitutional manner, that was *discov-*

ered as the result of a constitutionally flawed practice, is in effect tainted fruit of a poisonous tree and is not admissible." *United States v. Kroesser,* 731 F.2d 1509, 1519 (11th Cir. 1984).

B. Policy: The courts suppress evidence obtained directly and indirectly by illegal police conduct in order to deter unlawful police activity and to maintain judicial integrity.

1. "[T]estimony as to matters observed during an unlawful invasion has been excluded in order to enforce the basic constitutinal policies.... [The aims are] deterring lawless conduct by federal officers,...[and] closing the doors of the federal courts to any use of evidence unconstitutionally obtained...." *Wong Sun v. United States,* 371 U.S. 471, 485-86 (1963).

2. "[The exclusionary] rule has primarily rested on the judgment that the importance of deterring police conduct that may invade the constitutional rights of individuals throughout the community outweighs the importance of securing the conviction of the specific defendant on trial." *United States v. Caceres,* 440 U.S. 741, 754 (1979).

3. "The deterrent purpose of the exclusionary rule necessarily assumes that the police have engaged in willful, or at the very least negligent, conduct which has deprived the defendant of some right. By refusing to admit evidence gained as a result of such conduct, the courts hope to instill in those particular investigating officers, or in their future counterparts, a greater degree of care toward the rights of an accused. Where the official action was pursued in complete good faith, however, the deterrence rationale

loses much of its force." *Michigan v. Tucker,* 417 U.S. 433, 447 (1974).

4. "[U]nbending applicaton of the exclusionary sanction to enforce ideals of governmental rectitude would impede unacceptably the truth-finding functions of judge and jury.... After all, it is the defendant, and not the constable, who stands trial." *United States v. Payner,* 447 U.S. 727, 734 (1980).

5. "[T]he exclusionary rule should be invoked with much greater reluctance where the claim is based on a casual relationship between a constitutional violation and the discovery of a live witness than when a similar claim is advanced to support suppression of an inanimate object." *United States v. Ceccolini,* 435 U.S. 268, 280 (1978).

6. "[I]t is not deterrence alone that warrants the exclusion of evidence illegally obtained—it is 'the imperative of judicial integrity.' . . . The exclusion of. . .illegally procured [evidence] obtained in its wake deprives the Government of nothing to which it has any lawful claim and creates no impediment to legitimate methods of investigating and prosecuting crime. On the contrary, the exclusion of evidence casually linked to the Government's illegal activity no more than restores the situation that would have prevailed if the Government had itself obeyed the law." *Harrison v. United States,* 392 U.S. 219, 224 n.10 (1968).

7. "[T]he Supreme Court base[s] its application of the exclusionary rule on the need for deterring unlawful police conduct.... The theory of deterrence operates 'only if an excludable piece of evidence is the target of policy activity.' . . . It is clear that the confession. . .was the 'target' of [Defendant's] unlawful detention.... [T]he mere passage of time [cannot] serve to 'dissipate the taint' of an

unlawful arrest. If this were so, the police would be free simply to keep a suspect 'on ice' for a day or two before beginning an interrogation. This would postpone the tasting of the fruit but would not diminish its temptation." *Collins v. Beto,* 348 F.2d 823, 827-28 (5th Cir. 1965).

8.   "The purpose of the rule against admission of illegally seized evidence is the protection of the right to privacy; by quarantining evidence gathered in this manner it is hoped that the zeal of enforcement agencies for such methods of procuring evidence will be curbed.... [C]onsistent with this broad purpose the rule extends beyond evidence directly seized in an unlawful search, to prescribe use of all evidence obtained as an indirect result of such illegal activity—the 'fruit of the poisonous tree.'" *United States v. Paroutian,* 299 F.2d 486, 488-89 (2d Cir. 1962).

C.   Independent Source Exception: The "fruit of the poisonous tree" doctrine will not be applied if the government learns of evidence from a source separate and distinct from the illegal source.

1.   "Of course this does not mean that the facts thus obtained [from illegally procured evidence] become sacred and inaccessible. If knowledge of them is gained from an independent source they may be proved like any others, but the knowledge gained by the Government's own wrong cannot be used by it...." *Silverthorne Lumber Co. v. United States,* 251 U.S. 385, 392 (1920).

2.   "[T]he exclusionary rule has no application because the Government learned of the evidence 'from an independent source.' ... We need not hold that all evidence is 'fruit of the poisonous tree' simply because it would not have

come to light but for the illegal actions of the police. Rather the more apt question in such a case is 'whether, granting establishment of the primary illegality, the evidence to which instant objection is made has been come at by exploitation of that illegality or instead by means sufficiently distinguishable to be purged of the primary taint.'" *Wong Sun v. United States,* 371 U.S. 471, 487-88 (1963).

3.   "The exclusionary rule enjoins the Government from benefiting from evidence it has unlawfully obtained; it does not reach backward to taint information that was in official hands prior to any illegality.... The pretrial identification obtained through use of the photograph taken during respondent's illegal detention cannot be introduced; but the in-court identification is admissible...because the police's knowledge of respondent's identity and the victim's independent recollections of him both antedated the unlawful arrest and were thus untainted by the constitutional violation." *United States v. Crews,* 445 U.S. 463, 476-77 (1980).

4.   "By contrast, the derivative evidence analysis ensures that the prosecution is not put in a *worse* position simply because of some earlier police error or misconduct. The independent source doctrine allows admission of evidence that has been discovered by means wholly independent of any constitutional violation." *Nix v. Williams,* 467 U.S. ____, ____ (1984).

5.   "[E]vidence discovered during the subsequent search of the apartment the following day pursuant to the valid search warrant issued wholly on information known to the officers before the entry into the apartment need not have been suppressed as 'fruit' of the illegal entry because the warrant and the information on which it was based were unrelated to the entry and therefore constituted an inde-

pendent source for the evidence." *Segura v. United States,* 468 U.S. ____, ____ (1984).

6.   "An unlawful search taints all evidence obtained at the search or through leads uncovered by the search. The rule, however, extends only to facts which were actually discovered by a procedure initiated by the unlawful act. If information which could have emerged from an unlawful search in fact stems from an independent source, the evidence is admissible." *United States v. Paroutin,* 299 F.2d 486, 489 (2d Cir. 1962).

7.   "The independent source rule is to be applied strictly. If the article is found initially as a result of the wrongful conduct, it is insufficient to show that it *could* have been found independently, it must be shown that it *would* have been." *United States v. Palumbo,* 742 F.2d 656, 660 (1st Cir. 1984).

8.   "[W]hen a search warrant is based partially on tainted evidence and partially on evidence arising from independent sources, '[i]f the lawfully obtained information amounts to probable cause and would have justified issuance of the warrant apart from the tainted information, the evidence seized pursuant to the warrant is admitted.'" *United States v. Smith,* 730 F.2d 1052, 1056 (6th Cir. 1984).

9.   "Of course, a witness' identity may be derived solely or principally from illegally obtained evidence and warrant a court in disallowing his testimony.... But the taint of the unlawful search may be removed if there are independently sufficient 'leads' by which the government may discover the identity." *United States v. Resnick,* 483 F.2d 354, 357 (5th Cir.), *cert. denied,* 414 U.S. 1008 (1973).

10. "An independent source could consist of information obtained through authorized discovery proceedings or otherwise from co-conspirators lacking standing or from other states which had instituted similar litigation or from any other legitimate independent sources." *Standard Oil Company v. Iowa,* 408 F.2d 1171, 1177 (8th Cir. 1969).

11. "A statement is inadmissible if it was obtained through the exploitation of a prior, illegally obtained statement.... But if the totality of the circumstances shows that the accused confessed of his own free will, his confession is admissible even though his earlier statements were procured illegally.... [S]everal factors that are important in determining whether a prior statement tainted a later one [include] the break in time between the two statements, whether the same conditions that rendered the first statement inadmissible persisted, whether the defendant was given renewed *Miranda* warnings, and whether the defendant initiated contact with the police before making his later confession." *Robinson v. Percy,* 738 F.2d 214, 221 (7th Cir. 1984).

D.   Attenuation Exception: The courts will admit derivative evidence if there is no significant causal relationship between the unlawful police conduct and the discovery of the evidence.

1. "Sophisticated argument may prove a causal connection between information obtained [unlawfully] and the Government's proof. As a matter of good sense, however, such connection may have become so attenuated as to dissipate the taint." *Nardone v. United States,* 308 U.S. 338, 341 (1939).

2. "In the typical 'fruit of the poisonous tree' case,...the challenged evidence was acquired by the police *after* some initial Fourth Amendment violation, and the question before the court is whether the chain of causation proceeding from the unlawful conduct has become so attenuated or has been interrupted by some intervening circumstance so as to remove the 'taint' imposed upon that evidence by the original illegality." *United States v. Crews,* 445 U.S. 463, 471 (1980).

3. "[S]ince the cost of excluding live-witness testimony often will be greater [than the cost of excluding inanimate evidence], a closer, more direct link between the illegality and that kind of testimony is required. [Here,] the degree of attenuation was...sufficient to dissipate the connection between the illegality and the testimony. The evidence indicates overwhelmingly that the testimony given by the witness was an act of her own free will in no way coerced or even induced by official authority as a result of [the illegal police conduct].... Substantial periods of time elapsed between the time of the illegal search and the initial contact with the witness, on the one hand, and between the latter and the testimony at trial, on the other. While the particular knowledge to which [the witness] testified at trial can be logically traced back to [the illegal search], both the identity of [the witness] and her relationship with the [Defendant] were well known to those investigating the case." *United States v. Ceccolini,* 435 U.S. 268, 278, 279 (1978).

4. "[A] confession obtained through custodial interrogation after an illegal arrest should be excluded unless intervening events break the causal connection between the illegal arrest and the confession so that the confession is 'sufficiently an act of free will to purge the primary taint.'... If *Miranda* warnings were viewed as a talisman

that cured all Fourth Amendment violations, then the constitutional guarantee against unlawful searches and seizures would be reduced to a mere 'form of words.'" *Taylor v. Alabama,* 457 U.S. 687, 690 (1982).

5. "The Miranda warnings are an important factor...in determining whether the confession is obtained by exploitation of an illegal arrest. But they are not the only factor to be considered. The temporal proximity of the arrest and the confession, the presence of intervening circumstances...and, particularly the purpose and flagrancy of the official misconduct are all relevant." *Brown v. Illinois,* 442 U.S. 590, 603-04 (1975).

6. "There are well-established guidelines to aid in determining whether the connection between the illegal arrest and the confession or search has become so attenuated as to dissipate the taint and ensure the admissibility of the evidence. Among the factors to be considered are (1) the temporal proximity of the arrest to the procurement of the evidence; (2) the presence of intervening circumstances between the arrest and discovery of the evidence, *e.g.,* giving of *Miranda* warnings, guidance of an attorney; (3) circumstances surrounding the arrest, *e.g.,* intensive questioning, continuous interrogation, coercion and other official misconduct." *United States v. Wilson,* 569 F.2d 392, 395-96 (5th Cir. 1978).

7. "The cocaine later discovered upon a search of [Defendant's] person must be suppressed as the tainted fruit of the illegal arrest unless [his] consent to the search in the airport office was both (1) voluntary, and (2) not the product of the illegal detention. The factors considered in this inquiry are (a) the temporal proximity of the arrest and the consent to the search, (b) intervening circumstances, and (c) the purpose and flagrancy of the official miscon-

duct." *United States v. Robinson,* 690 F.2d 869, 877 (11th Cir. 1982).

8. "Several factors can be considered in determining whether the testimony of a live witness is attenuated of the taint of an illegal search. One factor is whether the witness came forward 'by his own volition, regardless of his identification by the illegal search.'... The fact that a witness is not anxious to testify may not render his testimony involuntary.... Another factor is 'evidence that the witness was completely uncooperative when originally discovered by the illegal search but later changed his attitude and supplied the necessary information.'" *United States v. Parker,* 722 F.2d 179, 185 (5th Cir. 1983).

E. Inevitable Discovery Exception: If the derivative evidence would have been discovered through lawful means, it is admissible.

1. "While neither [Defendant's] incriminating statements themselves nor any testimony describing his having led the police to the victim's body can constitutionally be admitted into evidence [because they were illegally obtained], evidence of where the body was found and its condition might well be admissible on the theory that the body would have been discovered in any event, even had incriminating statements not been [unlawfully] elicited from [Defendant]." *Brewer v. Williams,* 430 U.S. 387, 407 n.12 (1977).

2. "When the challenged evidence has an independent source, exclusion of such evidence would put the police in a worse position than they would have been in absent any error or violation. There is a functional similarity between these two doctrines in that exclusion of evidence that

would inevitably have been discovered would also put the government in a worse position, because the police would have obtained that evidence if no misconduct had taken place. Thus, while the independent source exception would not justify admission of evidence in this case, its rationale is wholly consistent with and justifies our adoption of the ultimate or inevitable discovery exception to the Exclusionary Rule." *Nix v. Williams,* 467 U.S. ____, ____(1984).

3.   "The ultimate or inevitable discovery exception to the Exclusionary Rule is closely related in purpose to the harmless-error rule.... The harmless-constitutional-error rule 'serve[s] a very useful purpose insofar as [it] block[s] setting aside convictions for small errors or defects that have little, if any, likelihood of having changed the result of the trial.' The purpose of the inevitable discovery rule is to block setting aside convictions that would have been obtained without police misconduct." *Nix v. Williams,* 467 U.S. ____, ____n.4 (1984).

4.   "[E]videntiary fruit that has a reasonable probability of subsequent discovery through 'normal police work investigation' [has been admitted]. Although that evidence has been found in fact through the illegal source of an excluded confession, the illegally acquired evidence was not the indispensable source of the identification.... Deterrence is only marginally served by suppression of testimony derived from illegally obtained evidence if such testimony would have been discovered without the illegal actions, because the motivation for the illegal search or interrogation was not the quest for derivative evidence that the police were already pursuing and would probably have been discovered in any event.... Like other circuits that have adopted the [inevitable discovery] rule, we do not require absolute inevitability of discovery but simply a reasonable probability that the evidence in question would have been discovered

other than by the tainted source. Unlike precedents from those circuits, the ruling in this case is based on two additional factors: first, that the prosecutor demonstrated that the leads, which made discovery inevitable, were possessed by the police and were being actively pursued by the police prior to the occurrence of the illegal police conduct; second, that the evidence in question was the voluntary testimony of a witness." *United States v. Brookins,* 614 F.2d 1037, 1042 n.2, 1045, 1047 (5th Cir. 1980).

5. "It was inevitable that, even had the police not [illegally] entered appellant's apartment at the time and in the manner they did, the coroner would sooner or later have been advised by the police of the information reported by the sister, would have obtained the body, and would have conducted the post mortem examination prescribed by law.... Thus, the necessary causal relation between the illegal activity and the evidence sought to be excluded is lacking in this case." *Wayne v. United States,* 318 F.2d 205, 209 (D.C. Cir.), *cert. denied,* 375 U.S. 860 (1963).

6. "[There are] danger[s] in...a broad inevitable-discovery exception whenever a court is satisfied that any government illegality was not the but-for cause of the discovery of any incriminating evidence.... A broad but-for exception...encourages speculation on whether a blunderbuss constable *might* eventually have developed a lawful basis for his investigation. A judge would have to conjecture about what the police would have done, or might have done, or could conceivably have done, in deciding whether illegal conduct which led to incriminating evidence was the but-for cause of the seizure. And these determinations would have to be made retrospectively, after the inculpating evidence has been incorporated into the government's

case, a time when the purposes of the Fourth Amendment and the exclusionary rule may seem least compelling and the need for a conviction may seem paramount." *United States v. Alvarez-Porras,* 643 F.2d 54, 63-64 (2d Cir.), *cert. denied,* 454 U.S. 839 (1981).

F. Burden of Proof: Once the defendant has made a *prima facie* showing of government illegality, the prosecution has the burden of proving an independent source by a preponderance of the evidence.

1. "The burden is. . .on the accused in the first instance to prove to the trial court's satisfaction that wire-tapping was unlawfully employed. Once that is established. . .the trial judge must give opportunity. . .to the accused to prove that a substantial portion of the case against him was a fruit of the poisonous tree. This leaves ample opportunity to the Government to convince the trial court that its proof has an independent origin." *Nardone v. United States,* 308 U.S. 338, 341 (1939).

2. "The United States concedes that when an illegal search has come to light, it has the ultimate burden of persuasion to show that its evidence is untainted. But at the same time petitioners acknowledge that they must go forward with specific evidence demonstrating taint." *Alderman v. United States,* 394 U.S. 165, 183 (1969).

3. "[T]he government has the burden of proving by a preponderance of the evidence. . .that the evidence has not been tainted either indirectly or directly." *United States v. Falley,* 489 F.2d 33, 41 (2d Cir. 1973).

4. "[W]hile the ultimate burden of proof is on the Government to show the absence of taint, the defendant must first establish a factual nexus between the illegality and the challenged evidence. The mere establishment of an illegal search does not place upon the Government the burden of affirmatively proving that each and every piece of evidence is free of taint." *United States v. Spetz,* 721 F.2d 1457, 1468 (9th Cir. 1983).

G. Limited Use of Illegally Obtained Evidence: Evidence which is obtained through illegal means may be used to impeach a defendant, and may be presented to a grand jury.

1. "[T]he use of evidence obtained in an illegal search and inadmissible in the Government's case in chief [may be] admitted to impeach the direct testimony of the defendant.... [S]tatements taken in violation of *Miranda*...and unusable by the prosecution as part of its own case [are] admissible to impeach statements made by the defendant in the course of his direct testimony.... [P]ermitted impeachment by otherwise inadmissible evidence is not limited to collateral matters.... [A] defendant's statements made in response to proper cross-examination reasonably suggested by the defendant's direct examination are subject to otherwise proper impeachment by the government, albeit by evidence that has been illegally obtained that is inadmissible on the government's direct case, or otherwise, as substantive evidence of guilt." *United States v. Havens,* 447 U.S. 620, 624-25, 627-28 (1980).

2. "[W]e [have] refused to require that illegally seized evidence be excluded from presentation to a grand jury.

We have likewise declined to prohibit the use of such evidence for the purpose of impeaching a defendant who testifies in his own behalf." *United States v. Ceccolini,* 435 U.S. 268, 275 (1978).

Chapter 33

Police Interrogation and Defendant's Statements

A. Warning Requirement: Suspects must be informed of their constitutional rights before they are interrogated.

1. "Prior to any questioning, the person must be warned that he has a right to remain silent, that any statement he does make may be used as evidence against him, and that he has the right to the presence of an attorney, either retained or appointed." *Miranda v. Arizona,* 384 U.S. 436, 444 (1966).

2. "The warnings, mandated by [*Miranda*] as a prophylactic means of safeguarding Fifth Amendment rights,...require that a person taken into custody be advised immediately that he has the right to remain silent, that anything he says may be used against him, and that he has a right to retained or appointed counsel before submitting to interrogation." *Doyle v. Ohio,* 426 U.S. 610, 617 (1976).

3. "One of the principal advantages of the doctrine that suspects must be given warnings before being interrogated while in custody is the clarity of that rule. 'Miranda's holding has the virtue of informing police and prosecutors with specificity as to what they may do in conducting custodial interrogation, and of informing courts under what circumstances statements obtained during such interrogation are

not admissible. This gain in specificity, which benefits the accused and the State alike, has been thought to outweigh the burdens that the decision in Miranda imposes on law enforcement agencies and the courts by requiring the suppression of trustworthy and highly probative evidence even though the confession might be voluntary under traditional Fifth Amendment analysis.'" *Berkemer v. McCarty,* 468 U.S. ____, ____ (1984).

4. "[A] person subjected to custodial interrogation is entitled to the benefit of the procedural safeguards enunciated in Miranda, regardless of the nature or severity of the offense of which he is suspected or for which he was arrested." *Berkemer v. McCarty,* 468 U.S. ____, ____ (1984).

5. "The purposes of the safeguards prescribed by Miranda are to *ensure* that the police do not coerce or trick captive suspects into confessing to relieve the 'inherently compelling pressures' generated by the custodial setting itself, 'which work to undermine the individual's will to resist,' and as much as possible to free courts from the task of scrutinizing individual cases to try to determine, after the fact, whether particular confessions were voluntary. Those purposes are implicated as much by in-custody questioning of persons suspected of misdemeanors as they are by questioning of persons suspected of felonies." *Berkemer v. McCarty,* 468 U.S. ____, ____ (1984).

6. "[T]he admission of testimony...obtained in the absence of the required warnings was a flat violation of the Self-Incrimination Clause of the Fifth Amendment...." *Orozco v. Texas,* 394 U.S. 324, 326 (1969).

7. "*Miranda*...[is not] applicable only to questioning one who is 'in custody' in connection with the very case under

investigation. There is no substance to such a distinction, and in effect it goes against the whole purpose of...Fifth Amendment rights." *Mathis v. United States,* 391 U.S. 1, 4 (1968).

8. "*Miranda* requires a clear and unequivocal warning to an accused of his constitutional rights, prior to the taking of any statment, whether exculpatory or inculpatory, during interrogation occurring after an accused is taken into custody." *United States ex rel. Williams v. Twomey,* 467 F.2d 1248, 1250 (7th Cir. 1972).

9. "Civil as well as criminal interrogation of in-custody defendants by INS investigators should generally be accompanied by the *Miranda* warnings.... Not all civil questioning constitutes interrogation.... We hold that in-custody questioning by INS investigators must be preceded by *Miranda* warnings, if the questioning is reasonably likely to elicit an incriminating response." *United States v. Mata-Abundiz,* 717 F.2d 1277, 1279, 1280 (9th Cir. 1983).

10. "A principal purpose of the *Miranda* warnings is to permit the suspect to make an intelligent decision as to whether to answer the government agent's questions.... In deportation proceedings, however—in light of the alien's burden of proof, the requirement that the alien answer non-incriminating questions, the potential adverse consequences to the alien of remaining silent, and the fact that an alien's statement is admissible in the deportation hearing despite his lack of counsel at the preliminary interrogation—*Miranda* warnings would be not only inappropriate but could also serve to mislead the alien." *United States v. Alderete-Deras,* 743 F.2d 645, 648 (9th Cir. 1984).

B. When Required: An individual who is in custody or otherwise significantly restricted in freedom of action must be advised of his constitutional rights before interrogation.

1. "By custodial interrogation, we mean questioning initiated by law enforcement officers after a person has been taken into custody or otherwise deprived of his freedom of action in any significant way." *Miranda v. Arizona,* 384 U.S. 436, 444 (1966).

2. "[T]he *Miranda* safeguards come into play whenever a person in custody is subjected to either express questioning or its functional equivalent. That is to say, the term 'interrogation' under *Miranda* refers not only to express questioning, but also to any words or actions on the part of the police...that the police should know are reasonably likely to elicit an incriminating response from the suspect. The latter portion of this definition focuses primarily upon the perceptions of the suspect, rather than the intent of the police.... A practice that the police should know is reasonably likely to evoke an incriminating response from a suspect thus amounts to interrogation. But, since the police surely cannot be held accountable for the unforeseeable results of their words of actions, the definition of interrogation can extend only to words or actions on the part of police officers that they *should have known* were reasonably likely to elicit an incriminating response." *Rhode Island v. Innis,* 446 U.S. 291, 300-02 (1980).

3. "The considerations calling for the accused to be warned prior to custodial interrogation apply with no less force to the pretrial psychiatric examination at issue here. Respondent was in custody...when the examination was ordered and when it was conducted. That respondent was questioned by a psychiatrist designated by the trial court to

conduct a neutral competency examination, rather than by a police officer, government informant, or prosecuting attorney, is immaterial. When [the psychiatrist] went beyond simply reporting to the court on the issue of competence and testified for the prosecution at the penalty phase on the crucial issue of respondent's future dangerousness, his role changed and became essentially like that of an agent of the State recounting unwarned statements made in a post-arrest custodial setting.... [Defendant] was given no indication that the compulsory examination would be used to gather evidence necessary to decide whether, if convicted, he should be sentenced to death. He was not informed that, accordingly, he had a constitutional right not to answer the questions put to him." *Estelle v. Smith,* 451 U.S. 454, 467 (1981).

4. "The similarly noncoercive aspect of ordinary traffic stops prompts us to hold that persons temporarily detained pursuant to such stops are not 'in custody' for purposes of *Miranda.*" *Berkemer v. McCarty,* 468 U.S. ____, ____ (1984).

5. "It is settled that the safeguards prescribed by *Miranda* become applicable as soon as a suspect's freedom of action is curtailed to a 'degree associated with formal arrest.'... If a motorist who has been detained pursuant to a traffic stop thereafter is subjected to treatment that renders him 'in custody' for practical purposes, he will be entitled to the full panoply of protections prescribed by *Miranda.*" *Berkemer v. McCarty,* 468 U.S. ____, ____ (1984).

6. "There is no requirement that police stop a person who enters a police station and states that he wishes to confess to a crime, or a person who calls the police to offer a confession or any other statement he desires to make.

Volunteered statements of any kind are not barred by the Fifth Amendment and their admissibility is not affected by our holding today." *Miranda v. Arizona,* 384 U.S. 436, 478 (1966).

7. "[I]nvestigation may include inquiry of persons not under restraint. General on-the-scene questioning as to facts surrounding a crime or other general questioning of citizens in the fact-finding process is not affected by our holding." *Miranda v. Arizona,* 384 U.S. 436, 477 (1966).

8. "[There is] a four-factor test for determining whether a declarant is in custody, to wit: (1) the existence of probable cause to arrest; (2) the subjective intent of the police; (3) the subjective belief of the defendant; and (4) the focus of the investigation.... The former Fifth Circuit...recognized a clear exception to the *Miranda* rule for voluntary unresponsive statements." *United States v. Castro,* 723 F.2d 1527, 1530, 1531 (11th Cir. 1984).

9. "No *Miranda* warning was necessary before the officers questioned defendants...as to their identity and places of residence. Disclosure of name and address is an essentially neutral act. It identifies but does not by itself implicate anyone in criminal conduct." *United States v. Jackson,* 448 F.2d 963, 970 (9th Cir. 1971), *cert. denied,* 405 U.S. 924 (1972).

10. "While it is established that the *Miranda* safeguards come into play when an individual is in custody and subjected to interrogation, the *Miranda* safeguards are not applicable to private citizens who conduct an investigation unless they have some connection with the government." *United States v. Pullen,* 721 F.2d 788, 790 (11th Cir. 1983).

11. "The interrogation herein amounted to no more than routine customs and immigration inquiries, such as are conducted at a border crossing.... This court has recognized that *Miranda* warnings need not be given to one detained at the border and subjected to a routine customs inquiry.... *Miranda* warnings are required in border interrogations when the questioning of the official becomes an interrogation that is custodial in nature and is one in which 'information is sought for the purpose of using it against [a] person in a criminal proceeding.'" *United States v. Silva,* 715 F.2d 43, 46, 47-48 (2d Cir. 1983).

12. "*Miranda* warnings are required only where there has been such a restriction on a person's freedom as to render him 'in custody'.... This circuit employs an objective reasonable person test in determining whether a person is in custody. Factors to be considered are the language used to summon the defendant, the physical surroundings, the extent to which the defendant is confronted with evidence of his guilt, and the pressure exerted to detain him." *United States v. Crisco,* 725 F.2d 1228, 1231 (9th Cir.), *cert. denied,* ____U.S. ____ (1984).

C. Public Safety: The police need not give *Miranda* warnings in situations posing a threat to public safety.

1. "We conclude that the need for answers to questions in a situation posing a threat to the public safety outweighs the need for the prophylactic rule protecting the Fifth Amendment's privilege against self-incrimination. We decline to place officers...in the untenable position of having to consider, often in a matter of seconds, whether it best serves society for them to ask the necessary questions without the *Miranda* warnings and render whatever proba-

tive evidence they uncover inadmissible, or for them to give the warnings in order to preserve the admissibility of evidence they might uncover but possibly damage or destroy their ability to obtain that evidence and neutralize the volatile situation confronting them." *New York v. Quarles,* ____ U.S. ____, ____ (1984).

2. "[T]here is a 'public safety' exception to the requirement that *Miranda* warnings be given before a suspect's answers may be admitted into evidence.... [T]he availability of that exception does not depend upon the motivation of the individual officers involved. In a kaleidoscopic situation...where spontaneity rather than adherence to a police manual is necessarily the order of the day, the application of the exception which we recognize today should not be made to depend on *post hoc* findings at a suppression hearing concerning the subjective motivation of the arresting officer.... [W]e do not believe that the doctrinal underpinnings of *Miranda* require that it be applied in all its rigor to a situation in which police officers ask questions reasonably prompted by a concern for the public safety." *New York v. Quarles,* ____ U.S. ____, ____ (1984).

D. Waiver: Suspects may relinquish their constitutional rights, but the government must establish that the waiver is made voluntarily, knowingly and intelligently.

1. "After...[the required] warnings have been given, and such opportunity [to exercise these rights] afforded him, the individual may knowingly and intelligently waive these rights and agree to answer questions or make a statement. ... Any statement given freely and voluntarily without any

compelling influences is, of course, admissible in evidence." *Miranda v. Arizona,* 384 U.S. 436, 478, 479 (1966).

2.   "However, [i]f the individual indicates in any manner, at any time prior to or during questioning, that he wishes to remain silent, the interrogation must cease...[and], [i]f the individual states that he wants an attorney, the interrogation must cease...." *Miranda v. Arizona,* 384 U.S. 436, 473-74 (1966).

3.   "[An] accused,...having expressed his desire to deal with the police only through counsel, is not subject to further interrogation by the authorities until counsel has been made available to him, unless the accused himself initiates further communication, exchanges or conversations with the police.... [I]t is inconsistent with *Miranda* and its progeny for the authorities, at their instance, to reinterrogate an accused in custody if he has clearly asserted his right to counsel." *Edwards v. Arizona,* 451 U.S. 477, 484-85 (1981).

4.   "An accused in custody, 'having expressed his desire to deal with the police only through counsel, is not subject to further interrogation by the authorities until counsel has been made available to him,' unless he validly waives his earlier request for the assistance of counsel. This 'rigid' prophylactic rule embodies two distinct inquiries. First, courts must determine whether the accused actually invoked his right to counsel. Second, if the accused invoked his right to counsel, courts may admit his responses to further questioning only on finding that he (a) initiated further discussions with the police, and (b) knowingly and intelligently waived the right he had invoked.... Where nothing about the request for counsel or the circumstances leading up to the request would render it ambiguous, all questioning must cease. In these circum-

stanes, an accused's subsequent statements are relevant only to the question whether the accused waived the right he had invoked. Invocation and waiver are entirely distinct inquiries, and the two must not be blurred by merging them together." *Smith v. Illinois,* ____U.S.____, ____(1984).

5. "Although ambiguous, the respondent's question in this case as to what was going to happen to him evinced a willingness and a desire for a generalized discussion about the investigation; it was not merely a necessary inquiry arising out of the incidents of the custodial relationship. ... Since there was no violation of the *Edwards* rule in this case, the next inquiry was 'whether a valid waiver of the right to counsel and the right to silence had occurred, that is, whether the purported waiver was knowing and intelligent and found to be so under the totality of the circumstances, including the necessary fact that the accused, not the police, reopened the dialogue with the authorities.'" *Oregon v. Bradshaw,*____U.S.____(1983).

6. "If the interrogation continues without the presence of an attorney and a statement is taken, a heavy burden rests on the government to demonstrate that the defendant knowingly and intelligently waived his privilege against self-incrimination and his right to retained or appointed counsel." *Miranda v. Arizona,* 384 U.S. 436, 475 (1966).

7. "[A] valid waiver will not be presumed simply from the silence of the accused after warnings are given or simply from the fact that a confession was in fact eventually obtained." *Miranda v. Arizona,* 384 U.S. 436, 475 (1966).

8. "An express written or oral statment of waiver of the right to remian silent or of the right to counsel is usually strong proof of the validity of that waiver, but is not inevitably either necessary or sufficient to establish waiver.

The question is not one of form, but rather whether the defendant in fact knowingly and voluntarily waived the rights delineated in...*Miranda*.... As was unequivocally said in *Miranda,* mere silence is not enough. That does not mean that the defendant's silence, coupled with an under-standing of his rights and a course of conduct indicating waiver, may never support a conclusion that a defendant has waived his rights. The Courts must presume that a defendant did not waive his rights; the prosecution's burden is great; but in at least some cases waiver can be clearly inferred from the actions and words of the person interrogated." *North Carolina v. Butler,* 441 U.S. 369, 373 (1979).

9. "[O]nce a suspect has invoked the right to counsel, knowledge of that request is imputed to all law enforce-ment officers who subsequently deal with the suspect." *United States v. Scalf,* 708 F.2d 1540, 1544 (10th Cir. 1983).

10. "If a suspect is indecisive in his request for counsel, law enforcement officials must cease the interrogation unless they ask the suspect further questions to clarify whether the suspect wants to consult with an attorney before continuing with the interrogation. However, such questioning is to be limited to this clarification and cannot be used as a means of eliciting any incriminating state-ments from the suspect relating to the subject matter of the interrogation." *United States v. Cherry,* 733 F.2d 1124, 1130 (5th Cir. 1984).

11. "[T]he waiver of constitutional rights must be consid-ered in light of the background, experience, and conduct of the accused. That defendants were police officers at the time their statements were given is therefore relevant to a determination of the voluntariness of their statements."

United States v. Charles, 738 F.2d 686, 697–98 (5th Cir. 1984).

12. "A promise that cooperation by an accused would be made known to the appropriate authority is insufficient inducement to render an incriminating statement involuntary." *United States v. Packer,* 730 F.2d 1151, 1158 (8th Cir. 1984).

E. Silence: An individual's exercise of his right to remain silent cannot be used against him.

1. "[W]hen a person under arrest is informed... that he may remain silent, that anything he says may be used against him, and that he may have an attorney if he wishes,...it does not comport with due process to permit the prosecution during the trial to call attention to his silence at the time of arrest and to insist that because he did not speak about the facts of the case at that time, as he was told he need not do, an unfavorable inference might be drawn as to the truth of his trial testimony." *United States v. Hale,* 422 U.S. 171, 182-83 (1975) (White, J., concurring).

2. "[W]hile it is true that the *Miranda* warnings contain no express assurance that silence will carry no penalty, such assurance is implicit to any person who receives the warnings. In such circumstances, it would be fundamentally unfair and a deprivation of due process to allow the arrested person's silence to be used to impeach an explanation subsequently offered at trial." *Doyle v. Ohio,* 426 U.S. 610, 618 (1976).

3. "It is well established that in a situation where a defendant makes no statement to law enforcement officials

after the giving of the *Miranda* rights, evidence that a defendant has invoked his right to remain silent or requested an attorney is not admissible evidence at trial.... The reason for this is that a defendant should not be penalized for exercising his constitutional rights and a jury should not be allowed to draw an inference of guilt from such exercise. However, in certain atypical situations such evidence is properly admissible." *United States v. De La Luz Gallegos,* 738 F.2d 378, 382 (10th Cir. 1984).

4.   "However, when a defendant sponsors a defense at trial to the accusation laid against him, which common sense and good reason assert is totally inconsistent with pretrial silence of the testifying defendant or his witness, the pursuit of truth may allow penetration of what is otherwise shielded, to test the credibility of the defense he offers." *United States v. Harp,* 513 F.2d 786, 790 (5th Cir.), *cert. denied,* 423 U.S. 939 (1975).

F.   Impeachment: Statements made by a defendant in circumstances violating the strictures of *Miranda* are admissible for impeachment if they are shown to be trustworthy.

1.   "[E]vidence inadmissible against an accused in the prosecution's case in chief is [not] barred for all purposes, provided of course that the trustworthiness of the evidence satisfies legal standards." *Harris v. New York,* 401 U.S. 222, 224 (1971).

2.   "[T]he shield provided by *Miranda* is not to be perverted to a license to testify inconsistently, or even perjuriously, free from the risk of confrontation with prior inconsistent utterances.... [I]nadmissibility would pervert the constitu-

tional right into a right to falsify free from the embarrassment of impeachment evidence from the defendant's own mouth." *Oregon v. Hass,* 420 U.S. 714, 722, 723 (1975).

3.   "But *any* criminal trial use against defendant of his *involuntary* statement is a denial of due process of law even though there is ample evidence aside from the confession to support the conviction. . . . If. . .[Defendant's] statements to [the] [d]etective. . .were not the product of a rational intellect and a free will. . .his conviction cannot stand." *Mincey v. Arizona,* 437 U.S. 385, 398 (1978).

4.   "[T]he government can use *pre-arrest* silence to impeach a defendant." *United States v. Nabors,* 707 F.2d 1294, 1298 (11th Cir. 1983), *cert. denied,*____U.S.____ (1984).

NOTES

NOTES

NOTES

NOTES

NOTES

NOTES

NOTES